LOW ON GAS
HIGH ON SKY

Also by J. B. Rivard

Handful of Air

Illusions of Magic: Love and Intrigue in 1933 Chicago

Illusions of Magic: The Movie
(with Anya Carlson)

Nick Mamer by J. B. Rivard (ink wash)

LOW ON GAS

HIGH ON SKY

Nick Mamer's
1929 Venture

J. B. Rivard

ISBN: 978-0-9968363-4-0
Library of Congress Control Number: 2018914129

Impressit Press
1452 S. Ellsworth Rd #3017
Mesa, AZ 85209

Includes notes, references and index. For information on special discounts for bulk
purchases, please contact Sales at the above address.

Photos: Courtesy Mamer Family Archives
Illustrations by: J. B. Rivard

Printed in the United States of America

Design by Gray Dog Press, Spokane, Washington

First printed in 2019

Again for Anya and Ivy

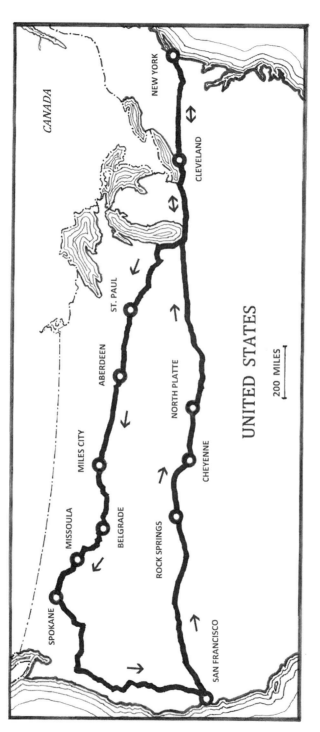

The path of the *Spokane Sun God* flight showing aerial refueling locations (circles).

CONTENTS

Part IV: A Life Aloft

Low on Gas

High on Sky

INTRODUCTION

They're flying west toward Kylertown. Everything outside is velvet black. The big motor up front churns with nine-cylinder vigor, allaying fear. But the pilots tug at their parachute straps.

In a split-second, a streak of jagged, cloud-to-cloud lightning reveals towering thunderheads—everywhere ahead. As low to the ground as he dares, Nick Mamer seeks a path between the bulges of vapor, as great rushes of rain blot his vision.

Close by, a bolt of white-hot lightning flashes. The sudden explosion of superheated air rocks the airplane sideways. Nick corrects. The two men are almost deafened by the roar.

Recalling that night over the Allegheny Mountains, Nick Mamer later writes, "...we encountered one of the severest electrical storms I have ever seen..." "We were ready to jump any minute."

It all began when Nick Mamer, a thirty-one-year old aviator, considered the flight of four military men in a Fokker tri-motor named *Question Mark*. During the first week of January, 1929, that three-motored airplane took off at 7:26 a.m. and stayed aloft for more than six days over an airfield at Van Nuys, California. It was a major demonstration of aerial refueling, in which *Question Mark* was refueled in the air forty-three times by supply planes.

What intrigued Nick Mamer was the idea that refueling afforded an opportunity to extend the distance flown beyond what the on-board supply of gas allowed. With aerial refueling, an airplane could "reduce gasoline loads [and] increase payloads," he said. In other words, he believed aerial refueling was a key to extending an airplane's range.

To provide a demonstration, he, the Buhl Aircraft Company, Texaco, and the businessmen and citizens of Spokane, Washington, planned a flight across the U.S. continent and return, without landing. Specially-equipped airplanes with extra fuel would be stationed at locations along the flight path from which they could launch and refuel the long-range airplane's tanks.

The idea seemed straightforward enough, and on August 15, 1929, the just-named airplane, the single-engined *Spokane Sun God*, with Nick Mamer piloting and Art Walker assisting, took off from Felts Field in Spokane, to attempt the transcontinental, nonstop, round trip. The story of that venture, the unlikely adventure that it became, is told in Parts I, II, and III. Part IV, titled "A Life Aloft," is a brief account of the life of the man who led it.

It is some measure of the importance of Nick Mamer's venture that in 1948, the United States Air Force activated its first refueling units. The next year, Air Force Capt. James Gallagher flew nonstop around the world in 94 hours and 1 minute in a refueled B-50. From the KC-97s of the early 1950s through to jet-powered KC-135 workhorses, the Air Force depends on these aircraft that now dispense jet fuel to extend the reach and capabilities of the U.S.'s armed forces.

Today, the defense posture of the U.S. depends upon its ability to launch military aircraft from air bases within the continental United States, yet handle missions anywhere on earth and return safely to airbases in the homeland. This capability relies heavily upon the aerial refueling pioneered by Nicholas B. Mamer during the flight of the *Spokane Sun God*.

On August 21, 2009, a KC-135 named Spokane Sun-God II was launched from Fairchild Air Force Base. The launch, attended by dignitaries and military leaders from across the nation, celebrated the 80th anniversary of Nick Mamer's five-day venture.

This nonfiction book is based on historical records. It contains no invented dialogue or scenes. Unless otherwise attributed, words between quotation marks are cited from a certificate, letter, telegram, newspaper, magazine, book, handwritten notes, or similar source, as discussed and documented in the Notes.

Where possible, and in keeping with its daring and dangerous nature, events of the 1929 flight are related in present tense. While adhering closely to the historical record—see the extensive Notes and References—I have sometimes in these three Parts added less significant aspects which probably occurred, but for which no historical record exists. For example, I report that Art Walker wore helmet and goggles during the North Platte refueling. No source reported this. Actions of this kind were added to bring living and breathing life to a story that might otherwise tend toward a dry recitation of fact. Be assured that during the writing I avoided falsifying the basic underlying events and circumstances as reported in the References.

Part IV, on the life of Nick Mamer, adheres strictly to biographical standards and avoids any undocumented additions. It is written in traditional past tense.

In choosing sources ("References"), I have preferred those closest to the event, both in the choice of person and/or in its time of creation. For example, I quote from Nick's actual handwritten note rather than from a news account of what the note said.

This book depends heavily upon contemporaneous newspaper reports and clippings. The reader should always be aware that news accounts in this 1900-1940 era, especially those appearing in newspapers, are sometimes less than reliable. For example, it is often reported that Nick Mamer served in France during World War I. This is false; Mamer did not enter that country during his World War I military service.

Where sources disagreed, I have chosen what I judged to be the most likely event, sequence, or timing. In rare instances, I have simply excluded a contentious issue from the narrative.

During his life, Nick Mamer and his wife Faye kept scrapbooks, albums and envelopes of newspaper clippings, articles and photographs documenting Nick's exploits and achievements. Faye continued this, with less intensity, following his unexpected death. Some additions were made by their only child, Patricia Ann Mamer Lee (1927-1995). These records were retained by Patricia's husband Leo R. Lee, Jr. (1928-2009) and their living children, Georgia Maye, David Scott, and Stephen Nicholas, Lee. It is important to note that much of the information contained herein could not have been made available except for access to this trove, herein referred to as the Mamer Family Archives, most generously granted by Nick Mamer's grandchildren.

For those less-acquainted with aviation jargon, a Glossary follows the text, as do the Notes, References, a brief Bibliography and Index.

PART I

TO SAN FRANCISCO

1. A New, Blue Home

"Will they make it?" That's the crowd's, and the reporters' question as the motor of the bright red biplane roars to life. Followed by a cloud of dirt caused by its whirling propeller, the plane pulls out and away from its position near the hangars. It bounds across the sod of Felts Field, recoiling heavily with each bump. The reason, the pilot knows, is the added weight of 320 gallons of gasoline, totaling more than a ton. It all takes place at the Spokane, Washington, airport, where a large crowd has gathered.

One last time, pilot Nick Mamer glances across the brownish stubble, at the place that might as well be home—his hangar office, his airplanes, his workers, his *life*. But now, it's crammed with cheering, waving crowds, fluttering flags, wool-suited politicians on a bunting-shrouded reviewing stand, the Chief and his costumed tribesmen, and an overflow of raucous hullabaloo. All this spectacle lacks, perhaps, are jugglers, trapezes and acrobats.

But now, there is business.

At the extreme east end of the field, Nick slows the plane. He swings it around to face the breeze, and stops. The weeds below the fuselage tremble, flexing in the propeller's wash. It is 6:00 p.m., Thursday, August 15, 1929.

Nick scans temperature, pressure and electrical indications. The needles of the gauges quiver, excited by the shaking of the big motor up front. He tests first one magneto, then the other. Swinging the stick side to side, he notes the aileron's motion, then tests the rudder and elevator.

Thinking ahead, Nick knows the challenge of this takeoff. With more than a ton of gasoline on board with all the additional supplies, the plane is overloaded. Worse, the 200-gallon tank was installed on the right side of the cabin, making it an unbalanced load that will make the aircraft tend to dip to his right.

Now, feet hard on the brakes, he moves mixture to rich and advances throttle.

Blue smoke shoots from the motor exhausts. The roar increases to that of a tornado.

Nick glances at the tachometer and releases the brakes. The craft jerks forward. The airplane bounces across the uneven ground.

Speed comes slowly, twenty six, thirty-four, forty-one miles an hour. The tail wheel bounces some, and lifts. Nick feels the control stick press into the palm of his hand.

The craft veers to the right. It's the unbalanced load. Quickly, Nick applies left rudder.

The airplane skips across the ground, as if it were somehow shedding its weight.

Abruptly, the jouncing and rattles cease. The plane is airborne. The right wing sinks a little. Nick jogs the stick left, then adjusts until the wings are level. He relaxes that input. Seemingly slowing, the airplane grunts up and over the fences and scrub at the west end of the field.

Finally, the needle of the altimeter ticks past one-hundred feet. Nick banks the plane to the southwest. The environs of Spokane, Washington roll beneath.

The meetings, the planning, the palaver, the packing, the checking, the well-intentioned ceremonial froth—all are over now. Nick Mamer exhales a long, easy breath. A familiar feeling suffuses his body: it's the elation of flight—the exhilaration of commanding a chariot that rides on air.

At cruise level, Nick adjusts the motor and the control surfaces for the long flight ahead. This plane, with "Spokane Sun God" in white letters on its side, is a metal-framed, wood-winged, single engine sesquiplane—similar to a biplane but with a much smaller lower wing. It's been modified from a commercial model by its builder, the Buhl Aircraft Company, especially for this flight. Modifications include a more powerful motor and a 200-gallon tank with a hand pump for transferring gasoline from this tank to two 60-gallon gas tanks in the upper wing.

Although the airplane is fabric-covered, the fully-enclosed cabin is covered by aluminum sheet, with a windshield and real windows on its sides. The cabin is three and a half feet wide and about four feet high—sitting room, you'd guess, except it's mostly occupied by the big 200 gallon gas tank.

The presence of the tank on the right shrinks the space to only about two feet of width on the left, barely enough for a person to traverse. Nevertheless, this is the crew's new home, a home, so to speak, in the blue.

Behind the cabin itself, in the narrowing space near the tail, is a slim mattress, equipment and supplies. Wriggled onto the mattress is Art Walker, Mamer's crewmember. Younger than Mamer by eight years, he's a mechanic employee of Mamer's aviation company at the field. Although only 23, he was chosen for this venture by Mamer for his mechanical abilities, piloting skill, and general compatibility.

Walker checks his equipment—the blackboard and chalk, the five pairs of canvas gloves, the pair of grappling hooks, the hand tools, all the extra flashlights, the canned food and more. Is it all there? Is something missing? How will they know, until the last contact is complete? And that cut on his arm, from bumping into sharp metal on Tuesday—it's doing well, healing up fine.

The sun is low and sinking. Up front, Mamer peers down and aligns the plane's path to the sun's reflections off the rails of the Northern Pacific Railroad track.

To his left, the struts and wires connecting the upper and lower wings vibrate in the swift air like tuning forks, fabric flutters on the wings, each sound and sight as familiar as lies to a judge.

Because of its heavy load, the craft responds slowly as Nick nudges the stick. Apparently there's little headwind. Soon they'll have to work the hand pump, propelling gasoline from the big tank to the overhead tanks that feed the motor. But only in time will they discover the rate at which their gasoline is being consumed.

Mamer's thoughts turn to the five test flights he and Walker flew, two days ago on Tuesday. They proved the airplane's worth and capability, as well as demonstrating the skills of the two refueling planes that left Spokane yesterday to await their later contacts with the Sun God.

This route is the new airmail airway to Pasco, Washington. Airmail service arrived in Pasco in the mid-1920s. Varney Air Lines had signed on to what was known as Contract Air Mail (CAM) route 5, to supply planes and pilots to deliver the Post Office Department's new mail service. Using Pasco's original airfield east of the Northern Pacific rail yards, the service grew and expanded such that Varney eventually became part of United Airlines.

Without warning, the motor of the Sun God stumbles. It misfires, as though short of gas. Mamer franticly scans gauges and valves, searching for the cause. He yells at Art, who can't hear his call. The pilot does not find fault in the readings or settings. After a few anxious minutes, the motor picks up its monotonous rhythm and rumbles on as though the misfires had never occurred. Mamer makes a mental note to talk to Robin Harris of the Wright factory about this event. Later, shaking their heads in hesitant gratitude, the two men agree they don't understand what happened. Still, it might have ended their venture—even their lives.

At Umatilla, on the south bank of the Columbia River in Oregon, Mamer swings the Sun God west into the Columbia River gorge.

It's now past sunset, and both men strap on their parachutes. The dusky sky ahead glows a dull red, and below, a brown haze obscures the landscape. Forest fires have devastated this region of the Northwest. The fires to the west and north of the Sun God yield giant plumes of dark smoke. Despite difficulty in seeing, the men are able to sight through a single break in the gloom the dim outlines of Mount Rainier.

Lacking visibility, the pilot is occasionally forced to fly blind—on instruments alone—for minutes at a time. Mamer describes the occasional spectacle of fire: "Thick smoke...in dense clouds beneath us, pierced now and then with red tongues of flame."

Just before 9:00 p.m., the blurry lights of Portland appear through the haze. Nick does a quick mental calculation. "Our speed has been around 100 miles an hour," he says, boding well for their arrival early tomorrow at San Francisco.

2. THE FIRST REFUELING

The *Spokane Sun God* turns south. It seems to float effortlessly on the growl of its motor. The ghostly sparkles of Portland below and behind fade slowly into the night. By moonlight the craft glides over the broad and mostly clear Willamette valley. The pilots, exchanging places at the controls occasionally, follow the flashing beacons of Silverton and Brownsville to Eugene, where citizens are extinguishing their lights and anticipating their pillows.

While Mamer guides the craft, Art Walker lies on the mattress in the tail of the cabin. On the right side of the narrow space, close at hand, is the radio. An Atwater Kent receiver, it's big and heavy—probably 60 pounds—crammed with glass tubes, transformers, capacitors. It won't serve to communicate, but will enable the fliers to receive radio broadcasts.

Behind the radio are batteries. Back in Spokane, before Thursday's takeoff, the crew was advised to tune to local ABC and NBC broadcasts along their route. Hourly bulletins will tip them of bad weather ahead.

Walker, headphones plugged into the set and cocked over his ears, checks to see that the batteries are connected to the different voltage taps. He turns the set on. The tubes warm to a pink glow in the dim light. He refers to the paper that lists station frequencies for their route. He also glances at the log of the receiver, which lists the set's dial positions and frequencies that were documented before the flight.

They're over Oregon, so Art decides to try radio station KGW. Based on the log, the receiver's three knobs should be set around 64. He adjusts the knobs. All he hears is a whoosh of static. Lowering the tuning frequency, he recalls, requires turning the dials to higher numbers. He selects higher numbers, but receives no signal. Next he tries clicking the antenna coupling switch to different positions, but nothing changes.

On the suspicion there's a problem with lower frequencies, he dials to higher tuner frequencies, but still receives no broadcasts. Next he tries a different coil tap to adjust how the antenna is coupled. That doesn't help.

Nothing seems to work.

Following an hour or so of sweat, Walker wriggles from his cramped location and crouching, advances to the pilot's station. Despite everything he's tried, he tells Mamer, the set doesn't respond. The pilot understands, but mentions that it worked on the ground in Spokane. Art shrugs. Maybe something came loose or was displaced during takeoff. Mamer nods and says if they can't fix it, they'll transfer the radio to one of the supply planes to lighten their load a little.

Now they are over the Siskiyou Mountains, the east-west snow-capped peaks that intermingle with the Coastal Range to the west and the Cascades to the east. This represents some of the most difficult flying terrain in the United States. Icing conditions are a danger, summer or winter, daytime and especially at night. And it is midnight, with haze.

Mamer later writes, despite its height of over 14,000 feet, "It was then so hazy we could not see Mount Shasta." There's little time to gape, anyway.

As Nick flies the plane, he also exercises the auxiliary oiling system, and perhaps balances a cup of cold coffee on his lap. Art, on his knees at the 200-gallon tank, jogs the handle of the fuel pump back, forward, back, forward, back, forward—ounce by ounce impelling gasoline up the pipe to a tank in the wing overhead. As he wags the handle with one hand, he possibly grabs at a sack of peanuts with the other. Meanwhile the tail section of the cabin is collecting a few shards of cardboard, a wad of paper, and an empty food tin, evidence of living at 10,000 feet.

It's 1:15 Friday morning. The Sun God passes over Red Bluff, California, and the two men agree to exchange piloting duty. This time they squeeze to pass each other in the gap between the side of the cabin and the gas tank, and become jammed.

Neither man can move. The aircraft is stable, purring along in level flight, but without a pilot. What now?

They attempt to separate by turning, squeezing and pushing on each other's bodies. After moments of anxiety, shallow breaths and tussle, they manage to part, Art to the front, Nick to the rear. Breathing heavily, Art tumbles to the controls, grasps and sinks into the seat. They'll traverse the passageway singly from now on.

Around two a.m., Mamer resumes his seat at the controls, this time avoiding the jostle with Walker. They are flying at 4,000 feet. A slow right turn brings the lights of San Francisco and the expanse of San Francisco Bay into view ahead.

Before the flight, Texaco had arranged for Aviation Accessories Corporation of San Francisco to supply an experienced crew to refuel the Sun God. Pilot Donald Templeman and hoseman James M. Warner wait at Mills Field, the site of present-day International Airport of San Francisco. It is close to three o'clock in the morning. Their roomy and well-equipped Travel Air 6000 monoplane, named *Californian,* sits nearby, awaiting its refueling duty.

Although Templeman's small crew at Mills Field searches the air, darkness and mist prevent them from spotting the red airplane as it arrives. Overhead, as Nick Mamer flies lazy circles over the Bay, he recollects the first appearance of the plane he's now flying, the *Spokane Sun God.*

At 9:45 a.m. the previous Monday the special Buhl CA-6 appeared in the eastern sky near Spokane with the Buhl company's pilot, R. M. Wilson, at the controls. It powered smoothly to a landing at Felts Field and touched down in a graceful three-pointer.

When the Buhl drew to the flight line, a small crowd of spectators applauded. Mamer himself could hardly wait for the propeller to stop spinning. First out of the cabin was pilot Wilson, followed by Robin Harris of the Wright engine factory. They were all smiles as Nick ducked in, looked around, emerged from the cabin and declared, "It's a wonderful job...I'm sure of success after looking it over."

The success Mamer imagined that day was to be the culmination of a plan. Its idea originated with Major Clarence M. Young, aeronautical director of the U.S. Department of Commerce. The plan called for a coast-to-coast nonstop flight fueled in air by refueling aircraft. The planned flight, the first ever attempted, was enthusiastically backed by a group of thirty Spokane businessmen headed by Victor Dessert. The group's nucleus derived from the great success, two years earlier, of the National Air Derby & Races their association had sponsored.

Over the past few months Nick Mamer had been managing the flight of his new, 14-place Ford Trimotor about the country. As part of what was called the Mamer-Ford Tour, the Mamer Air Service's tri-motor flew more than 18,000 miles, appeared in more than thirty-six cities across the country and had made more than 1,500 landings. It was no surprise, then, that at the group's organizing session at Dessert's hotel in downtown Spokane, Nick Mamer was the unanimous choice as the pilot to execute the transcontinental attempt.

According to Nick, the plan had "aroused much interest over the country," which prompted Texaco and other companies to join the effort. Herbert

Hughes, vice-president of Buhl Aircraft Company, sent a telegram saying the company would supply a new Buhl sedan of the latest type, equipped with a 300-horsepower J-6 Whirlwind engine for the attempt at a record.

Mamer announced to the supporters that Art Walker would be his choice for co-pilot. Walker, eight years younger, had co-piloted the Ford Trimotor on the Mamer-Ford Tour. He had also spent several weeks at the Ford airplane factory in Dearborn, Michigan, studying Wright Whirlwind motors and learning about their features and repair. Nick added he thought the best means for carrying out Major Young's idea was to turn the coast-to-coast flight into a round trip.

At the next Wednesday's meeting of the supporters, Nick reported a second telegram. It said that if the factory could "obtain prompt delivery" of the improved Wright motor, the Buhl company would deliver a new CA-6 for his use, equipped with a 200-gallon fuselage tank, "in eight days."

It seemed to Nick he'd come a long way in a very short time. This plan for record-setting was certainly a change from a couple of years ago, when he'd taken on the role of winged delivery man.

The winter had been unusually cold in the Northwest. Snow came often and grew deep in the wrinkles of the Clearwater Mountains of Idaho. The village of Orofino became snowbound. With its roads impassable, the transport of goods stopped. Citizens of Orofino received no mail and no supplies.

Food was still available, but they'd run out of bread. Compounding the lack of bread was a lack of yeast. No one seemed to have anticipated that yeast might be handy when there was no more bread. Over the telephone, someone complained to a friend in Spokane. "We aren't starving," the complainer said, "but we do need yeast mighty badly,"

The word spread.

The next morning, an airplane zoomed over Orofino. It swept over downtown, right down the main street. Dangling from the plane was a rope, and at its end, a box. At the precise right moment, the box dropped. It struck in the depths of a snowdrift, but was hurriedly rescued by townspeople. Nick Mamer had delivered a box of yeast cakes and ended Orofino's bread famine.

Two hours after the arrival of the Sun God over Mills Field, in the dim light of dawn, Mamer guides the craft lower through the mist. Over the outer perimeter he takes the plane on a low trajectory. As the plane passes a hangar, Art tosses a packet over the side, a message for Templeman's ground crew. It requests 250 gallons of gasoline for the Sun God's flight to Cheyenne, Wyoming, the next-scheduled refueling location.

A bit later, at about 5:30, flying over Dumbarton bridge, Nick sights the *Californian* at altitude, a mile or so away. Good, he thinks, they've joined us over the pre-arranged landmark. In the aft section of the cabin, Art Walker yanks on his helmet, thrusts his hands into his canvas gloves and lowers his goggles. Crouching, he moves forward to the opening in the top of the Sun God's fuselage and peers out.

Nick, at the controls, greets the newcomer at about 4,000 feet with a waggle of the Sun God's wings, and takes the craft lower. Now, he wonders, will they set a good course?

Walker stands up in the opening in the fuselage, next to the 200-gallon tank, with his head, shoulders and one arm outside in the 80-miles-per-hour wind. He waves at hoseman Jim Warner, although the monoplane is probably too far away for the hose-handler to see him.

Templeman guides the *Californian* on a straight and level course at about 80 miles an hour. With his hand nudging the throttle, Nick guides the Sun God toward the monoplane at a slightly-faster speed. The Sun God, below and well to the right of the supply plane, slowly closes on it. With fine adjustments, Nick prods the Buhl up, below and behind, yet close to the other airplane. Reducing throttle, Nick slows to match the speed of the Californian.

Meanwhile Warner feeds line and hose out of the right side of the supply plane. The fifty-foot, weighted hose drops to within the reach of Art Walker, who grasps the nozzle and shoves it into the Sun God's big tank. The *Californian* leading, the planes are now separated by about thirty feet.

Art yells "Okay" at Mamer and signals Warner by waving his arm. Warner opens the valve that sends gasoline gushing down to the Sun God.

The refueling process is a tense dance between the two aircraft. Not only do the pilots need to maintain their critical positions despite gusts and air turbulence, they must compensate for weight changes. As gasoline is transferred, the supply plane becomes lighter and the Sun God grows heavier. If either airplane changes its position relative to the other airplane, the hose may either be sliced in two by the Sun God's propeller, or the nozzle-end may be jerked from the Sun God's tank. Either way, gasoline sprays around the Sun God, and may be ignited by sparks or the high temperature exhausts of the Sun God's motor.

Engrossed, Nick squints, his focus shifting, first to the airplane above, second to the wavering hose, then back. Muscles tighten, nerves buzz.

Minutes later, Nick's concentration and skill pay off when Warner signals that their supply tank is empty. He retracts the hose.

Nick breathes easier as he watches the *Californian* slip away for its return to Mills Field. Such has been his concentration that he has no idea how long the transfer took.

Later, the supply plane appears again over Dumbarton bridge, and again, a successful catch and drain is made by Warner and Walker. The crews now estimate that a total of about 175 gallons has gone into the Sun God's tank. Ten gallons of oil are also transferred.

Later, a third refueling is attempted. "[T]he hose choked," a spokesman for Aviation Accessories later explained. Almost no gas is transferred. "The hose had lain out in the weather for a week...Examination revealed corrosion... probably a result of gasoline left in the hose after the test."

Because of this difficulty, and the time the refueling has taken—it is now near 7:30 a.m.— Mamer tells Art to break the connection. Nick banks the Sun God away, abandoning the contact. The Sun God heads eastward, toward the high Sierras.

PART II

TRANSCONTINENTAL

3. CLIMBING THE SIERRAS

The Sun God had circled the 150-acre cow-pasture known as Mills Field in the dark for hours. When not at the controls each man had retreated to the mattress at the rear of the cabin to catch a little sleep, but the wariness, the roar of the motor and the vibrations, all interfered.

Now, 7:30 a.m. on Friday, August 16, with the sun shining brightly, they rechecked everything. The weather forecast for Oakland and vicinity had predicted fair and mild, with coastal fog, but the pilots did not notice any fog over the bay. The schedule for today, although not simple, was straightforward. From here over San Francisco bay, they would begin the long eastward segment to New York City, 2,665 miles distant.

The plan was to fly the same route flown by airmail pilots. The Transcontinental Airmail Route had been established four years earlier by the Post Office Department. Although not a 'great circle,' or shortest route, it comprised a sequence of airfields and connecting courses, or directions, that led from San Francisco to an airfield outside Newark, New Jersey. It was designed to aid pilots of the new 'airmail' service flying the mail from New York to San Francisco. The courses, called 'airways,' connected an airfield with a subsequent airfield, all the way across the country.

Before the establishment of the airway system, letters sent via so-called 'airmail' hopscotched their way across the country. By daylight and in good weather, airmail pilots flew them. But at dusk the pilots landed and transferred the mail to a steam train that sped them through the night toward their destination. After dawn another rendezvous took place. The mail was taken from railcar and loaded onto another airmail plane. The pilot of that plane flew the next leg, and so on. This hybrid method avoided the very real hazards of attempting to transport the mail in the air at night. And it succeeded in speeding the mail coast-to-coast in an hour short of three and a half days, a record for 1922.

Prior to this, statistics suggested airmail pilots had a one in ten chance of dying while attempting to satisfy the postal service's airmail initiative. They'd become lost in darkness or bad weather, run out of fuel, and crash. Emergency landings, often with injuries, damage to the brittle aircraft of the time and lengthy delays in mail delivery, were common. A better, safer way was needed, a system for secure flying at night and in bad weather.

Beginning in 1923, the government developed an array of airways defining a route across the country. Colored maps were printed on which each airway was indicated by a dashed line. Alongside the line was its associated magnetic compass heading. Beacons, spaced 15 to 25 miles apart were constructed, with flashes and brightness enough to aid night-flying pilots to navigate from airfield to airfield. When finally completed, it allowed airmail pilots—in good weather—to fly the complete distance across the country. This shortened the time for coast-to-coast airmail to arrive at about 33 hours, a new record.

Now, over San Francisco Bay, Nick advances the throttle that sends the Sun God away from Mills Field and the Dumbarton Bridge. With the bay and the city fading behind them and sunlight glinting off the whirling propeller, Nick smoothes the fold in Air Navigation Map No. 35, the map he'll depend upon for navigation.

Art Walker is again busy with the hand pump, transferring some of the new supply of gasoline from the big tank in the cabin to a nearly-empty overhead wing tank. Nick has selected the other overhead tank by operating a valve that directs fuel to the Wright motor by gravity.

The map is labeled "RENO, NEV. TO SAN FRANCISCO, CALIF." With his finger, Nick traces the dashed line from the left, going in the opposite direction. This line represents the 'airway,' the path he would try to follow to Reno, 185 miles distant, on a magnetic heading of 33 degrees, 08 minutes.

Nick is aware they'd departed San Francisco with less than the full load of gasoline that Templeman, the pilot of the refueling airplane out of Mills field, had on board. But ahead are the Rockies, the Sierra Nevada range nearest. The map's gradations of color from pale green to rusty orange illustrate changes in elevation from sea level to more than 10,000 feet, a steep rise.

From years of mountain flying in the Northwest, Nick knows that climbing to the height needed to clear the mountains may be difficult if the Sun God carries full wing tanks and 200 gallons in the big tank in the cabin. Although the refueling crew probably did not understand, Mamer saw the Sun God facing a most demanding leg ahead, where too much gas might be as much of a hazard as too little gas. He therefore feels the decision to cut away early from Templeman, with only about 180 gallons of fresh fuel on board may be a wise action considering the timing and the circumstances. Though he sees no need to worry Art about it, he wonders if today's progress may be more difficult than had been planned, back in Spokane.

The Sun God crosses over Richmond, California and Nick sets the thirty-three degree course on the compass dial. Banking slightly, he turns the airplane to that number. It feels good to be underway, to fly a course, an airway, after those many hours circling the bay area.

Nick eases the stick back. As the craft noses up, he focuses on the vertical speed dial and the airspeed. Adding an increment of power with the throttle and glancing below, he observes an industrial area where smoke pours from several factory smokestacks. The view strikes him as peculiar—it brings to mind his studies at Princeton's School of Military Aeronautics back in 1918. In a class titled "Cross-Country and General Flying," the instructor had forcefully emphasized the importance to pilots of scrutinizing events below, on the ground over which their aircraft passed. From these observations, he stressed, pilots could learn facts that would aid them in arriving safely at their destination. Conversely, a failure to account for telltale clues on the ground might result in a dangerous outcome.

The peculiarity Nick noted below was that the smoke from the smokestacks appeared to drift westward. Was this only a local phenomenon? He wondered.

At this time, however, he needed to consider their climb rate, speed, and fuel usage. Map No. 35 showed Truckee, California, 160 miles ahead. Dozens of peaks near Truckee jutted near 11,000 feet into the air. He'd need to juggle the Sun God's airspeed and rate of climb over the 160 miles to assure they'd gain enough altitude to surmount this mountain range. At the same time, he wanted to avoid using too much fuel. It's a tricky balance, as he had learned and experienced over the past decade. *If you just throttle up to attain a rapid climb rate, you might reach the required altitude in advance of the need. But that costs extra fuel, or a slower speed—it's not smart piloting. On the other hand, if you choose a climb rate that's too low, you can go faster, but you may not have the required altitude when you need it. Try for a balanced approach between climb rate, throttle setting and airspeed that's efficient, but that assures you of a safe flight.*

Winds aloft shift airplanes from their intended course, despite a pilot's accuracy in steering his craft. The only way to determine the plane's adherence to a planned course is to see if observed landmarks are where the map indicates they should be. But Air Navigation Map No. 35 shows few landmarks ahead. Other than the tracks of the Oakland, Antioch and Eastern Railway and a tiny hamlet called Montezuma, the delta between San Francisco and Sacramento holds no easy-to-recognize landmarks. Navigation by landmarks is impossible without landmarks, so Nick must wait to see how close they are to maintaining the thirty-three-degree course to Truckee. When Sacramento comes into view, he'll be able to ascertain any off-course drift.

Later, with Art at the controls, Nick puts pencil to paper. He figures time and distance, and the rate at which their load of fuel is decreasing. With Salt Lake City 430 miles beyond Reno, and Cheyenne another 380 miles farther, it's vital to see if their supply of fuel is adequate, with a safety margin, to take them to Cheyenne where another refueling is planned.

Over Sacramento, Nick hastily writes down the figures. As they pass over the prison city of Folsom, he notes the elapsed time and the distance they'd flown from San Francisco. He purses his lips.

Pilots usually enjoy a tailwind when eastbound out of San Francisco. Now it has become obvious they were bucking a substantial headwind, exactly what he'd feared when he'd earlier observed the drift of smoke over Richmond. It looks like the day's planned trek of almost 1,000 miles might be impossible with the gasoline they have left in the big tank and the two wing tanks.

Back at San Francisco, Art Walker worked feverishly during the refueling operations. He'd stood in the specially-framed opening in the top of the Sun God's cabin with his head, arms and shoulders outside. Despite the push of high-speed air, he'd wrestled the dangling refueling nozzle from the *Californian* inside and kept the flailing hose from pulling out of the Sun God's filler hole during each refueling operation.

Although the fliers are now confined inside a cramped cabin only about four and a half feet high, Walker had at least had a brief opportunity to stretch his body and exert his leg, arm and other muscles. Nick, on the other hand, had not had any such exercise. He had been hunched over the controls much of the time since he and Art had left Spokane. It's not difficult to understand how numb one's buttocks became and how achy one feels after hours behind the stick.

It is nevertheless becoming obvious that both men are starting to suffer aches and stiffness from hours squeezed into tight, somewhat uncomfortable positions.

An additional danger looms: noise. The big 9-cylinder Whirlwind motor is less than a yard in front of the aircraft's controls. Its flaming exhausts are not muffled, so they roar loudly, monotonously and continuously. It's now known that this unrelieved assault on one's hearing is deleterious. At minimum it causes hearing loss. Ringing may occur. It creates physical and psychological stress and contributes to errors and potential injury. Although the extreme racket means the fliers have to shout to communicate, the men try hard to ignore this pernicious and possibly injurious, hazard.

Now, south of their line of travel, Lake Tahoe shimmers into view, its great depth lost in the reflection of the late-morning sun.

Nick selects the next map, No. 34, to view the airway and courses they'll take from Reno to Elko, Nevada. From Elko, Cheyenne is 584 miles distant. There, at the Cheyenne airfield, the Buhl refueling plane piloted by R. M. Wilson awaits the Sun God, as earlier arranged by Spokane's Derby committee.

After passing over Reno, where the Truckee River meanders lazily through the squares of the small mountain town, Nick swings the Sun God to the right, to the new course of forty-seven and-a-half degrees that takes them toward remote Elko, an oasis in the heart of Nevada's alkali flats. But scribbles on the scratch pad next to him prove all is not evolving according to plan. Enough elapsed time and distance numbers have now been accumulated to prove the rate at which the Sun God's fuel is being consumed. The indications are unmistakable: the Sun God's fuel will not allow them to reach the refueling contact at Cheyenne, Wyoming.

4. Running on Empty

A big sign, U. S. AIR MAIL ELKO NEV, black paint on a white background, looms below. Nick banks the Buhl and side-slips to lose altitude. The scrub of pale desert vegetation comes rushing up to meet the Sun God as Nick levels out.

Nick reduces the Whirlwind's power and at a few hundred feet above ground, the airplane glides, its nose aimed skillfully at the airfield dead ahead. Shimmering heat waves blur the men's vision of the dusty landing strip and hangar. A few years earlier, this field had been the base for the first scheduled airmail service, so Nick is confident it's still manned.

Now's the time Nick's days with Federated Flyers pay off.

Clarence Hinck, a Minneapolis business man, was smart when the Armistice was signed. World War I airplanes became surplus, and their price plummeted. Hinck bought 18 surplus Curtiss Jennys (JN-4s) from Aero Mechanics School in St. Paul. They came in crates, but his crew soon had them assembled and flyable. Hinck then hired itinerant pilots to perform. He had in mind making money with them as a traveling aerial circus, but it didn't catch on at first. Nevertheless the outfit, called Federated Fliers, kept at it.

Typically, a Federated Fliers' show began with a series of motorcycle races, often including the pilots as contestants. Then the boys began their JN-4 stunts, swooping low over the crowds doing rolls, loops and other tricks. Finally they succeeded and made a name for themselves performing at county fairs around Minnesota, and elsewhere in the Northwest.

Following his discharge from the Army in 1919, Nick Mamer joined this diverse group of experienced fliers known for their barnstorming stunts and aerobatics.

The main hangar with the big sign U. S. AIR MAIL ELKO NEV appears ahead and a dangerous few feet below. Nick levels the Sun God and brings the craft low over its roof. The roar of the Whirlwind motor easily rattles the hangar's rafters, and workers quickly pour outside.

As he gains altitude for a second pass over the hangar, Nick smiles a barn-stormer's smile, and Walker makes ready with a weighted packet. On the second pass, Art tosses the packet over the side. It flutters to the field and lands in a cloud of yellow-tinged dust.

Nick makes another low pass over the field to make sure the workers below retrieve the packet. As he thrusts the throttle forward and climbs out toward the east, both pilots wave at the men below, who return their waves.

Within a short time, at Derby Association headquarters in Spokane, Washington, a telegram arrives from the Elko airport. It says the Sun God has dropped a note. The note says the Sun God will run out of gas before reaching Cheyenne. Further, it says Mamer wants Bob Wilson, who is waiting at Chey-enne, to hurry his Buhl refueling plane *west* to the Rock Springs, Wyoming airfield, where they'll meet for a refueling contact to enable the Sun God to reach Cheyenne.

A message conveying the urgency is quickly relayed by wire to Wilson at Cheyenne, and he hastily takes off with hoseman Al Coppula heading for Rock Springs.

It's 1:15 p.m. (Friday).

The Sun God now begins climbing. Nick, once more navigating, consults Air Navigation Map No. 33, which gives a magnetic compass course of 72 degrees 39 minutes to Salt Lake City, 195 miles distant. They'll again have to climb to about 10,000 feet to clear the mountains ahead.

The Buhl Company's specifications for the CA-6 Airsedan with the Wright Whirlwind motor give its cruising airspeed as 115 miles-per-hour. But the worrisome thing now is ground speed—the distance actually traversed in the time taken to span it. From long experience on cross-country flights, Nick knows how a headwind can rob you of ground speed.

The airspeed indicator on the instrument panel registers the airplane's progress *through the air*. But with a headwind, air moves opposite the airplane's progress, so the indicator fails to show the true speed over the ground. Mamer calculates that the Sun God has so far averaged much less than 115 miles-per-hour. Partly that's due to the speed lost climbing to achieve the height needed to pass over the Sierra Nevada Range and, more generally, the Rocky Mountains. The other reason is the wind, which apparently opposed them most of the time. Now he scratches his head wondering if they'll even make Rock Springs, Wyoming by dark.

Off to the left, the twin tracks of the Western Pacific and Southern Pacific railroads snake between the mountains of the East Humboldt Range, where

Mt. Bonpland (now called Hole in the Mountain Peak) pierces the sky at over 11,300 feet. As they pass near the remains of the town of Tobar, they begin to parallel the Victory Highway stretching toward the tiny settlement of Shafter. Wendover and the Great Salt Lake Desert lie ahead.

With the Western Pacific Railroad and Victory Highway now on their right, they fly over the south end of the Great Salt Lake and on over Salt Lake City. Lengthening shadows below forecast the swift approach of night on the desert—and sharpen the crew's unease.

Across the Wasatch Mountains, they set a course of 41 degrees 30 minutes based on the airway of Air Navigation Map No. 14.

With the sun sinking in the west, they leave Utah and pass south of the Wyoming town of Evanston, and shortly, Fort Bridger. Nick switches the navigation lights on and checks that all the fuel has been pumped to the wing tanks. Here the Sun God accommodates a slight realignment of the airway that skirts the high peaks of the Uinta Mountains to the south.

Nick squints hard through the failing daylight to identify the reflections of the Green River flowing south below. Slight pinpoints of light in the distance—mere twinkles—suggest they may be closing on their destination. The men glance anxiously at the wing tank fuel gauges, the floats of which now sink toward 'empty.'

Darkness converges. At the Rock Springs airfield, 6,760-ft. elevation, floodlights come on. The airport is five miles north of the small town of Rock Springs, Wyoming, on flat acreage where sagebrush has been cleared to provide useable landing area. The wind sock on top of the hangar flaps briskly at changing angles, suggesting unstable, gusty winds.

A restless group has gathered between the hangar and the parked airplanes of Bob Wilson and Vern Bookwalter. Those two pilots talk, amble about, then search the sky. Others of the group converse on diverse topics, stop, grow silent and scan the western sky.

On a cage atop the airport's hangar, an employee mans a powerful electric-arc searchlight. Swinging it through an elevated, curved path centered on the western vista, he searches for the speck of an airplane.

The western sky, dullish red in a day-ending sigh, remains empty.

A hushed but audible "Look!" and "There!" rises from the group. The fleck in the west slowly grows into a red biplane. The pilots and the group gab excitedly. By the time the man aiming the arc-light finds the incoming aircraft, the circled red "Texaco" stars on the underside of the *Spokane Sun God's* wings are visible.

As he trots to the Buhl aircraft, Wilson hails hoseman Al Coppula. Coppula begins pulling the propeller through by hand. Soon, with a rush of blue smoke from its exhaust and a surge of wind from its prop, the airplane shakes a little, as though in anticipation.

 Overhead, and descending from its cruise level, the Sun God approaches. Nick banks the plane, levels out a few hundred feet above the edge of the airfield and begins a circle. Eagerly searching, Nick and Art identify the large winged icon and horizontal striping of the Rock Springs hangar in the illumination of the floodlights. The painted image with a "U.S." centered between wings, identifies the field as an official stop for the transcontinental Airmail Service between Cheyenne and Salt Lake City. The fliers in the Sun God acknowledge their success in reaching Rock Springs, glimpse the refueling airplanes, and make quick note of the flapping wind sock, also distinct in the field's floodlights.

Onlookers wave at the Sun God. They shut their eyes and turn away from a giant cloud of grit ballooning behind the Buhl as Wilson taxies onto the field. Well out on the field, he brakes and swings the craft into the wind. As he pauses to run the propeller up, a ragged cloud of dirt behind the plane races across the field and disappears into the blackness at its edge. Less than two minutes later, the Buhl is airborne, its navigation lights fading from the view of the workers below.

Despite the fuel gauges' display of a dwindling supply of gasoline, Nick has shown, and continues to exercise, patience. At reduced throttle, he banks shallowly in a large circle around the airfield awaiting Wilson's arrival at altitude.

In the planning days back in Spokane, Nick and the refueling pilots had agreed to cruise at about 8,000 feet at Cheyenne—elevation, 6,060-ft—for the refueling of the Sun God. No plans had been drawn for Rock Springs, 700 feet higher and 230 miles distant from Cheyenne. Nor had anyone seriously considered refueling at night. Conscious of the delay and of the many difficulties attending refueling in the dark, Nick nevertheless confidently advances the throttle to follow Wilson's Buhl to their rendezvous.

In the rear of the cabin, Art Walker wipes his goggles and selects a pair of gloves. Nick told him they'd follow Wilson with the expectation that the other pilot would level out at a height where the air was smoothest. Art adjusts the goggles on his cap and shoots a glance up at the refueling hole in the top of the cabin. He has no idea how he'll see to find and grab a thrashing fueling hose in the black of night.

The two aircraft bounce erratically in the unstable air. The blackness of the desert sky, contrasting strongly with the floodlit airfield below, causes Nick difficulty in sighting Wilson's navigation lights. At times he loses sight of the lights and has to back away until he finds them again. Despite this, he keeps his plane a hundred or so feet behind and below Wilson's Buhl.

In the Buhl, Wilson is fighting his own battle. The extra load of 105 gallons (660 pounds) of gasoline in the refueling tank makes gaining altitude extremely tricky, as the Buhl threatens to stall in the thin air over Rock Springs. Finally he manages to level out close to 8,000-ft. altitude.

The Sun God, cruising to the right of Wilson but now thirty feet lower and fifty feet behind, also levels out. At an airspeed of not quite 80 miles per hour, Nick struggles to preserve these distances to the Buhl as Art positions himself in the opening in the top of the Sun God.

"I see 'em," Art shouts over the rushing air and the roar of the motor, but Nick can't hear him.

Shortly the hose tumbles out of Al Coppula's hands. Its nozzle, weighted by lead, pitches down and to the right of the Buhl. As Al feeds more of it out from inside the Buhl, the hose, driven by the wind, flails wildly, up, down and from side to side. In a few moments, most of the fifty feet of the fuel hose waves and whips freely in the air. Wilson, perhaps the most-skilled pilot at Buhl Aircraft Co., contends with the rough air, trying for a level and steady speed.

To Walker, squinting into the night sky from the Sun God, the hose is invisible. All he can make out is an occasional spark that seems to wobble across his vision. The spark looks to him like a star, yet it flicks and moves, unlike a star. Inside the Sun God's cabin, Nick stares intently at the faint exhaust flames from the Buhl's motor, and yaws his craft leftward. As adroitly as the bumpy air permits, he moves the Sun God ever closer to the refueling plane.

Coppula, stretching against the life belt that attaches him to the cabin floor of the Buhl, leans far out of the doorway. (The door had earlier been removed.) Although he can easily see the Sun God, he strains to discern Walker in the dark.

By a miracle that can never be explained, Walker somehow catches the hose. It is then that he spots the 'star,' a lit flashlight that Coppula has taped to the end of the hose. Gripping it with hands and underarm, he attaches its copper wire to the Sun God's ground wire. This is necessary to forestall the buildup of static electricity, and possible sparking. He thrusts the hose's nozzle into the filler hole in the Sun God's tank, and grabs a lit flashlight. Popping back out the refueling opening into the swift night air, he waves frantically with the flashlight, hoping Coppula understands the signal to start the flow of gasoline. At the same time, he screams to Nick, saying he's captured the hose.

Coppula reaches for the handle of the valve that allows gasoline to stream into the refueling hose and swings it open. He can almost hear the downward gush of fluid as gas from the Buhl's refueling tank streams by gravity into the Sun God's tank.

The pilots of the two aircraft are now fearful. They're anxiously aware that a sudden movement—for example, a drop or bounce in the unstable air over Rock Springs—may cause Walker, who's entangled in his grasp of the hose, to be yanked out of the Sun God and into the night. This would be followed by the freeing of the hose and a cloaking of the aircraft in a shower of gasoline. If gasoline vapor were to contact the hot exhaust of the Sun God's engine, a giant ball of flame engulfing both planes is a real possibility.

As gasoline flows through the hose to the Sun God, without warning Art Walker is abruptly inundated. Liquid slams into his face and over his shoulders. His goggles smear before he can move. He can't see what happened. But the smell identifies: it's gasoline!

He ducks, but too late, and yells in panic at Nick.

Nick, as yet unsure of the problem, maintains the Sun God's position. When he smells the telltale odor he steers the Sun God away. Realizing the possibility of fire, he drops the nose, and the Sun God plunges downward and away from the Buhl.

Walker, still gripping some hose, is stunned. What happened? He ducks inside the cabin, discards his goggles and struggles to shuck his saturated jacket. He and Nick scream back and forth trying to understand what occurred.

Walker senses that the hose he holds is not attached. He tugs the piece that leads outside, and pulls a few feet of it inside. Frayed threads at the ragged end show that the hose has separated at an apparent weakness.

Coppula, in the Buhl, also sees that the hose has come apart. He closes the valve as quickly as possible and yells an explanation at Wilson, who turns the Buhl left, away from the Sun God. After some confusing moments, Coppula retrieves the remainder of the hose and the men realize they'll have to land for repairs.

It seems a miracle. Despite the nearness of the hot exhausts of the Sun God's motor, gasoline spurting from the break had not caught fire.

Circling the Sun God about a thousand feet above Rock Springs, Nick watches the Buhl aircraft's silhouette descend toward the floodlit airfield and land safely. Then he glances at the cabin tank's fuel gauge. It looks about the same as it looked before the contact with the Buhl.

On Art Walker's fuel-soaked advice, Nick begins to descend. He will guide the Sun God low over the Rock Springs airfield so that Art can toss the remains of the hose, with its nozzle, attached lead weight, wire, and flashlight out of the Sun God onto the ground. They'll also drop messages instructing Wilson to use what he can to repair the hose as quickly as possible.

The dropped messages include urgent scribbles making plain that for lack of gasoline, the Sun God is now perilously close to landing.

5. Severed Connections

Update: It's the middle of the night at the Rock Springs, Wyoming, airfield where the refueling planes of Bob Wilson and Vern Bookwalter have converged. Overhead, the Sun God is running out of gas. Wilson and Coppula attempted to refuel the Sun God but failed when the hose came apart. Mamer flew low over the airfield and Walker tossed the separated end with the nozzle onto the field. Also dropped were messages urging Wilson to fix the hose so the Sun God could be refueled. Coppula, a trained mechanic, has managed to join the nozzle, weights and flashlight onto the remaining length of refueling hose. He says it 'will do the job.' With the shortened but functional hose and Wilson piloting, the Buhl takes to the air to refuel the Sun God.

At the controls of the Buhl, Wilson bobs uncomfortably in his seat. On the deck behind him, Coppula has anchored his lifeline—the device that permits him to lean far out the opening in the side of the Buhl without falling. At this moment, however, he simply holds down the fuel hose to prevent it from slipping out.

Flying slow, large circles over the 6,760-ft. elevation of the airfield, Nick switches his attention between the diminishing level of gas in the wing tank and the activity below on the field. Even with judicious adjusting of the fuel and mixture, each quarter-hour of flying sees gallons of precious gasoline disappear. The wait is the most nerve-wracking event the crew has yet experienced.

The inky night air is now chilled, and the Buhl's rate of climb at the thin altitudes over Rock Springs is embarrassingly slow. Turbulence makes it even less comfortable—and more worrying for the success of this refueling contact. After what seems an interminable wedge of time, Wilson's Buhl surpasses the Sun God's altitude. Wilson hopes he'll encounter calmer air before he reaches the Buhl's altitude ceiling, not long from now.

Behind the Sun God's windshield, Mamer stares into the blackness at the faint navigation lights of the Buhl, then glances again at the fuel gauge. The Whirlwind motor drones steadily. With his left hand, Mamer nudges the throttle, adjusting his speed to stay with Wilson, yet always seeking the lowest power setting. Where, he wonders, will Wilson level out?

Finally, Wilson retards his throttle and brings the Buhl to level flight. He hollers at Coppula that this is the calmest air they'll find.

Mamer, staring out and up, spies the orange glow of the Buhl's exhaust against the black sky. Has Wilson leveled? Yes, so he maneuvers the Sun God, seeking to close while staying twenty to thirty feet below the Buhl. Coppula is now dimly visible dangling out of the Buhl's open doorway.

Wilson, unable to see the Sun God, feathers the controls to maintain straight, level flight, despite the lumpy air. Coppula begins feeding the hose toward the Sun God. As though alive, the hose dances a snaky whirl in the turbulence below the Buhl. He slows its downward slither as the Sun God appears to bolt toward the Buhl.

Walker can see the Buhl above, but doesn't see the hose until the glow of the attached flashlight happens to angle perfectly. It appears not more than a flickering spark against the blackness. Straining outward over the Sun God's wing against the force of the wind, he grasps, but catches only air. Again and again, he bends and snatches with fingers spread but fails to capture the hose.

Mamer, preserving the Sun God's position relative to the Buhl, is too engrossed with flying to notice Walker's struggle behind him. But he counts the seconds, knowing that an extra minute at this close alignment could result in a deadly crash into the other plane.

Exclaiming aloud, Walker finally traps the hose under an arm, where it wriggles like a greased snake. He crouches inside, and while clutching the hose with desperate strength, connects the grounding wire and plunges the nozzle into the tank. With one hand grasping the hose, he thrusts his arm out the opening and waves his flashlight at the Buhl.

Coppula, gripping the hose with both hands, senses that Walker has control. He prays that the planes stay locked in close, parallel flight. Noting Walker's signal, he flips the valve handle. As he again clasps the hose in both hands, gasoline flushes down to the Sun God.

Walker, now inhaling a full whiff of the pungent vapor, smiles. When the splashing inside the tank ceases, he removes the hose and tosses it over the side. The nozzle bounces off the wing.

Coppula has shut the valve. Noting the wild flailing of the hose, he quickly pulls it to him, hand over hand, coiling it onto the Buhl's deck. When the Sun God drops away to the right, Coppula signals Wilson, who banks off and begins his descent to the airfield.

Walker now works the wobble pump, sending gas to the near-empty wing tank. Working the pump in the cramped cabin is exhausting, although Mamer later remarks that during the planning phase he thought the exercise would "keep us limbered up during the flight."

Shouting back and forth as Walker pumps, he and Mamer debate and then agree: the hose is far too difficult to see and capture in the dark, endangering the men and the flight. Mamer drops the Sun God to a few hundred feet and guides it over the hangar. As the plane passes overhead, Walker tosses a bag onto the field. It contains three flashlights and a note telling Coppula to attach them to the hose.

Coppula and Wilson had already discarded their parachutes to lessen the weight, but the limited power of the Buhl in the thin air means they can load only a reduced amount of gasoline into the Buhl's 150-gallon refueling tank. Thus, despite the reduced weight, the climb to the altitude needed for refueling seems agonizingly slow.

With four flashlights now lit and taped to the hose, Wilson commences a third refueling run. The improved visibility of the four flashlights makes Walker's capture earlier and easier. The connection is successful, and more gas is transferred to the Sun God.

Night refueling is not simply unexpected, it is difficult and fraught with danger for both aircraft crews. Communicating with the ground and with the refueling crew, by dropped notes, hand signals, or by messages scratched on board, adds complexity to every aspect of the operation. The added flashlights help Walker find the waggling nozzle, but catching and securing the hose remains a significant trick.

The Buhl makes more refueling flights that night. The actual number is uncertain; various numbers are reported (see Notes). What is certain is the toll these repeated fuelings take on the participants, especially Walker and Mamer, now well into their third day aboard the Sun God.

As midnight passes with replenishment of the Sun God's gas supply, the calendar turns to Saturday, August 17. The Sun God has now been airborne for more than fifty-four hours.

Despite the hour, the Rock Springs searchlight operator continues to beam his light on the drama above the airport. During one refueling, the beam is angled such that the arc's intense light, reflected by the Buhl's propeller, flashes before Mamer's eyes, causing him momentary blindness. The airplanes close, and the refueling hose contacts the Sun God's propeller, slicing it in two.

Before Walker can react, the severed lower section slaps backward around him and the remaining section dangling from above sprays him with gasoline. Once again, a shower of fuel engulfs the Sun God. And Walker is awash in gas!

Coppula, fortunately realizes what's happened and flips the release valve off. But Walker is already drenched. Mamer, alerted to the danger, quickly steers away. Had the spreading cloud of gasoline vapor contacted the extremely hot exhaust surfaces of the Sun God's motor, a huge ball of fire might have engulfed the planes. Fortunately, that doesn't happen.

Reacting to this near disaster, Mamer later pencils a note which the Sun God drops to the airfield. Directed to "the floodlight gentleman," it requests that he "cut off his artificial sun."

Because Mamer needed daylight to fly the next leg to Cheyenne, the Sun God' crew is now forced to delay departure until after dawn, a few hours from now. This, plus delays caused by the multiple refueling contacts, contributes to a significant overall delay in the schedule.

The original schedule, published in *The New York Times*, called for refuelings at Cheyenne yesterday (Friday) afternoon and New York this (Saturday) afternoon, culminating in a return to Spokane Sunday evening, August 18. Although the delay undoubtedly disappoints Mamer, he is experienced in sustained flight and the unexpected. As he is quoted at one point, "...difficulties are to be expected in a pioneer undertaking like this..."

Mamer and Walker had earlier in the flight said they'd tried to sleep but been unsuccessful. They blamed the loud noise of the motor, vibration, their parachutes, and the cramped quarters. The year 1929 was one of extraordinary enthusiasm for celebrating endurance, and aviators weren't the only ones fighting sleep. Flagpole-sitting was the rage. Joe Rock and his sister Mary won a dance marathon at Chicago in a time of 1,245 hours, and Jerry McDonnell and Ed Williams set a bicycle endurance record of 175 hours.

No doubt the Sun God pilots' initial fervor for their mission led to reduced awareness of any impediment, including being deprived of sleep. After two-and-a- half days, however, their bodies displayed the symptoms of a lack of regular sleep. Although it's impossible to say, the crew may have benefitted from naps of a few minutes or longer duration that reset their alertness and allowed them to at least feel refreshed.

During early-morning hours, after an absence of sleep for a period longer than two days, people experience an overwhelming desire for sleep and remaining awake becomes very difficult. Research shows that after two days without sleep, the human body compensates by shutting down for microsleeps—half-second to multiple-second periods of sleep, during which the person experiencing them is often not aware of their occurrence.

Regardless of how they rested, cat-napped, slept, or simply carried on with microsleeps, Mamer and Walker prepared that Saturday dawn to receive—by daylight this time—a hundred more gallons of gas from Wilson's Buhl. During this final refueling, the Buhl also lowered a gallon of water, probably for drinking, and two gallons of oil.

The Sun God aviators had little time or notion to reflect on these risky and unplanned accomplishments in the night sky over Rock Springs. Yet the refueling feats of this day would quickly be noted world-wide, and aviation record books would henceforth note the first-ever successful air-to-air refuelings at night. They also happen to mark the first refuelings accomplished at such high altitudes.

For now, though, the weary fliers had but one goal: to reach their next refueling at Cheyenne, Wyoming, 245 miles to the east.

6. Hazards on the High Desert

In a short piece in Saturday's *The Spokane Daily Chronicle* topped by the heading DEMPSEY TALKS TO SCHMELING, former world champion boxer Jack Dempsey refused to reveal what was said. Another breathless heading on the page proclaimed "Local Cops Claim Capture of Champion Chicken Thief." But the prominent coverage, the headline news, was accorded the flight of the Sun God. Comments were reported by Art Walker: "Everything's O.K., the only inconvenience is the loss of sleep. We haven't slept but two hours so far."

"Whirlwind 9 sure [is] knocking 'em off," Walker wrote in a dropped note, referring to the Sun God's nine-cylinder motor. "[It's] just as smooth and even as the day we left Spokane." There seemed no disappointment on board the Sun God as it flew toward the rising sun on Saturday, August 17. The delay for the night refueling and daylight over Rock Springs was quickly forgotten as they soared over Wyoming's Red Desert.

Resting from working the wobble pump, Mamer pores over a Section map. It outlines the airmail route from Rock Springs to Medicine Bow that would lead them over auxiliary airfields at Bitter Creek, Red Desert, and Cherokee. After Rawlins, Wyoming, the airway crosses the North Platte River, then the Parco and Dana airfields. At Medicine Bow, Wyoming, it detours around the Snowy Range. After that the course turns southeast, passing over Laramie on the way to Cheyenne.

Later in the day it would warm, but now it was cold, cold enough to justify donning the sheepskin-lined coats they'd packed. They'd also packed cord (1 ball), two grappling hooks, a hatchet, and three hacksaw blades, but so far they'd had no need for these items.

Mamer notes that this airway follows the Lincoln Highway, an only-partly paved road in this part of the West. Occasional autos below, trailed by clouds of dust, confirm the presence of the highway. As envisioned by Carl G. Fisher in 1912, this road constitutes a "Coast-to-Coast Rock Highway" from Times Square in New York City to Lincoln Park in San Francisco.

Fisher was an early auto enthusiast, a racer, and the builder of the famous Indianapolis Speedway, home of the "Brickyard '500 mile' Race." He promoted the Lincoln Highway idea among interested men from the automobile industry. The group evolved into the Lincoln Highway Association with the mission: promote a toll-free "continuous improved highway from the Atlantic to the Pacific..." Although some critics called it "peacock alley," it later became the premier highway in United States. Just short of a year before the flight of the Sun God, on September 1, 1928, Boy Scouts across the nation place some 3,000 markers along the road's right-of-way dedicating it to the memory of Abraham Lincoln.

Two men, encaged in the aluminum-sheathed Sun God, are pulled along, even in this lean, high air, by a roaring lion of a motor. Below them passes the continental divide, unnoticed. The emptiness, an emptiness full of crumpled ridges and scoured gulches, rolls onward, onward and onward in unrelieved sameness.

Nick looks up. He's in the kitchen, and his mother is at the stove. She's telling him about his father, the victim of an accident before he was born. Speaking warmly, she tells him what a fine and brave man his father was, and that when he is grown he should always remember that his father, dead now a half-dozen years, was a fine and brave husband . . . a fine and hard-working father.

The scene dissolves. Before Nick are the old brick buildings of East Second Street in downtown Hastings, as two school chums round the corner. He hails them, but for a reason he can't understand, they don't respond.

"Oh!" Nick says, abruptly alert. Induced by lack of sleep and mesmerized by the passing landscape's monotony, he's lost touch; his mind has taken a rest.

Mamer knows of this danger—he's read of the difficulty that Lindbergh experienced in keeping focus across the Atlantic. Several times, on previous flights, Nick fought off this drift, yet now without warning it had overcome him. From now on, he promised, he'd need to practice a determined and disciplined approach to counter this growing hazard.

From high above, on the landscape here nothing larger than sagebrush grows. It resembles a gray and tan wrinkled bedsheet spattered with stains of chalk and blots of slate. Only the odd truck, an oil rig, or wild horses, specks against a parched colossus, betray its scale, its vastness.

A hundred miles ahead, Vern Bookwalter's Ryan airplane sits on the edge of the Cheyenne Airport. With only 50 gallons of gasoline in the refueling tank, he awaits the arrival of the Sun God. Bookwalter worries. The plan all along was for a major refueling at Cheyenne, and he knows that the aviators are expecting to fill the Sun God's tanks to their 320-gallon capacity. But because of Cheyenne's elevation, 6062-feet, the underpowered Ryan can carry only 50 gallons each flight and still gain the needed altitude for refueling.

At about eight this morning, Mamer spots a tiny settlement ahead and to the left of the Sun God. It's a dry rectangle of a dozen dirt streets amid the looping meanders of the Medicine Bow River. Here he swings the Sun God to the right, as they pass over a vacant airfield to the southeast of town. On the craft sails, below the top of 11,156-foot Elk Mountain, where, in the Snowy Range, the Medicine Bow River flows out of North Gap Lake northeast toward its namesake town of Medicine Bow.

About an hour later, at 9:11 a.m., the Sun God appears in the northwest sky above Cheyenne. Bookwalter's Ryan churns a tornado of brown dirt as it lifts off and labors to make the rendezvous. Fortunately, this refueling will be take place by daylight. But at altitude, Bookwalter experiences difficulty in maintaining the 80 miles-per-hour needed to keep a steady course in the thin air for the refueling. Nevertheless, hoseman Neil O'Connell is able to transfer the 50 gallons. When the Ryan has landed, Mamer glides over the field and drops notes.

"We know you think we are late, but...'Save the old mill' is our motto," is the thought in one, referring to the Sun God's Whirlwind motor as 'the old mill.' In another note, the aviators warn, "Be sure to watch the slack in the hose. We cut the one on the Buhl with our blade last night."

A half-hour later, a second refueling is cut short when a persistent kink in the Ryan's refueling hose allows only 20 gallons to be delivered, plus eight gallons of oil. The Sun God drops a note, this time displaying irritation.

Seemingly balked by the delays over the two towns in Wyoming, Mamer finally directs Bookwalter to take on a full load of gas and follow him to North Platte, Nebraska, where the airfield's elevation is only 2,777 feet. Once there, he tells Walker, they should be able to fully top off their tanks in preparation for the next leg, the 988 miles to Cleveland, Ohio.

Advancing the throttle, Nick turns east, toward the Nebraska border. Bookwalter's Ryan, however, does not follow. Shortly, the Sun God returns to Cheyenne, circles within sight of the Ryan and speeds off again toward Nebraska.

Possibly confused by the change in plans, Bookwalter at first appears to believe the Sun God will remain at Cheyenne for another try at refueling. But after circling and noting the absence of the Sun God, Bookwalter speeds eastward, hoping to catch the *Spokane Sun God* short of North Platte.

7. "WE MADE A BEAUTIFUL CONTACT"

Heading eastward from Cheyenne, Nick and Art feel good. In less than a half-hour's flying time, they'll cross from the high plateau of Wyoming onto the wheatlands of Nebraska. That's important, because within the next hour or so the height of the land below them will drop two-thousand feet.

Ahead stretches the Great Plains, a wide basin free of mountains and high valleys, where the risky trick of refueling will ease. At North Platte, Nebraska, they'll refuel before pushing east to Cleveland.

Is Bookwalter behind them? Mamer tells Walker to pop out of the opening in the top of the cabin and take a look. Sure enough, the morning's light reveals the high wing of the Ryan not far behind them. Does Bookwalter have a full load? Mamer hopes he'd got the message that they needed to leave North Platte with their tanks full for the long haul to Cleveland.

Now over Burns station, Mamer glances down and spots the beacon tower and its shed, with "SL-O" and "44" painted on the roof. The letters SL-O identify the route—in this case, the Salt Lake-Omaha section. Built starting in the early 1920s, beacon stations are located ten-to-fifteen miles apart over the Transcontinental Airway from New York (Newark, New Jersey) to San Francisco, more than 2,000 miles.

The beacons were installed to aid airmail pilots, especially at night and in bad weather, when the revolving and flashing searchlights on elevated towers helps guide them safely to their destination. The numbers painted on the shed roofs increase consecutively from west to east. As of the year before the Sun God flight, there were a total of 185 beacons on this airway. Mamer's plan calls for the Sun God to navigate with their aid, in the dark, all the way from North Platte, Nebraska to Cleveland, Ohio.

Bookwalter's Ryan, speeding a little faster than Mamer's plane, draws even with the Sun God. Pilots and hosemen wave and gesture obscenely, laughing at each other's antics. Then, getting to business, the Ryan hoseman signals their tank is ready and they'll try for a refueling on this leg. Bookwalter's Ryan climbs to gain more height, and hand-over-hand, hoseman O'Connell pays out hose from the Ryan's doorway.

Walker, in helmet and goggles, stands in the Sun God's opening, facing the gusty blast of air. Now that there's daylight and he can see, he's eager to catch the hose's nozzle. He hopes the earlier kink problem has been solved.

At the controls of the Sun God, Mamer eases the plane upward, keeping a careful watch on the weighted nozzle end of the hose. It flails crazily above him, jostled up, down and side to side by the turbulent air in the wake of the Ryan. If he approaches wrongly, the Sun God's propeller can easily slice the hose to pieces.

After an uneasy moment, the Sun God powers to about thirty feet below, and less than twenty feet behind, the Ryan. Mamer calibrates the throttle position and nudges the stick to maintain these distances and angle to the Ryan. Such precision flying takes all the skill Nick has learned in more than a decade of flying. He wishes he could see the nozzle, but it's now behind him. All he can see by craning his neck is O'Connell, the hose and the underside of the Ryan.

The nozzle bangs against the fuselage. Nick can only hope there is no damage. Has Art grabbed it yet? The commotion behind him means activity.

Walker hangs onto the hose and attaches the ground wire. He next dunks the nozzle in the tank and, while grappling with the hose, signals to O'Connell. Within seconds, new gasoline pours from the Ryan into the fuselage tank of the Sun God.

About a hundred gallons are delivered and Bookwalter is pleased. He'd finally understood Mamer's request at Cheyenne. He wouldn't need to climb nearly as high in Nebraska as he had in Cheyenne to transfer a hundred gallons. All he had to do was get into the air from Cheyenne with the added weight in the refueling tank, which the Ryan had the power to do.

The two planes now pass over the beacon at Potter. The nearby village lies in the heart of the Nebraska panhandle, a region populated by emigrants and others who settled the land provided by the Homestead Act of 1862 and other government grants aimed at "settling the west." Now, following a series of wet years, increased demand and rising prices for grain, farmers here have plowed, planted and harvested more and more acres of winter wheat. They can't imagine that a few years in the future, much drier weather will set in, and thousands of acres of topsoil will disappear in the brown blizzards of the Dust Bowl era.

To the east, south of the town of Sidney is its airfield and the No. 51 beacon. Looking north, however, Nick spies a green belt. It's the fertile lowlands of the North Platte River, sweeping down from Scottsbluff. Passing Chappell, Big Springs and Ogallala, the Sun God soars ever closer to the River. Nearby was the terminus of the famous cattle drives of the 1870s, where drovers met the Union Pacific Railroad at Ogallala. It means that North Platte, Nebraska is less than an hour away.

Bookwalter's Ryan pulls ahead of the Sun God. Each plane now follows the North Platte River, as the Paxton beacon (No. 60) and the Sutherland (No. 61) pass beneath them.

Bookwalter arrives at North Platte before the Sun God, and a note in his hand flutters to field. The note is intended to be sent to the Air Derby Association in Spokane, which is the official sponsoring organization behind the flight of the *Spokane Sun God*, with able assistance from Texaco and the Buhl Aircraft Co.

In 1927 the enthusiastic local group of businessmen had assembled and financed the National Air Derby and Air Races in Spokane. The group, headed by Walter Evans, with Victor Dessert and Harlan Peyton as vice-presidents, put on the very successful Derby and Air Races, billed as a "World's Premier." It saw the fastest racing planes, cross-country races, generous cash awards to the winners, along with air circus stunts and aerobatics. Its international success led directly, under the leadership of Vic Dessert, to the planning, sponsorship and management of this 1929 Sun God flight.

Bookwalter's note, hand signed by him says, "Nick is going to mill around field here for about two hours. He has 90 gallons of gas. I will give him more when he is ready to leave for Cleveland. He wants to make Cleveland in the morning. He is taking ice-cold watermelon and fried chicken. I gave him 100 gallons of gas on way to North Platte."

The Sun God arrives over the North Platte Field at 3:25 p.m., central-standard time, as Bookwalter's Ryan makes its approach to landing.

In 1921, this airfield at North Platte saw the lighting of flaming barrels of fuel across the turf after sunset on February 22. This guided a de Havilland Four airmail pilot to land safely at 7:48 p.m. The occasion was the first night-time flight of the U.S. airmail service. The plane took off for Omaha later that night following some emergency repairs.

Once on the ground, Bookwalter's plane takes on a load of 100 gallons, and returns to the air a half-hour later. He immediately notes that the climb to refueling altitude is easier.

Notes now drop from the circling Sun God. One of them says Nick and Art expect to leave North Platte around eight o'clock this evening and reach

Cleveland by daybreak tomorrow, August 18th, flying by way of Omaha and Chicago.

So the Sun God settles into a circling pattern during which the pilots refresh with some food and continue their cycles of refueling. As described later by Mamer himself, "This time we made a beautiful contact, having perfected our technique through practice, and we took one-hundred gallons aboard in twenty minutes. Three more contacts were made and we succeeded for the first time…in taking on a full load…"

Between refuelings they exercise the wobble pump to fill and refill the overhead tanks. Finally, after undergoing the fourth refueling, the Sun God pilots wave goodbye at 8:15 p.m. and disappear eastward into the gathering night.

8. A Night of Hypervigilance

Now, in the fading gleam of August, a rotating light atop a beacon at a landing field ahead sweeps around toward the approaching Sun God. A brief flash follows. Then the searchlight's beam, a pencil of white against a dusky sheet of ground, sweeps on, completing one rotation every ten seconds.

Nick Mamer is in the pilot's seat of the *Spokane Sun God*. His eyes are night-adjusted. Although the almost-full moon rose earlier, before they left North Platte, it's now often hidden by clouds.

Below is a town, a few dozen squares of flicker within an expanse of lightless fields. It's Gothenburg, Nebraska, divided by the tracks of the railroad, kneeling at the silvery veins of the Platte River. Gothenburg's airfield, designated by the Department of Commerce as one of more than ninety "intermediate," airfields on the Transcontinental Airmail route, provides a potential landing field for aircraft in trouble. Nick won't consider the possibility of landing. Instead, he envisions arriving over Cleveland at dawn, where gasoline, oil, and—yes!—breakfast, will be waiting.

The path ahead, lit by the necklace of airmail beacons, entices. At first it parallels the curves of the Platte River, but by Grand Island it abandons the river to bend east, favoring York and the capitol of Lincoln.

But Mamer cannot allow his attention to be distracted by town lights or activities. To achieve the quickest arrival in Cleveland, he seeks to fly swiftly, accurately and safely. During daylight, he uses visual clues: not only to identify landmarks, but also to sense his aircraft's attitude and position relative to the earth, and to its horizon.

At night, senses of position, altitude and attitude essential to control of the airplane's flight are compromised. It's possible to lose sight entirely of the earth's horizon, risking confusion about whether the plane is in level flight or in an unsafe, or unwanted, attitude. During night flight Nick places considerably more dependence on the aircraft's instruments, several of which substitute for the visual cues that are now absent. Attention shifts from outside the plane to the cockpit panel with its dials, gauges and controls.

One of these, an instrument called the "artificial horizon" ("attitude indicator" today) substitutes for the earth's horizon. It indicates whether the nose of the Sun God is tilted up, or down, and whether its wings are level. It's termed a "primary" instrument.

Mamer also checks the altimeter. Is it steady? If not, he's either climbing or descending. Another instrument called the "vertical speed indicator" shows how fast the climb or descent is progressing. If the aircraft is banking, turning or slipping, the "turn and bank indicator" or "turn and slip" registers this. Used together, these instruments inform the pilot of the airplane's flight path, and deviations that may be unwanted or unsafe.

Corrections to unwanted or unsafe deviations are made using the throttle, stick and rudder pedals, which alter the aircraft's motive power and its behavior relative to the airstream outside. These corrections help the pilot achieve straight and level flight, safe climb and descent, and controlled turning, as well as takeoff and landing.

Is his speed steady at the 'cruise' speed he's selected? If the needle of the airspeed dial reveals deviation, he alters the craft's attitude and/or throttle to achieve the desired speed.

Having completed what's called the "flight instrument scan," he glances at the other indicators. The tachometer, temperature and pressure gauges, mixture controls and fuel gauges. These instruments yield information on the performance of the motor as it propels the plane forward. If required, he makes adjustments.

One by one, in a sequence made habitual by practice, the pilot scans all instruments. As quickly as he finishes the scan, Mamer glances outside and down, to see if the aircraft is following the lighted airway. Once assured of that, or correcting back onto the airway if it isn't, he returns again to scanning the instruments.

Over and over, as the Lincoln, Union, Ashland and Gretna beacons roll beneath the Sun God, Nick scans first inside and then peers out, first to the instruments and then to the airway.

Ahead, growing from a glimmer to bright sparkles of lights and color, is the city of Omaha.

Art Walker is behind, in the dim cave of the fuselage's tail section. Nick hopes he's sleeping—or at least resting, for hours will pass before the men will enjoy breakfast.

Unknown to Mamer, officials at Boeing airfield in Omaha have placed two-hundred gallons of aviation gasoline in storage for possible refueling of the Sun God. The officials admit, however, that there is no airplane in Omaha equipped for refueling, so they await the aircraft's arrival with some trepidation.

Flying high, the Sun God skips across Omaha, Nebraska, without notice. The craft leaves Omaha, and within minutes, the pilot sights the beacon at Oakland, Iowa, and further on, the beacon at Adair.

Soon the Sun God skims over downtown Des Moines, then on to Newton, Grinnell and Iowa City. From there, the pilot's airway map reveals, it's 191 miles to Chicago. It's tedious and grueling, and Nick grits his teeth to counter the dazing effects of its repetitive nature.

The routine of endless alertness contrasts with piloting in the 21st century. When on course and at altitude, modern pilots' duties are largely assigned to computers. These efficiently monitor the aircraft's speed, attitude, altitude, etc., relative to assigned inputs and the external environment. Needed corrections are determined and performed by an autopilot. In 1929, however, there was no relief from the anxiety-producing and tiring mode of constant alertness and attention to all aspects of flying.

On the exact day Nick Mamer and Art Walker left Spokane on this momentous flight, a differing event, but one of importance to aviation, occurred at the Detroit home of Mrs. Evangeline L. Lindbergh, the mother of Charles A. Lindbergh.

Less than two years earlier Lindbergh had crossed the Atlantic Ocean, alone. He'd returned to unprecedented glory and acclaim throughout the U.S. "The receptions given to Lindbergh in the United States, first in Washington, then in New York and St. Louis, were among the most lavish that any human being in history had ever received," writes Robert Wohl. Now, in a Detroit interview on topics of the past, the present, and the future of aviation, the boyish Lindbergh, recently appointed a Colonel, weighs his words carefully before answering.

"How do you regard the present position of the United States in regard to aviation?" he's asked.

"Much more lies ahead for aviation than has appeared in the past," says Lindbergh. "Looking at aviation from that standpoint, it is just emerging from infancy, although much has been accomplished already. The next few years will see much greater developments than has the past."

Asked for specifics, Lindbergh says, "There is more flying by private individuals in the United States at present than in the rest of the world combined. There will be a development of larger transports and faster planes. There will be a development of more efficient airplane motors and the development of planes requiring less skill for safe operation."

The interviewer writes that Colonel Lindbergh views altitude attempts and endurance flights, when conducted for the purposes of scientific experiment and the testing and demonstrating of new equipment, anything but stunts. Lindbergh also expresses warm admiration for pilots carrying on such pioneer flights for definite scientific purposes.

Lindbergh speaks of the marking of towns and cities. Aviators, he says, know how important it is for navigation that they are able to get their bearings. While much has been done along this line since three years previous (1926) when he was flying airmail routes, many towns today remain unmarked.

In commenting on the growing chain of airports being extended north and south, east and west, Lindbergh says every important city in the country either has, or is constructing an airport. "The time will come," he continues, "when the town without an airport will be in the same position as the town without railroad connections has been."

Passing now over Clinton, Iowa, with the pale glint of an almost-round moon reflecting from the Mississippi River, Nick Mamer is too busy to be reminded of Lindbergh's influence on America's enthusiasm for aviation. Yet the Sun God's mission itself owes much of its genesis to Lindbergh's flight and the subsequent spread of aviation interest across the continent and into the hearts of citizens—especially those in Spokane, Washington, where they've contributed so generously to its support.

The Sun God has now entered Illinois, where it flies over Franklin Grove, Waterman, Aurora, and then on to the immensity of Chicago, shimmering with a million lights that end at the lips of Lake Michigan. The trail of airway beacons here turns southeast, into Indiana at McCool, then over Goshen, Indiana and on into Ohio. In less than a half-hour, the sparkle of water between Lake Erie's islands gives notice that Toledo and Lorain are not far off.

At Cleveland Municipal Airport, Dan Robertson and James Buchanan of St. Louis, with their refueling aircraft, await the arrival of the Sun God. They are there by arrangement of the Texas Oil Company. Captain Frank Hawks, current (1929) holder of the transcontinental speed record in both directions and a Texaco employee, arrived the previous day. He's at Cleveland Municipal to assist in the refueling operations for the Sun God flight.

Upon learning of the flight's delays, Hawks suggests that Mamer and Walker could, after refueling, follow him to New York. "I have a radio receiver tuned to the directional radio broadcast and can guide them over the route," he says. This offer would take advantage of one of the newest developments of the time in aviation technology, the use of radio signals to aid navigation. As it later turns out, however, this doesn't happen.

Now, as the Sun God approaches from the west facing a Sunday sunrise (September 18), Mamer, fighting drowsiness, fumes, noise, aches and the mind-numbing routine, can't wait—Cleveland is less than an hour away!

9. Unheard Cheers

Dan Robertson strides from the terminal building at Cleveland Municipal airfield with James Buchanan. The two men had toured the almost-new building, with its first-of-a-kind control tower. They'd learned nothing of the Sun God's progress.

They walk to the hanger near their parked Curtiss Robin airplane, where they'd stored their gear. Although it is still early, it's now light. The men loiter outside, scanning the partly-cloudy skies to the west. Buchanan rubs his chin, and wipes the palm of his hand on his pants leg. In a low voice, he says something to Robertson. Dan either doesn't hear, or doesn't acknowledge. They're about to enter the hanger when they hear the low purr of a motor. They move away from the hangar, and strain to see over the airport's buildings. They hope to pick out an image, a red-colored airplane.

Within moments, the Sun God powers into view, its red paint appearing dusky from below. The roar of the Whirlwind motor sets Robertson and Buchanan in motion. They duck inside, grab their gear and jog toward the Curtiss.

In the cramped cabin of the Sun God, Nick hollers at Art over the engine noise, announcing their arrival at Cleveland. He reduces throttle and aims the craft at the airfield. They'll swing over the hangars a couple of hundred feet above ground to make sure the crew sent here by the Texas Oil Company knows of their arrival.

Art Walker checks the location of his gloves. He pulls on his leather helmet, and adjusts his goggles in their rest position above his forehead. Crouching to clear the low ceiling of the cabin, he moves forward close to Nick.

Pilot Robertson and his hoseman Buchanan had earlier met with Frank Hawks, head of Texaco's Aeronautical Division. They'd been chartered, along with the Wassall-Chaffee crew, after the record endurance flight in July of the *St. Louis Robin* piloted by Jackson and O'Brine. During that flight of 420 hours, it was fueled by the Curtiss monoplane of Ray Wassall, with "Shorty" Chaffee on the hose.

At the meeting, Captain Hawks related how smoothly the Templeman and Warner refueling had gone two days earlier in San Francisco. He gave Robertson and Buchanan some tips on how best to conduct the upcoming contact with the *Spokane Sun God*.

In response Robertson and Buchanan assured Hawks they were eager to demonstrate their flying and hose-handling skills to benefit the Sun God's mission.

In New York meanwhile, an official of the National Aeronautical Association had received a telegram from the N.A.A. office in Seattle. Dated two days previous on August 16, the message requested "time arrival and departure over your city Mamer non-stop orange Buhl plane NR9628."

The National Aeronautical Association, the record-keeping organization for United States aviation, was following the flight of the *Spokane Sun God* from its inception on August 15. The west coast message continued, "Plane due over your city 3:30 P.M. Eastern Standard Time." The official at the Seattle office had not foreseen the delays that occurred over Wyoming, and therefore expected the Sun God to arrive at New York yesterday (Saturday) afternoon.

Completing the 'fly-by,' Mamer advances the throttle and starts a climbing turn. Clearing his throat, he notes the dryness. He and Walker drank the last of their supply of water shortly after leaving North Platte.

Thinking about the upcoming contact with Robertson's supply plane, Nick glances again at the brown-stained windshield. Too bad the Buhl factory hadn't foreseen what would occur on a long flight: emissions from the Whirlwind engine's rockers deposit a smeary, oily mess over the front of the Sun God and on the windshield, clouding the pilot's vision.

As he watches Robertson's Curtiss climb out of Cleveland Municipal to meet them, Mamer flicks his portfolio open. He's reminding himself of its contents. In particular, he verifies the official letter that he is to deliver in New York is safely inside. Part of the publicity arranged by Texaco, it was transferred to the Sun God during the San Francisco refueling. It's a greeting from San Francisco Mayor James Rolph, Jr. to the colorful 'Jimmy' Walker, Mayor of New York.

Mamer and Walker know that arrival of the Sun God over New York will provide the opportunity for a celebration. The New York newspapers are alerted, and radio broadcasts of the Sun God's completion of the transcontinental crossing are planned. The event will no doubt be played to the advantage of the Texas Oil Company, a sponsor of the flight.

Nick sighs. He realizes he has writing to do during this next leg from Cleveland to New York. It's not that he dislikes writing, rather it is a lack of time that provides the difficulty. Piloting the plane, pumping gasoline, tending the oiling and keeping the flight log, not to mention minimal breaks for eating and bodily functions, leaves little time for writing. But notes dropped to airfields as well as the written reports he'd agreed—before the flight—to supply to the North American Newspaper Alliance and the Spokane newspapers are unwritten.

In addition he is sometimes obliged by the flight's sponsors in Spokane to respond. The following telegram came from 'Frenchie,' (Ellsworth C. French) of the Sun God Flight Committee:

WILSON PLEASE DELIVER THIS TELEGRAM TO
MAMER...NICK YOU AND ART ARE CERTAINLY TO BE
CONGRATULATED AS WELL AS REFUELING CREW
STOP MAKING AVIATION HISTORY WITH NIGHT
REFUELING STOP NICK BE SURE AND TELL US
WHERE YOU WANT WILSON AND BUHL TO GO FROM
ROCKSPRINGS SO WE CAN GIVE HIM ORDERS STOP
WILSON HAS ASKED FOR NEW REFUELING HOSE AND
WE WANT TO KNOW WHERE TO SHIP IT STOP=

The first refueling over Cleveland by Robertson and Buchanan is completed by midmorning, but Mamer and Walker are hungry and thirsty. They're hoping food and water might be transferred by Buchanan during this run, but it didn't happen. However, they're happy that the refueling plane's actions are smooth, safe and fairly predictable, and that Buchanan knows how to handle the hose.

The second contact is successful as well, completing the transfer of 200 gallons of gasoline and filling the Sun God's tanks to capacity. Fortunately, this latter transfer includes the drop of a gallon or so of drinking water, an extra the thirsty Sun God pilots eagerly accept. They are now ready for the next leg, their trip across Ohio and Pennsylvania and on into New York.

With Walker at the controls, they embark for Parkman, Ohio. Fortunately, the plane is gaining ground speed—for the first time on the flight they have a tail wind.

The pilots navigate using a combination of visual sightings and so-called "dead reckoning." This phrase, derived from nautical practice, means determining one's current location by adding a calculated advance to the previous (known) location. The advance is based on one's estimated course (the direction flown) and the estimated forward speed. Suppose the flight passes City A, while heading a certain direction, say east. The pilot thinks he's flying 100 miles per hour. Combining these means that in a quarter of an hour he will arrive 25 miles east of City A. This is his new location, calculated by "dead reckoning." Of course this new location is subject to error because neither the direction nor the speed over ground, is known *precisely*.

Piloting has become more difficult because the Sun God's Earth Inductor Compass—a newly-developed instrument installed before the flight and successfully employed for the first time in the record attempt by Lindbergh—has failed. Thus the Sun God's pilot can no longer set a course into the Inductor's controller dial and maintain the plane's heading simply by keeping the needle on the "L-R" meter centered; instead he must rely on compass readings which are difficult to obtain and subject to deviation.

Behind Art, Nick scribbles notes to Frank Hawks at Roosevelt field in New York. Each sheet of bond paper used for these messages had been prepared in advance of the flight for dispatches to news outlets. Each has pre-typed text at the top of the page: "Dear Sir: Will you kindly deliver this message to all news services in your city thereby accommodating 'Spokane Sun God'? Nick Mamer".

Nick begins by crossing out the pre-typed message with his pencil. Then, in a looping, Palmer Method-inspired handwriting, he writes,

> Frank – I know I hav'nt said much on this flight simply
> because I hav'nt time, honestly we hav'nt had a minute to
> spare – I told you about the wobble Pump – taking all our
> time – I believe I will load up to the top with gas here – and
> go straight to St. Paul, without refueling, I can make it O.K.
> without bad head winds. If I cannot I will drop message to
> Cleveland Refuel Crew and ask them to meet me Chicago
> dawn Municipal field – Will you personally thank the
> Cleveland refuel Crew right away for us – We did not send
> them a word – I had to fly, and Walker, work the pump so we
> could get as much gas with our Wing tanks – I have only sent
> one message to Spokane, so you see how crowded we are – In

fact I don't think we even read all we get =

Confidential this is a Hell of a night flying ship, no provision to Wipe Windshield which becomes oil soaked and utterly impossible to fly blind even for short periods – No instrument arrangement – our earth Inductor is out – and if possible send up an Altimeter

Nick is writing to Frank Hawks in New York, who will receive Nick's notes when they're dropped to the airfield upon the Sun God's arrival there. (In his reference "*top with gas here*," the "*here*" refers to Roosevelt field on New York's Long Island, the next refueling stop.) Nick's capitalization possibly emphasizes the importance he attaches to certain words such as "pump," "crew," "wipe," "inductor" and "altimeter." Also, his abrupt changes of topic, rushed grammar and odd punctuation reveal the urgency and strain he feels as he hurriedly prepares these messages.

The pilots cross from Ohio to Pennsylvania heading near Mercer, where the afternoon's heat closes in. They shed their shirts, and push on to Bellefonte. But before Bellefonte and the low peaks of the Allegheny Mountains that rise in the southwest and range to the northeast, the air turns unsteady. The Sun God now seems to ride like a truck bumping over 'corduroy' ruts.

Nick searches for a more favorable altitude, but to no avail.

It's not long before all of the onboard supplies that are not tied down are airborne part of the time. Lightweight items dance across the cabin, migrating downhill. Even well-stowed supplies loosen. At the controls, Nick struggles to keep the wings level while the sudden lift and abrupt halt of an updraft unseats him. That's followed by its opposite, a stomach-stirring downdraft that jams him into his seat. Winds with a side component force the airplane into unintended skids.

Nick knows about this. It is "hell stretch," the name awarded by airmail pilots flying this Airmail route over the past years. As described in a 1927 article in *Aviation*:

"... the airway ... is distinguished as having the worst weather in the country — by common consent, the New York-Cleveland division of the U. S. Air Mail Trans-Continental route. Its diabolical propensities arise from the diverse influences of the Atlantic Ocean, the Allegheny Mountains, and the Great Lakes, and from the fact that

all storm roads lead to the St. Lawrence valley, and the
majority across this airway. Seldom does favorable weather
extend from end to end of this section of the route for more
than twenty-four hours."

After a half-hour of the rough weather, Nick wishes he could take his hand
from the stick, but it's not possible. Nor can he find a comfortable way to
avoid being bounced around on his seat. Higher or lower altitudes fail to avoid
the terrible air. About all he can do now is keep the aircraft on an approximate
east-southeast course toward New York.

Behind him, Art Walker is as well subject to the erratic motions that toss
him, and every loose item in the cabin, up, down and sideways. In between
work pumping gasoline, he scrambles to secure essential supplies, but there's
no place for them where they'll stay put.

Over Numidia, Pennsylvania, the rough air gets somewhat worse. Updrafts
originate on craggy mountainsides, then fall away with breathtaking speed.
Drifting clouds cause the air below to cool, kicking off spasms of contraction.
The unexpected motions are maddeningly unending.

After hours of this, the Sun God fliers perceive dense tracts of houses,
roads and buildings. And within minutes they see large, irregular rims of
shimmering water—the bays of the Atlantic Ocean to the south. Mamer turns
northeast, toward what appears as a large urbanized part of the New Jersey-
New York area. But the scene before him, because of its extent and immensity,
lacks easily-identified landmarks that could aid in identifying its location.
It's undifferentiated city, carved and dimpled by bays, waterways and ocean.
Mamer now realizes, he's not sure how to reach Roosevelt field.

Ahead, on the ground at a tiny airfield near Armonk, New York, a test
pilot for the Wright Aeronautical Corp. has landed his personal airplane. Leon
Allen intends to contact a passenger at that location. As he is busily engaged,
he notices a red airplane overhead. The Sun God appears out of the southwest
sky, swooping low over the airfield. A weighted packet flies out and flutters to
the airfield.

Worried that the aircraft is in trouble, Allen rushes to pick up the packet.
Its message turns out to be benign: signed by Nick Mamer, it simply asks
for directions to Roosevelt field. Pilot Allen, fully aware of the record-setting
flight of the Sun God, rushes to his airplane, starts it up and joins the Sun God
in the sky above, where he leads them due south, across Westchester County,
over Long Island Sound, and on over to Roosevelt field.

A large crowd of spectators, estimated at 10,000, peers into the sky at Roosevelt field. The Sun God, led by Allen's plane, appears in the northwest sky, and circles the airfield. First one, then another weighted packet flutters to the ground from the plane. Spectators cheer as mechanics and other airfield workers scurry to gather the notes.

"This is a wonderful thrill," reads one of the notes from the Sun God pilots. "After three nights and three days of fighting – New York! The temptation to land is sure great, but our friends are waiting for us in Spokane, and besides, we are so grimy and soiled you would not care to see us."

Also enclosed are letters to Frank Hawks, the letter to New York's Mayor Walker, and a letter to Bruce Leighton, chief of Sales for the Wright Company, informing him that the J6 Whirlwind motor functions perfectly. In another note directed to "Dear Capt. Hawks," Mamer writes positively of the contribution of Texaco's gasoline and oil to the Sun God's performance.

But Ray Wassall is already taxiing the St. Louis Curtiss Robin to Roosevelt's runway. Noting the NR81H on the Robin's wing, Nick turns east and throttles down to a modest speed to await the refueling plane's arrival.

Other airplanes follow the Curtiss Robin into the air. Responding to the national publicity about the Sun God's flight, several of them have been chartered by news and newsreel photographers, who will record the refueling missions from the air. Other airplanes simply fly nearby to observe.

One of the dropped notes, addressed to Frank Hawks, reads in part:

> Now on tonights Schedule I would like to get away from
> New York soon as possible to get away from Pennslyvania
> before dark – if the weather looks doubtful to St. Paul I would
> rather Cruise over an airport & fly that by day – let me know
> about this ... Would appreciate if you will fly as far with us as
> possible, so Art can follow giving me an opportunity for rest
> before the dark sets in. If you do this when you leave us be sure
> and be on the beacon course –, We had a hell a time last night
> – No visibility, out of the front account oil on Windshield and
> no wipers Speed up refueling crew Please send up some tomato
> juice –Just use an ordinary sack to put these things in like oil
> food water tomatoe Juice ect – Frank if it is not too much
> trouble send up some food, Ice Cream, Chicken Watermelon,
> almost anything but don't delay a minute if this is not handy –
> lets get gassed up and get going west quick as Possible.

This part of Nick's letter appears to show, in addition to the rushed handwriting, frustration, anxiety and impatience. No doubt these feelings were driven by three days without significant sleep, lack of adequate time for required duties, problems with the plane and its equipment, hunger, and a growing realization that this venture is much more difficult and riskier than anticipated. It's interesting to note that these frustrations, feelings and problems were never publicly aired after the flight.

On this fairly clear, sunny day, fueling will begin when Wassall establishes level flight with a speed of 85 miles-per-hour at the refueling altitude. In helmet and goggles, Shorty Chaffee positions his upper body outside the hole in the upper fuselage of the Robin.

When Nick guides the Sun God to within range behind and below the Robin, and Walker is seen waiting in the opening in the top of its fuselage, Shorty leans out over the side and begins threading a cord tether, followed by the weighted refueling hose, out of the Robin and down toward the Sun God. The cord tether is attached to the hose about ten feet above the nozzle end of the hose. Naturally, the 85 miles-per-hour wind causes the tether and hose to belly out well behind and below the Robin, where they writhe and twist unpredictably.

By skillfully manipulating the tether while feeding out hose, Shorty Chaffee is able to roughly guide the nozzle to within distance of Walker's waiting arms.

When Walker is able to grasp, control, and insert the hose into the Sun God's tank, he signals Shorty. Shorty then opens the valve from the supply tank to the hose, sending a supply of gasoline down to the lower airplane. When all the gas has been transferred, the tether and hose are hand-over-hand retrieved by Chaffee.

Sometimes, the Sun God crew attaches messages to the hose before it is retracted. Two messages attached to the retracted hose were written on the reverse of yellow pages torn from a "Periodic Inspection Report." One says, simply: "Something to eat to please hungry as hell."

A series of these transfers results in the Sun God receiving more than 200 gallons of gas, thirteen cans of oil, an altimeter, and parts for the Earth Inductor Compass.

On an oil-stained, roughly torn page received by the Curtiss Robin, is the following: "Dear Frank Will you show us to Cleveland after this refueling - Nick."

PART III

TO THE NORTHWEST

10. Kylertown Fusillade

Nick rests now. At the controls, Art Walker keeps the Sun God behind, and off to the right of Frank Hawks' airplane. Although the Sun God flew over these Pennsylvania hills and boroughs on their way east, that jostling journey allowed little time for observing Allegheny landmarks. Now, westbound from New York, Art is glad for Hawks' experienced navigation over this leg of the trip. All Walker has to do is match Hawks' speed and altitude.

As the sun lowers, Art finds Hawks' aircraft, silhouetted against the failing light, a little harder to follow. But the Wright motor churns along with nine-cylinder vigor, sponsoring a comforting feeling of security. Only the bumpy air is intimidating.

Night encroaches. They pass near Allentown and Walker spots blooms of lightning in the cloud-shrouded distance.

Nick, bending at the waist, comes forward behind Art. The pilots squeeze by each other to exchange control. As Art moves aside he points ahead, beyond Hawks' airplane, and shakes his head. Nick's lips gather into a pugnacious pout. He forces a slight nod. He grasps the stick and levels the airplane. Scanning the instruments, he ends on the fuel gauges. Fortunately, they have plenty of gas.

Nick follows Hawks as the latter climbs, exploring for smoother air. Now over Sunbury, Nick thinks he recognizes the flickering lights of the town, but the visibility is tenuous. Within minutes, Hawks changes his mind and descends. Height yields no smoother air, and clouds begin to obscure visibility of the ground.

The pitch blackness is broken by gray haze as the two planes approach Bellefonte. Beacon lights ahead confirm that Hawks has delivered them onto the Airmail's Airway. Hawks dips his wings first left, then right, a "goodbye, good luck" signal. In less than a minute he's out of sight, on his way east to New York.

Nick drops down and levels over the Bellefonte beacon. The airfield's hangar, with its shed office on one side brightly lit by more than a dozen outside lights, looks welcoming. Walker, positioned now behind the big fuel tank, scans the landscape out of the side window. He thinks he identifies a biplane inside the open front of the hangar. "Air mail," he yells at Nick.

Nick nods, but his gaze is directed ahead, at what the repeated flashes of lightning reveal: towering thunderheads.

In dry, matter-of-fact words, the Pittsburgh Press reports the weather: "...a trough...of low pressure extending from New England southwestward over the Ohio valley states to the far Southwest...[with] local showers...as far west as Ohio...".

Warm, moist air is boosted skyward by the Allegheny mountains. The moisture rises ever higher, into cooler and colder air, where it condenses into mountainous clouds. Now, these nocturnal cells are forming groups, feeding off other clouds' convection.

Nick continues flying.

Soon the Sun God approaches the hamlet of Kylertown.

With the exception of some flickers of light on the ground, everything outside the airplane is steeped in velvet black. Abruptly for a split second, jagged streaks of cloud-to-cloud lightning illuminate enormous banks of clouds ahead.

Nick tries to scan the horizon for a path between them. But the blackness quickly returns, instantly cloaking the view in a shroud of lightlessness.

Nick realizes the severe threat in the wall of storms ahead. He later writes, "Thirty miles west of that town [Bellefonte] we encountered one of the severest electrical storms I have ever seen..."

He banks the plane and completes a turn. They'll fly east, back toward Bellefonte. On course to return them to the Bellefonte airfield, he writes a quick note, and directs Walker to prepare a weighted packet.

Once again over the hangar at the Bellefonte airfield, Nick takes the Sun God low. Walker tosses the weighted packet onto the airfield. The message requests aid in identifying the airway to Cleveland in the worsening conditions. "...[I]t was difficult to get our bearings," he later writes.

Noting the lowering clouds, Nick takes the Sun God lower. Marking time, he flies a roughly triangular course over Bellefonte, awaiting improved conditions and help from the ground.

Somewhat later, the pilots observe "a great deal of flashing on and off of lights" at the Bellefonte airfield. Mamer interprets this as signalling danger ahead (west of Bellefonte), so he continues to fly the triangle.

The storm clouds approach Bellefonte and intensify. After enduring the turbulence and decreasing visibility for thirty minutes or so, Mamer decides they have no choice but to try to cut through it.

Flying as low as he dares, Nick seeks the least obscured canyons between threatening bulges of vapor. "At such moments up in the sky," he later writes, "you have to think quick and act quicker."

Indeed, decisions are forced by great rushes of rain that blot his vision. It drums on the planes' fabric and metal, matching the roar from the Wright motor up front. Nick reacts, banking off toward the brighter spots. Art simply hangs on, as the aircraft is buffeted by updrafts, down drafts and skidding movements.

Close, and off to one side, a bolt of white-hot lightning flashes. The airplane rocks sideways with the sudden explosion of superheated air. The sound assaults their ears, nearly deafening them. Nick feels control of the aircraft wash away. He struggles thrusting the stick. He adds power, and begins to recover from a near-stall. Glancing quickly at the altimeter, he realizes they came close to meeting an Allegheny hilltop.

Under these chaotic conditions, there's no time to think about crashing. Although during the Federated Fliers days Nick had thrilled the crowds at Minnesota fairs by skimming the field at a height of twenty feet and dared drowning by flying under bridges, the acrobatics of avoiding mishaps in the midst of thunderstorms is different. It requires instant decisions that subsequently may require extreme control of the aircraft to insure survival. Yet Walker, and Mamer too, take a bit of ease knowing of Nick's barnstorming expertise as well as years pioneering mountain flying routes in the Northwest, at night and in the winter, dodging deteriorating weather.

More than once, Nick reverses course to avoid sheets of rain and murderous lightning. A straight course for Cleveland is forgotten; it's now a matter of survival—escape from certain wrecking. Nick describes it in a dispatch the next day: "Twice we thought the severity of the storm would break us down..."

The Sun God veers and swerves to skirt the intense cores of the storms. Throughout the night, its path grows into a tangle of roundabouts and detours. "Repeatedly, we tried to break through, but the storm was too tough and too extensive," Nick says.

Eventually, "Nothing is quite comparable to the thrill of literally winging your way on top of the thunderbolts in a frail device of fabric and metal, while the lightning surrounds you with streaks of white-hot flame."

When finally the feeble light of dawn squeaks through the weakening squalls, the aviators wonder how they survived. They are completely spent, and spend the next miles across Ohio into Cleveland in thanksgiving for Nick's skill and the good fortune that allowed them to continue.

Over Cleveland, Ohio, they rendezvous once again with the Curtiss Robin refueling plane piloted by Dan Robertson, with James Buchanan handling the hose. The transfer of gasoline in two contacts is successful, and the pilots also take on breakfast, a most welcome gift after a most harrowing night.

The Sun God, its motor unaffected by the ordeal, powers monotonously on toward St. Paul, Minnesota.

11. Those Are the Brakes

Now, nearing Chicago, the pilots of the Sun God are surprised. A brisk tail wind has whisked them along, far ahead of their planned arrival. "As if to compensate," Nick writes later, "for the rough treatment of the night before," referring to their experience in the storms over Pennsyvania.

It's sunny—"...a marvelous day for flying," Nick exclaims as they guide the Sun God over the southern edge of glistening Lake Michigan. Here what grips the fliers is a sublime sense of freedom, the escape from earthly cares that breaks the knotty constraints of ordinary life.

Asked why they fly, true aviators can't answer. Seemingly they choose danger, yet danger does not explain why they fly. It's mysterious they know, a paradox, a question seemingly without an answer.

The *Spokane Sun God* turns north, passing first over Chicago Municipal, the Chicago River, and off to the left, Maywood Field, made notorious in the mid-twenties by the arrivals and departures of the Airmail Service airplanes.

Their route this morning of August 19 curves the western shores of Lake Michigan to Milwaukee, where they swing inland, over Oconomowoc. (The odd name Oconomowoc comes from a Potowatomi word for "waterfall.") Here they divert to catch Madison, Wisconsin.

Nick, whose hobbies include hunting and fishing, swoops low over the lakes on either side of Madison, circles the airfield north of the city, and drops a note:

> "Hello, boys at the airport. This time I'm not stopping for gas. Still have about 200 gallons on board. This wagon takes more than the Ford I stopped here with about a month ago. Those are keen lakes and we need a bath badly. How about a bath on the sly? Send up 499 gallons of lake water. (signed) Nick Mamer and Art Walker, Spokane endurance flyers."

Two other messages are dropped. One requests that the refuelers at the St. Paul airfield prepare a hundred and fifty gallons of gas, ten gallons of oil, and hot food for the Sun God's arrival. The second, addressed to the Spokane Aeronautic association, says the pilots expect to arrive in Spokane tomorrow, Tuesday, August 20.

At Spokane headquarters, right now, Vic Dessert and the committee puzzle over a telegram from St. Paul. "Weather report looks bad to me," begins the wire from refueling pilot Vern Bookwalter. "Tail wind to Dakotas, side wind to Montana and headwinds Montana to Spokane. Think your best bet is to move Wilson further east."

Dessert interprets this as Bookwalter's feeling the Sun God may run short of gas before arriving at Missoula, where refueling pilot Wilson's aircraft is currently located. Dessert understands that headwinds through Montana may cause Mamer to consume more fuel than anticipated. Yet he refrains from directing Wilson to move. Instead, he advises Wilson at Missoula by message to hold himself in readiness for further instructions.

Dessert is the son of Alsace-Lorraine natives. In this country, however, the senior Dessert becomes a successful hotel owner and operator. Upon his death in 1907, young Dessert is thrust into the family business, which he continues successfully. Later he is chosen as co-vice-president of the Association sponsoring the 1927 Spokane Air Races and Derby, the success of which places Spokane in the nation's aviation spotlight.

Dessert had earlier seen to it that a man from the Northern Pacific Railway had left Spokane for Helena, Montana with a new 65-foot refueling hose ordered by Wilson. Dessert's training and business experience helps him frame a reply to Bookwalter:

> "Thanks for the weather report. Suggest you advise Mamer as you advised us. Ask Mamer where he wants Wilson to be moved if Wilson is to be moved. Do not like to move refueling planes without approval of Mamer as Mamer may have different plans regarding storm. Have advised Wilson to hold himself in readiness for instructions. Suggest you give Mamer this wire on refueling hose so he will be in touch with the situation."

Afterwards he delivers a reassuring assessment to news reporters: "[E]very precaution will be taken to prevent any accident at this time," he says. "Mamer has been notified of the weather conditions and Wilson and his refueling ship is in readiness to go anywhere Mamer wants him."

The Sun God now is about to leave Wisconsin. At La Crosse, the pilot turns and follows the gently-curving Mississippi River into Minnesota. Less than an hour later, the plane appears over the river bluffs at St. Paul.

People gathered on the tops of buildings in St. Paul wave and cheer the arrival of the Sun God. According to an observer, Mamer and Walker pass low over several tall buildings and wave back at the spectators. The observer also reports "[N]o one in the Great Northern [railroad] building was doing any work at all...everyone was up on the roof watching the Sun God."

Slightly after 1:30 p.m., the Sun God swoops low over the St. Paul airport, and a note is dropped saying they're ready for refueling. "Be sure and let's go up pretty well in the contacts," it says (to Vern Bookwalter), "The air is pretty smooth about 4,000 above sea level."

Bookwalter takes the *Apple Blossom* to the sky, where he and Neil O'Connell deliver 75 gallons of gas, two gallons of oil, and two chicken dinners. As Bookwalter later returns to the St. Paul field, a cable controlling the brakes on the plane snaps. Brakeless, the Ryan coasts through a low fence bordering the flying field and rolls to a stop inches from a parked automobile. The airplane is tugged away from the car by ground personnel and pushed back to the hangars. There, the broken cable is removed and a new cable quickly installed. This takes less than an hour.

Meanwhile, unaware of the brake problem, the crew of the Sun God continues circling. A note is dropped. It's directed to Frank Geng, station master of the airport. "This is like home," writes Nick, referring to the Minneapolis area (he was born in nearby Hastings). "Sorry I can't spend more time with you. Will try and stay longer next time."

Another note is dropped that, perhaps due to the wind, is lost to the river. A third note dropped by the Sun God instructs Bookwalter to "take on as much gas as possible and follow us to Aberdeen."

At about this time, a third airplane (pilot unknown) is seen rendezvousing with the Sun God. It carries a large sign affixed to its side that reads, "Take on as much gas as possible and don't leave." This message to the Sun God pilots appears to tell them to not to leave St. Paul at this time, while Bookwalter's airplane is being repaired. It seems confusing, but is included in this narrative because it was reported by the press at the time.

Following the repair to the *Apple Blossom*, Bookwalter responds with a refueling contact at 4,000 feet altitude. O'Connell transfers more gas, about

125 gallons. After landing, Bookwalter reloads the Ryan's refueling tank with 125 gallons and takes off.

At close to 4 p.m., observers see the Ryan and the Sun God flying together toward the west, leaving St. Paul behind.

12. On to the Great Plains

Winging away, the Sun God leaves the Minneapolis-St. Paul area accompanied by the Ryan, with Bookwalter and O'Connell aboard.

They skew across Minnesota, passing over squared-off cornfields and towns nuzzled to rusty sidings, prairie lakes dappled with boats and skinny piers. Narrow roads hide between windbreaks and hillocks, then sweep by dome-topped silos clasped to board-sided barns. Watching below, the pilots are benumbed by the blueish shadow of their airplane as it crawls across the terrain, wriggling and wavering as if it were alive.

They'll follow the tracks of the "Milwaukee Road," the steam train's shiny rails that trace west to Granite Falls, then stream to the edge of Big Stone Lake where the tracks cross into South Dakota. This is also the route of the Yellowstone Trail, a well-graveled and occasionally paved cross-country auto road. As it happens, it's also well-promoted by one J. W. Parmley of Ipswich, South Dakota, a keen-minded man who foresaw an expansive future for automobile travel.

The rolling flatland invites speed. It's a compass course, a straight shot. Nothing much invites the eye, nothing much demands attention.

Despite the need for constant alertness, memories tend to percolate into consciousness. Days of sun, much like today, surface, with Master Signal Electrician Nick Mamer in the front seat of the open cockpit biplane and Lieutenant Winslow at the controls of the R-6. At about sixty miles an hour, the salty, humid air rushes not unpleasantly past them in their tandem seats. It's June 6, 1918, and they're crossing the Rio Chagres on their way out over the Atlantic Ocean.

They turn to a heading of eighty-degrees and pass over Point Toro and the two breakwaters in Limon Bay. To the south, if Mamer could see them, are the Panama Railroad, Gatun Locks and the Coastal Defense guns of Manzanillo. The Air Service hasn't converted this aircraft yet, so the observer's seat remains up front, where the downward view to the side of the biplane is blocked by the lower wing. Despite the observer's hindered vision, their mission is 'Reconnaissance and Patrol.'

In this lumbering, slightly improved Curtiss aircraft—it might break eighty miles per hour in level flight—they're looking for U-boats. Military planners think a German U-boat might try to sneak into Limon Bay and torpedo a ship at the entrance of the Panama Canal, intent on blocking it. But despite numerous attacks and sinkings by U-boats in the Atlantic, no U-boat has been sighted by patrols of the 7th Aero Squadron since their arrival on the Isthmus in early 1917.

Nick is delighted to be in the air, but staring at an empty ocean during this second patrol of the day is boring. It would be better if he were at the controls. That's why, in March, he has petitioned the Office of the Chief Signal Officer to be placed on flying status.

This letter petition (see Notes) displays his youthful eagerness and confidence in seeking to become an accomplished pilot in the Air Service. Thanks to the sincerity of his writing and the recommendations of his superiors, including his pilot this day, in July of 1918 his petition is successful. He's sent to Princeton, New Jersey, to the Military Aeronautics School at Princeton University, from which he graduates. The war ends shortly thereafter. Later, after his promotion to 2nd Lieutenant, he becomes a flight instructor for the U.S. Army.

In a slight mist ahead lie the by-now familiar outlines of the coast of Panama.

But in a blink, the scene reverts to the arid plains of South Dakota. With a tail wind, this leg to Aberdeen will take the *Spokane Sun God* less time than expected.

Had the Sun God pilots been reading the latest papers (newspapers were delivered to them at North Platte), they would know that the news of other record attempts is less than encouraging. Kaesar and Luescher, two Swiss aviators attempting to reach New York from Lisbon, are sighted circling a village on the Island of Terceira (Azores). But the latest report is that they and their snow-white airplane, Jungschweitgerland, are overdue in Nova Scotia and presumed lost.

At the same time, the *Boston Globe* reports "[four] ranchers...saw a plane... dive into a thick growth of cottonwood trees a short distance from the Gila River [Yuma County, Arizona]." When found, the wreck is identified as an airplane flown by Miss Marvel Crosson, an entrant in the Santa Monica to Cleveland women's air derby. The smashed airplane's clock is stopped at 12:16.

A Yuma County deputy later locates the pilot a hundred yards away, crushed in an isolated ravine. Her wristwatch, with its strap broken, is stopped at 12:16:30. Miss Crosson, a 25-year-old, is enveloped in her parachute, which partly deployed. It is surmised she bailed out when her airplane malfunctioned, but was too close to the ground to have been saved by her 'chute.

Now, skipping over Blue Dog Lake, Nick Mamer and Art Walker pass the Day County town of Andover, South Dakota. Next is Groton, South Dakota, another town oddly named after the ones in Massachusetts.

In the near distance, past the 98th Meridian, is Aberdeen, where the Great Plains stretch westward before them. This is also where Vern Bookwalter and Neil O'Connell finish transferring seventy-five gallons of gas into the tanks of the Sun God, to continue its long journey home.

It's now almost 6:30 p.m., Monday, August 19, four full days since they left the sod at Felts Field in Spokane.

13. UNDER A RED MOON

The story of the journey of the Sun God from Aberdeen, South Dakota to Miles City, Montana, is not a tale of fire—and yet it is. Any tale in which flames threaten the deaths of men can be called a story of fire. The difference here is not the danger, only the pilots' distance from the flames.

From Dayville, Oregon, to the Umatilla reserve, to the Rainier National forest, to the Wenatchee forest, to Maggie Butte and the Musselshell zone of the Selway, to Yakinikak creek west of Glacier, to Gypsy creek in the Kooksia forest, to Moyie creek northeast of Bonner's Ferry, to Granite creek in the Coeur d'Alene forest, fires rage. Near Cedar lake west of Columbia Falls, Montana, forty men are trapped by fire on this nineteenth day of August, 1929.

But to the airmen flying west from Aberdeen, South Dakota, the sky overhead appears at first pristine. From Ipswich to the Missouri River, following the gleaming rails of the Milwaukee Road, they face the glare of the lowering sun. The benign land below glows daylight-distinct.

The railroad parallels, and sometimes intersects, the Yellowstone Trail. On five iron spans easily identified from the air, the Trail's auto road crosses the Missouri on an almost-new bridge. Built in 1924 over a nearly mile-wide part of the river, its heritage of earlier transportation is recalled when it is described by the highway department as "the new wagon bridge."

Beyond the Missouri River, the iron rails of the Milwaukee Road veer to the north. Now almost an hour west of Aberdeen, Nick calculates the fuel used and the distance covered. The figures show they face a strong headwind slowing their progress. The wind not only hastens the exhaustion of their supply of gasoline, but calls into question the stationing of Wilson's refueling plane at Missoula, Montana, more than 650 miles from their present location.

At the airport in Miles City, Montana, E. B. "Buck" Winter fingers a telegram, timestamped 7:00 p.m. It's from Aberdeen, South Dakota. It says Nick Mamer, pilot of the *Spokane Sun God*, has left Aberdeen and is coming to Miles City. It also says the Sun God may circle the Miles City airport and that if it does, to please notify Wilson to relocate: "Have R. M. Wilson at Missoula go to Belgrade. I will meet him there." Nick Mamer had apparently dropped this note at Aberdeen asking that the message be wired to Miles City, Montana.

After conferring with Miles City pilots Frank Wiley and Tom Mathews, Buck Winter wires Wilson at Missoula that he should relocate to Belgrade.

The Sun God passes the west bank of the Missouri River, leaving behind the Lakota enclave of Standing Rock. It enters the sparsely-populated southwest corner of North Dakota. The haze here is at first slight, but Nick notes the sky is graying and dimming. The haze tints the town below—Bowman, North Dakota—a dull shade of ochre. It smells like smoke, he tells Art, even as he mentally reviews the Sun God's position, speed, and gasoline supply.

U.S. Forestry headquarters in Portland, Oregon has reported twelve new forest fires. Eleven of these were caused by lightning. High winds, Chief District forester Granger says, are blowing embers into unburned areas, sparking new, more dangerous fires.

The airmen in the Sun God are of course unaware of these developments. Here, at the eastern edge of Montana, all they notice is the odor of smoke as it seeps inside the Sun God's cabin. Gradually, as the eight o'clock hour of sunset approaches, their vision ahead diminishes. The sun no longer glares—instead, the bright red disk is comfortably viewed without a squint.

The almost-full moon rose earlier. Its reflection in the artificial lake at Baker shows as a pale red disk. (This lake had been created early on by the railroad to supply water for the Milwaukee Road's steam engines.) Nick has been over this terrain between St. Paul and Miles City, Montana many times during the past decade. While he seems able to consult a detailed mental map of the territory as they traverse it, it's still necessary to confirm their progress with landmarks.

To compensate for the dimming by smoke drifting toward them from more distant parts of Montana, he takes the Sun God lower, at least temporarily prolonging their view of the railroad tracks through the dry farm country of Fallon County. With their gas running low and with smoke from forest fires becoming ever more dense ahead, what are their options?

It's late Monday when the Sun God arrives over Miles City, Montana. Here the Northern Pacific and Milwaukee Road main line tracks and yards lay side by side, making Miles City a "two-railroad town." But at ten p.m. this evening, the Road's lighted roundhouse and turntable, busy as usual, are barely seen by the pilots.

The Miles City airport is two miles from the city on the "bluff side," the low bluffs that face the city on the northwest side of the Yellowstone River. A single bridge across the Yellowstone connects the city to the field's two turf runways fronted by a big hangar. With news of the layer of smoke over eastern Montana, an earlier request had arrived from Spokane asking the airport to set out flaming cans of gasoline along its favored runway—in case the Sun God was forced to land.

Mamer now sights the river, and heads north, circling slowly. Although he believes they are over the airport, he's forced to swoop low to verify his belief. Worse, it seems that viewing landmarks to the west of Miles City, even if brightly lit, will be impossible. His hope "to boom right on home" from St. Paul is not to be. "We had to give up the idea," he later says, because the nighttime smoke "made the visibility so poor...we had...to remain in Montana overnight."

Because they can't leave, Walker pilots the Sun God in leisurely circles over the city and the airport while Nick composes a note he intends to drop to "Buck" Winter, the man in charge of the airport.

Meanwhile, as the Sun God roars overhead, the airfield's workers gather outside, near the hangar, peering at the sky without seeing anything except smoke. The group includes Buck Winter, Jack Hotaling, Roy Milligan and Tom Mathews. These air-minded men watch and wonder what is to happen with the Sun God, although they cannot see the airplane itself.

On its ninth pass over the airfield—the men are counting—the Sun God approaches, very low. With its navigation lights out, it is visible only by reflections from lights on the field. It skims a trajectory directly over the hangar and at the precisely-timed moment, a packet and attached flashlight hurtles to the ground. The packet lands forty feet in front of the hanger, where it is retrieved by Tom Mathews.

The gathered men eagerly read the enclosed note, which says:

"Buck: The visibility is hellish tonight. Smoke is haze. You cannot see a thing on the ground such as contours, mountains. I believe I had better spend the night circling the airport – and in the morning if you can have a ship on hand I would like to have you refuel me in the following manner:

"Get round five gallon cans, heavy ones – have the refueling man strapped in the ship and with half-inch rope.

Let the can about 25 feet below plane. When I draw up underneath he can let it down the rest of the way until the man in my ship grabs the can. Have the rope in 50 feet lengths. Now for the pilot. He flies straight and steady course and absolutely pays no attention to anyone. I do all of the maneuvering. It is simple. In the meantime have my man Wilson go to Belgrade Mont., as they have a fine field there and I will meet him there.

"If you can meet all these conditions, indicate by building bonfire on field and I will stand by for daylight. – Nick

"If you cannot arrange this blink the flood lights on and off three times in succession."

During the brief discussion that follows, the group works out a plan. Jack Hotaling and Roy Milligan will work through the night to gather the necessary supplies and equipment. Other interested people are contacted to help. Inside the airfield office, Buck Winter fields questions over the single telephone line from citizens who want to know about the airplane they hear circling over Miles City in the dark. Its Whirlwind motor is easily heard, but residents can't find the noisy airplane.

Frank Wiley, operator of the airport's flying service, had for days been following the flight of the Sun God. At the airport this evening, he interprets the dropped note to say the Sun God is low on fuel, and that Nick and Art will circle until either they are refueled or they will attempt to land. He and some helpers set up a fifty-gallon drum out near where the runways intersect. They build a big fire in the drum to signal the airfield's intent to refuel the Sun God in the air, or if that fails, to provide guidance and some illumination for the plane to safely land.

Wiley discusses a possible refueling with Tom Mathews. They think they can use the Eaglerock airplane for the attempt. Wiley's flying service flies a brand-new J-5 Eaglerock aircraft. Manufactured by the Alexander Aircraft plant in Colorado Springs, this three-place, open cockpit biplane is fitted with the Wright Whirlwind 220-hp motor. It gives good performance at the higher altitudes encountered in the Rockies.

Over the following six hours, volunteers take on other aspects of the rescue operation. One group procures five-gallon cans from a local creamery. Another makes rope slings with letdowns and snaps courtesy of the Furstnow

Saddle Shop. A third group prepares food for all hands, including the Sun God pilots.

After seeing the creamery cans filled with gasoline, and readying the Eaglerock, Wiley feels they are ready for the refueling attempt. As dawn breaks, workers load eight of the cans into the wide front cockpit of the Eaglerock, along with the roping apparatus. Then they attach Tom Mathews to the cockpit using a telephone lineman's belt that allows him to lean far over the side of the fuselage without falling out.

Once at the controls in the rear cockpit, Wiley starts the motor and takes off. It's not quite five o'clock in the morning (Tuesday). The smoke is still thick, but the feeble red of the rising sun provides enough light for Wiley to find the Sun God flying on a northwesterly course through the murky atmosphere. He climbs above it and sees Art Walker, in helmet and goggles, waiting in the opening in the top of the Sun God's fuselage.

"Indeed, the oil-streaked old Sun God looked as if it had really had a rough time," he later recalls, remarking as well on a rag stuffed in a hole in its windshield.

After attaching a rope to a wing strut of the Eaglerock, Mathews snaps on a sling holding a can of gas. He swings the can over and down off the rear of the lower wing. Facing toward the tail and hanging half out of the cockpit, he feeds enough line out to allow the can to swing down and behind toward Walker.

From his plane's position to the rear and below the Eaglerock, Mamer maneuvers the plane underneath and powers upward until Walker is able to grasp the can as it wobbles in the air at the end of its tether. He unsnaps the can and lowers it inside.

Each can of gas weighs a little less than forty pounds. Nevertheless, because of the strength and skill of the men handling the ropes and the two pilots' expertise, the delivery of each can in this manner takes less than five minutes. It is the first time a plane has ever been refueled in this manner.

"Oh boy," says Nick, "this refueling is sweet stuff!"

With the forty gallons aboard the Sun God and more daylight, both planes turn south, flying low enough to discern the Yellowstone River when it appears through the brown smoke. They turn left and follow the river downstream until they reach the bridge and the airfield to its left over the bluffs.

Meanwhile, about three-hundred people have arrived at the Miles City airport. They've come from the city and the surrounding area to take in the spectacle of the Sun God's refueling.

The airmen fly the same triangular course for the second refueling. It goes more quickly, during which Art attaches a note to the rope line saying one more can on a third load will be enough. Hot breakfast, hot drinks and a letter from Buck Winter are also received by the Sun God pilots. The letter, on behalf of Wiley, Mathews and the citizens of Miles City, congratulates Mamer and Walker. "You are making history. You are writing pages in the 'flying book' that have never before been written."

While Wiley is loading up gasoline, a visiting farmer inquires how the creamery cans are being returned. In his book, Wiley recalls the incident: "... we had a boy with a rowboat down by the bridge, and...the Sun God Crew dropped the cans in the river after they were emptied. The boy picked up the cans as they floated by and returned them to us. The farmer thought that was pretty ingenious, and so did I."

Now saved from a premature end of landing at Miles City, the flight of the Sun God continues toward Belgrade. In a final note to their airfield benefactors, Nick writes, "Miles City – Buck, Frank and Tommy: There is no way to express our appreciation, Nick."

Unfortunately, although the *Spokane Sun God* airmen have thus survived another low-on-gas crisis, their tale of fire is not yet ended.

14. SMOKE GETS IN YOUR EYES

With fresh gas in their tanks and a hot breakfast in their stomachs, the Sun God airmen nose their craft to the southwest. The sun, barely risen, is behind them. Here the pilot must navigate by the Yellowstone River and the Northern Pacific tracks that closely parallel it. So far, the crew has encountered eye-stinging haze, but have not lost their way.

"Smoke rises," we say. Burning provides smoke's energy—its hot gases expand and buoyancy forces them upward. But as they rise, mixing and diffusion spread and cool the gases, slowing the smoke's expansion and upward movement. While all this is happening, winds at different levels tear at the cloud, spreading, displacing, and distorting the plumes. Its appearance changes from roiling brown to paler, graying haze.

All smoke hampers vision, but the density of the smoke matters: visibility through a moderate haze is better than through a billowing brown cloud directly over a fire. The viewing angle also matters: Peering through miles of smoke ahead or behind is more difficult than looking downward through a quarter-mile of smoke.

In 1925, Nick Mamer and R. T. Freng had initiated the Region 1 forest fire patrol service, piloting DeHavilland DH-4Bs, biplanes loaned to the Forest Service by the U. S. Army Air Corps. The area covered by the two U.S. Forest Service pilots was 200 miles wide and 300 miles long, or 60,000 square miles. Six-hundred hours of flying over the timbered forests of northern Idaho, eastern Washington and western Montana was typical for a single season of fire patrol. Over the years since, Mamer had experienced months of smoke-filled flying. So he knew better than to push away from Miles City in the dark. He knew to wait for daylight, with its unknown risks but hoped-for improved visibility.

Those DH-4B forest service airplanes had wide, equal span wings, fixed landing gear, and two open cockpits just behind the wings. The twelve-cylinder, water-cooled Liberty motor drove a two-bladed propeller. Control was from the rear cockpit; the observer rode in the front seat. The "B" model fuselage was wood, rather than fabric-covered as in the war-era plane, and it incorporated improved compass, altimeter and pressure gauges.

Mamer later described the patrol: "The observer accurately marks down the exact position of the fire, accurate to the quarter section if the observations are correctly made, as they usually are." The fire's extent and the effectiveness of firefighting can then be monitored. "[The] action [taken] depends largely upon the severity of the fire and conditions which might lead to its spread…"

"We had to invent all sorts of ingenious ways to get in through the smoke. Sometimes, out of Missoula, headed from one fire, I would time myself, five minutes west, five minutes northwest, which if my calculations were correct, would put me directly over a canyon into which I could spiral and then follow through the canyon and its tributary to my objective."

"We always flew in early morning, because as soon as the sun got up, it caused such terrible turbulence in the air over the canyons, I was tossed about until I thought the air would tear the plane to pieces."

Piloting the open-cockpit, Liberty-motored De Haviland for hours over burning timber, through turbulent air with limited vision was, to say the least, educational. "Flying conditions in July over the area were the worst I have experienced in thirteen years in the game," Nick Mamer said of one season's duty.

Region 1 forests provided few fields clear enough of trees to land a plane. Should the motor of the De Haviland quit, the pilot and observer had little choice but to jump, count to three, and pull the parachute's rip cord. If fortunate enough to make it to earth without injury, they should expect to spend days in isolation before returning to civilization. Although Nick Mamer never previously gave much thought to wearing a parachute, he favored it for forest fire service. "I would not like to be without it over that country," he said.

Once, coming out of the Selway heading for Grangeville, Mamer flew low along Moose creek to the Selway River. "Suddenly, with no warning, I hit a tunnel of yellow smoke that blotted out all daylight, although it was only 5 o'clock in the morning.

"I couldn't turn around and go back, I couldn't climb above it. Some of the smoke clouds were 20,000 feet high. I just went on flying blind and eventually got out."

"Time and again, I would swear I would never make another flight in through the smoke, with so many hazards. But as soon as we would get back in safety with both feet on the ground, I would be ready to go back. Why? I don't know. Certainly it isn't for the money..."

Nick Mamer knows that daylight's rays, bent by haze and blocked by ash, die. Then all the pilot has are his daring and the multiple skills honed during all those smoke-filled flights.

Spread wider here, the landscape nods goodbye to the Great Plains and faces the looming Rockies. Below, in the rolling river valley carved from rimrock, sits Billings, Montana. Mamer is well known in Billings for his stops at its airfield on flights east and west over the years, but the Sun God's passing at 7:00 a.m. goes unheralded. Had local pilots and enthusiasts known of his arrival, they would have been out to cheer the Sun God on.

By the time the Sun God reaches Big Timber, Montana, the indistinct prominence of Crazy Peak, at more than 11,000 feet, and the Absaroka Range south of their flight path, signal the end of the prairies. Bozeman pass, at 5,712 feet, is next. Then it's down into the Gallatin valley and the small town of Belgrade, at 4,459 feet, where the Sun God crew hopes to refuel.

With eyes smarting, nostrils burning and nerves tingling, the airmen have survived and outmaneuvered the smoke and haze all the way from Miles City. Arriving over Belgrade, the *Spokane Sun God* circles the airfield.

Mamer had flown his tri-motored Ford *West Wind* into this six-runway airfield for its grand opening celebration in the spring of this year, so it is familiar to him. And fortunately, Wilson had received the Sun God's message in Missoula and relocated his refueling operation here. Within minutes of appearing overhead, the Sun God prepares to receive gasoline from Wilson's Buhl.

The contact is successful. Leaving Belgrade with 75 gallons of new gasoline, the Sun God heads northwest, where *The Missoulian* reports more than a million feet of logs have been consumed in the Cooper's Mill fire.

Nick will guide them on to Missoula, where the forests in the Blackfoot valley and across Lolo pass are ablaze. Are they perhaps now speeding crazily from smoke to flame?

15. Almost Home

After more than four days entrapped in the low and narrow cave of an airplane cabin, the crew of the Sun God claws their beards and scratches their moustaches. Fingers serve as combs. Forearm swipes clear sweat from foreheads. Cleanup following repairs means wiping black and greasy hands on already-soiled golf pants. Droppings from food and drink show as colorful shirtfronts. Dousings with gasoline have rendered Walker's body raw, his jacket barely wearable. Cycles of sweating and cold have turned both men's skin itchy and smarting, their surroundings stale, smelly, and uncomfortable.

Before they left Spokane, Mamer and Walker packed the tail section of the Buhl airplane with supplies they thought they'd need. Included was an alarm clock, a blackboard, chalk, a first-aid kit, a mattress, a calendar, flashlights, pen and pencils, matches, two jack knives. Also included were some items they never used—grappling hooks, for example. Things they might have craved were not included, such as shaving materials and skin lotion. Changes of clothing were not thought necessary. There was no basin in which to wash. Their toilet was simply a trap door in the cabin floor.

Interrupted naps have left both men more restless than rested. Fatigue has turned them moody and slow to respond. The motor's constant roar has caused misunderstandings, rude questions and hoarse voices. Muscles stiffen from lack of exercise. Crouching beneath the low ceiling of the cabin has delivered backaches and leg cramps. Lack of sleep keeps eyes stinging, burning, and rimmed with red. The pilots wish for an end to these torments.

But without doubt, resolve and mettle flourish.

With Tuesday morning's daylight glinting pale behind them, the aviators push the Sun God through veils of smoky haze, keeping to the known valleys of the Jefferson, Madison and Gallatin Rivers. Soon they will graze the crest of the Continental Divide at 6,500 feet and descend to the vicinity of Butte, Montana.

Officials at 5,550-feet-high Butte Municipal Airport expect the plane to refuel over their airfield.

At 9:30, with Walker piloting, the Sun God glides toward town. Workers at Butte's airfield see the red plane approach, descend and circle. From the far edge of the field, the plane straightens its path and skims low. As it nears the main hangar, ground crews see a figure emerge from the top of the fuselage. He tosses objects out of the airplane. Workers at the field hurry to gather the packets from where they land.

Shortly, the Buhl airplane of Bob Wilson appears in the eastern sky over Butte. He circles, turns and approaches the runway. After landing and taxiing to the hangar area, he explains to airport officials he's landed to pick up a load of gasoline.

Officials have opened the dropped packets and found notes. One is directed to Wilson. Scribbled in pencil on one side of crinkled paper, it reads, "Not necessary for service of any kind here. Proceed to Missoula. Give us 50 gallons over Missoula before you land."

Another note, addressed to the Associated Press, features a wistful message: "Sorry we can't land—the field looks so good—this sure looks like God's country again."

A short time later, Wilson succeeds in getting the Buhl's supply tank filled with gas. Straight away he taxis the craft to the end of the runway, turns into the wind, and takes off.

After circling while awaiting Wilson, the Sun God now bears north, accompanied by the Buhl. Passing the world's tallest masonry chimney (585 feet) at the Anaconda smelter, they follow the narrow valley of the Clark Fork River through Deer Lodge County, aiming for Missoula.

By this time, newspapers across the country, small-town dailies as well as metropolitan giants, devote hundreds of inches of print to the venture of Nick Mamer and the Sun God. Front page stories and banner headlines tell of what's now called the "historic flight" of the *Spokane Sun God*. The stories counter each other with hyperbole. They speculate, "Will the flight (when it reaches Spokane) continue until motor or men are exhausted?" Or will it "end as it began," there in Spokane?

These newspapermen, isolated from direct contact with the fliers, have no idea what Mamer or his backers intend, or what is likely. All they can do is guess—and tease.

Bob Johnson, a Missoula resident, had taken flying lessons under Nick Mamer a few years earlier at Felts Field in Spokane. Right now, though, the

36-year-old is impatient. He's pacing back and forth near his new Travel Air airplane parked on the flight line at Missoula Municipal Airport. He's arranged to take six paid passengers up in the Travel Air to view the Sun God as it is refueled in the air. He scans the gray clouds intently, but doesn't spot the red airplane with the Texaco stars on its wings.

A bit past 11:00 a.m., though, the Sun God appears over the hills to the east of Missoula and Bob Johnson cheerfully loads his passengers into their seats. The fully-loaded Travel Air is seen hurrying to the outlying runway and running up its motor, stirring a dusty cloud behind.

The Sun God circles the airfield twice. It sweeps low, glides over the hangars and drops a weighted bag. Inside is a message written on a piece of pasteboard—apparently the Sun God's supply of paper is exhausted.

Mamer writes,

> "Hello, Missoula:
> "We are sure glad to be this close to home—this is God's country again. We will pull off a little refueling just as soon as the boys show up with our refueling plane, it
> "Here he is now
> "Hello to Harry Bell, Bob Johnson—I mean everybody—
> "Nick"

The Sun God swings out over the city, circling. It's 11:25 Tuesday morning, and Wilson's Buhl now flies in from the east. After overflying the airfield it motors off over the Amalgamated Sugar Company factory—an easy-to-identify landmark because of its tall smoke stack.

Bob Johnson's sightseeing Travel Air lifts off and climbs to altitude where its passengers expect to view the unusual spectacle.

The Sun God trails Wilson's Buhl out past the sugar factory, and pulls close to the supply plane. It noses underneath, and within minutes, the hose fed out by Al Coppula trails down inside the Sun God. In a few more minutes, 50 gallons are offloaded to the Sun God's tank.

On the ground, hundreds of spectators search the sky. They've gathered at the airfield to see the refueling, but almost none of the airborne action is visible. Even the nearby hills are pale and blurry, obscured by forest fire smoke. The more distant peaks are nearly invisible.

Above, Bob Johnson maneuvers his Travel Air as close to the refueling planes as safety allows. The persistent haze causes such poor visibility, his passengers have difficulty in discerning the intricacies of the two men handling the hose. They are amazed that Mamer and Wilson are willing and skilled enough to refuel, considering the conditions.

As Al Coppula retrieves the hose, Wilson banks the Buhl off and returns to the Missoula airport. It's now about 12:30. The Sun God turns toward the western hills outside Missoula and vanishes into the smoky sky.

Greasy, bearded, dirty and tired, the men and their red machine are now almost home.

16. Wobbly Legs and Fanfare

The watcher waits. He stands in an empty field that lies between a river and a railroad. The field has a hard gravel base. It's known as a fast field, which may not mean much to the gathered crowd, but is important to the people who work here.

It is 2:00 p.m., Tuesday, August 20, 1929.

The watcher's gaze probes the sky.

Fluttering crazily like a stricken bird, a sack plunges from above. Before it strikes the ground, the watcher rushes to a waiting car and hops on the running board. With the watcher clinging to a door pillar, the driver accelerates across the field.

When the car returns to the platform, reporters converge, shouting "Give us the story!" and "What's it all about?" The watcher does not yield, but surrenders the sack to a man in a suit on the platform. He opens the sack, which divulges a pile of magazines, old newspapers, pieces of card and torn pasteboard, several with scribbles in pencil.

He selects this one: "Hello, Spokane. It is a real thrill to be back here. This is the finest airport we have gazed upon. (signed) Nick and Art." Nick Mamer is the pilot of the airplane that has arrived in the afternoon sky above.

Earlier in the day, long before two o'clock, thousands had parked their cars wherever they could find space. They'd filled a half-mile-long line behind the hangars at Felts Field, and spilled out in both directions along the railroad right-of-way. The road to the field was parked deep as well.

The Buhl refueling plane arrives before the Sun God. Piloted by R. M. Wilson, it circles the field several times before landing. The crowd cheers.

The Buhl pulls forward with its trail of dust, and parks before the hangars. Wilson turns off the power, and the propeller stutters to a halt. The crowd surges forward.

Over a battery of loudspeakers, Leon Boyle's voice rises as he announces Wilson's arrival. Wilson and Coppula step out of the plane, cameras click and shouts ring out. Photographers and reporters close to the pair like scraps of iron to a magnet. Reporters yell questions as the crowd's hats and arms wag approvingly. The men slow and pose for pictures but are quickly hurried to the speakers' platform.

At the microphone, the two aviators smile. Boyle introduces Wilson, a small fellow with receding hair, to the crowd. "[He is] is the only man who had ever refueled a plane at ten-thousand feet altitude—and at night." Wilson, grinning, leans into the microphone. "Don't let that ten-thousand feet business bother you," he says, "it didn't me."

Boyle turns to Coppula, lanky and taller than Wilson. Coppula regards Boyle with a crooked grin. Boyle asks about the night over Rock Springs, Wyoming.

"It was a pretty hard job," Coppula says, "with the beacon light shining up into our eyes." Warmed by the crowd's applause, he continues, "It was a little hard, after the hose had been cut, for we had to get close together. The way we did it was just to hand the hose down..." The crowd's gabble diminishes. "I'd hold it in my hands and jockey it past the propeller..." Now the crowd is almost silent. "...into the hands of Art Walker, who would be standing up with his head and shoulders out of the top of the gas tank on top of the ship."

Art Walker, the subject of Coppula's description, is at this moment exchanging his piloting position with Nick Mamer, who's been writing in the rear of the Sun God. They are minutes away from Felts Field—the moment they've anticipated for five days.

Art grasps the big sack of magazines, old newspapers, and messages, verifying that it's tightly closed and ready for dropping.

Nick sees Felts Field ahead, and begins his descent. Shortly he sees the hangars, one with "SPOKANE AIR PORT" in white on its roof, and the older one with "FELTS FIELD" on its top. Freight cars sit on one of the two railroad tracks next to the field, but he's quite amazed to behold the thousands of automobiles parked everywhere, and the huge crowds gathered outside the hangars.

The wavering throb of a motor and a red speck in the east are what the crowd arrayed along the hangars anticipates. When the plane appears and nears, their babble rises to a crescendo. "It's the Sun God!" is the throated yell.

Indeed, the journey from Missoula has taken its crew just over two hours, despite the choppy winds and obscuring smoke. Now, accompanied by two escorting planes sent up from Felts Field, the red biplane dips easily into a relaxed glide toward the field. With the white lettering "SPOKANE SUN GOD" on its side clearly visible, the plane flashes by, low to the ground.

The crowd screams, "Hurrah!" Hats, hands and handkerchiefs waggle and wave. Nick and Art wave back as their plane climbs out over the field.

Moments later, whistles and bells in nearby Spokane sound, acknowledging the arrival of Nick Mamer and Art Walker, and tolling their remarkable achievement: They have flown coast-to-coast in a round trip over five days without ever touching ground.

"Think of it!" Mamer later says, "Less than 50 hours ago we had seen another crowd back on Roosevelt Field on the Atlantic coast waving at us... just as frantically."

But now, as he circles the field, it is the curves of the Spokane River, its waterfalls and dams, the "GN" clock tower over the Great Northern rail terminal downtown, puffs of steam from a locomotive entering Union Station—the scenes of his favorite city, springing as remembered to his eyes. It is a fevered homecoming.

Nick flies low, turning large circles around the field. On the ground below, Leon Boyle faces the big microphone and reads the greeting from the aviators that was dropped to the field. A huge cheer springs from the crowd.

Meanwhile, officials of the Air Derby association huddle behind Boyle. They shuffle quickly through all the messages in the sack, passing them around and reading each. In excited tones they confer, attempting to match Mamer's reports and desires with their detailed program for the day's celebration. A general nodding of heads follows as they leave the platform to consider their decisions in private.

Boyle, maintaining the crowd's attention with practiced skill, introduces Nick's wife Faye Mamer over the loudspeakers. He also introduces Art's mother, Mrs. J. J. Walker of the town of Opportunity, Washington.

Now thrust into the scrutiny of the crowd, the two women blush and smile. Urged by Boyle to talk, Mrs. Walker says, "Friends, I cannot find words to tell you how I feel." Boyle continues urging. "I certainly feel very happy to be here," she says, "and see my son fly over the Spokane port again." Excited cheers and shouts issue from the crowd.

Once more the crowd is distracted by activities in the air overhead. Two trimotor aircraft are aloft carrying passengers to observe the Sun God from the air. At least one airplane cruises close to afford cameramen on board favorable views of the Sun God. And, during all of this, materials and messages are transferred back and forth between the Sun God and various supply planes.

At 6 p.m., after four hours in the air over the field, the Sun God glides to a landing. Cheers erupt into pandemonium following the three-point landing. The crowd of ten-thousand or more surges at the restraints.

The red biplane, its nose streaked by oil, approaches the hangars. Police shout and gesture, urging the crowd to retreat. When finally the plane's motor chugs off and the propeller stops, they form a cordon with interlocking hands to keep the crowd from it.

Escorted from the crowd, Faye Mamer rushes to the airplane. At the same moment, the left door opens, and Nick hops to the ground. Faye throws her arms around the aviator. He returns the embrace, even with his right arm, which is bandaged. In greasy golf pants and dirty shirt, he looks around, slightly confused by the hubbub. Balance impaired as a result of long confinement in the cramped space of the plane's cabin, he steps forward on wobbly legs. It also turns out he's cut his right arm while working on mechanical gear inside the airplane.

Next out the door is Art Walker, similarly dressed in greasy clothes, and similarly unsteady on his feet. Both fliers' hair is askew, their faces flushed, their eyes red and jaws whiskered with stubble. A car pulls up to the plane, and the men, with Mrs. Mamer, are rushed in it to the speaker's platform.

The stand is crowded with officials of the National Derby association, guests, and Mrs. Walker. Mrs. Walker, in a cardigan, glasses, necklace and a cloche, warmly embraces her son, Art.

The crowd presses against the bunting-draped stand, with its mounted battery of loudspeakers. Officials crowd the aviators, shaking hands and con-gratulating. The scene appears slightly comical, with officials in suits, vests, ties and hats greeting the arriving heroes in dirty knickers and oil-stained shirts, their faces grimy and whiskered.

The arriving celebrities shake their heads and point at their ears. They have difficulty in hearing because the constant roar of the Wright motor has rendered them partially deaf. Mamer is even heard complaining of a ringing in his ears.

After a few confused words into the mounted microphone, the two aviators sit down. Art puffs on a cigarette while a city politician delivers a welcome speech that booms over the loudspeakers.

A different spokesman reads a telegram received at 808 Sprague Avenue, Spokane:

"RXCB569 34 GOVT 4 EXTRA=THE WHITE HOUSE
WASHINGTON DC
"MR NICK MAMER AND MR ART WALKER=
"CARE NATIONAL AIR DERBY ASSN SPOKANE
WASH=
"CONTRATULATIONS ON THE SUCCESSFUL
COMPLETION OF YOUR NONSTOP REFUELING
FLIGHT ACROSS THE CONTINENT AND RETURN
IT IS A FURTHER DEMONSTRATION OF THE
EVERWIDENING SCOPE OF THE PRACTICAL UTILITY
OF AIRCRAFT=
"HERBERT HOOVER."

When the interviewing begins, Mamer stands before the microphone with his hands in his pockets. He smiles, and speaks calmly in such a low voice a few in the crowd holler, "Louder!" In answer to a question about the Sun God's recent delay, Nick says the main reason for circling the Miles City airport last night was to avoid crossing the Rocky Mountains during nighttime. Also, he adds, he wanted to avoid arriving in Spokane at an awkward hour.

Answering another question, he pays tribute to the refuelers from the eastern cities: "The boys were right on the job with their refueling ships. We had no sooner got into Cleveland than they were up and after us. At New York, about fifty planes chased us around with movie cameras."

"On the trip back, when we were in middle Pennsylvania, we ran into a lightning storm. We spent the night dodging from one storm to another. We got reports of bad weather east and when we started west we got reports of bad weather west. That was about the most discouraging experience in the whole flight."

Art Walker's answer about using parachutes is delivered with a boyish smile. "A parachute was too cumbersome for refueling. I left it off during the night contacts." But he ruefully admits they caused soreness when they had to "wear parachutes too much going over the mountains."

The questioner asks about the failure of the Sun God's radio receiver. "The radio worked fine," Nick says, "until the weight on the end of the aerial broke off. We didn't know at the time that that was the trouble."

Regarding lack of sleep, Nick says, "When one of us got so sleepy he couldn't stay awake any longer...we changed places at the controls. One reason we had to stay awake all the time was that we had to pump gas into the wing tanks with a hand pump."

With the fanfare slowing, scratchy music plays over the loudspeakers. Speeches have turned routine, handshakes have grown flabby. The weary aviators are escorted away, without any doubt looking forward to sleeping for a full night and probably more.

A brief examination by Dr. P. J. Gallagher following the celebration determines that the men's temperature and pulse are normal. Mamer lost eight pounds during the flight, while Walker weighs the same as before the flight. Mamer says the two men seem more tired on the ground than they were in the air. Also, "[m]y ears roar until I can hardly hear," he says.

Just after noon the next day (Wednesday), thousands line Riverside Avenue from Monroe to Washington and on the next street over (Sprague). Many simply lean out of office and store buildings along the route to celebrate. The crowds cheer wildly as Nick Mamer, sitting on top of the rear seat of an open automobile, moves slowly down Riverside. The only element missing from this version of the ticker-tape parade is the copilot of the Sun God. Bashful Art Walker is nowhere to be found.

Over the coming days, Nick executes a thoughtful plan recognizing the flight's supporters and documenting the flight's success.

A telegram to the Marysville aircraft builder thanking them for their airplane reads (in part):

> "Spokane, Wash.
> "August 21st, 1929
> "Please accept our sincere congratulations to the Buhl
> Aircraft Company and its engineer in designing a ship
> which possesses such remarkable features of durability
> stability and comfort stop Its performance at high altitudes
> under varying weather conditions...was noncomparable
> stop...Words cannot express our appreciation ...for our
> many needs which were foreseen and provided for by your
> company stop.
> "(Signed) Mamer and Walker"

During the next days and weeks, Mamer produces published articles that recall details of the flight, include technical analyses, and offer philosophical projections regarding its meaning to aviation.

Most notable are "Texaco Across the Sky, The Flight of the Spokane Sun God," a heavily-illustrated feature in the August 1929 issue of *The Texaco Star*, and "Introducing an Advanced Phase of Endurance Flying," in the October 1929 edition of *Aero Digest*. These articles include recognition of the contributions by the Spokane Air Derby association, Texaco, Buhl, Wright, Mamer Air Transport, Aviation Accessories Corp., their leaders, and all the refueling crews. The articles also function as memorials of the flight's highlights.

A banquet for two hundred is held at the posh Davenport Hotel to celebrate Mamer, Walker, and the Northwest refueling crews of Bookwalter and O'Connell, and Wilson and Coppula. With the president of the Spokane Chamber of Commerce presiding, Charles Hebberd explains the goals and achievements of the flight's sponsors. The main speech by Vic Dessert, president of the National Air Derby association, begins with this: "On the lips of air-minded Americans are three names, Nick Mamer, Art Walker, and *Spokane Sun God*. No wonder air officials of Cleveland are burning up the wires in urging them to come for the air races..."

Towards the end, Dessert reveals a surprise: "...on behalf of the association I present you a check for $1,000 for your expenses [for Cleveland]. I'm sure you will have more fun than on your grueling trip that brought so many records home."

Mamer, uncomfortable with the gift, rises and accepts the check. In a barely audible voice, he expresses his thanks. Flushed, he turns to Walker and, after an awkward moment, thanks the association on behalf of Art, too. Applause fills the dining hall.

Later, his composure recaptured, Mamer is able to give a short presentation that concludes with his support for what he calls "the northern route"—his favored airway from St. Paul through Aberdeen, Miles City, Butte, Missoula, and Spokane to Seattle. "Air travel to the northwest, and to Alaska and even to the Orient," he says, "will largely come by the northern route when it is better known and marked."

This prediction turns true, with the contrails of today's passenger jets crisscrossing the Northwest every hour of day and night, flying airways Nick Mamer pioneered. It has occurred perhaps sooner than he, that evening, had any right to expect.

Spokane Sun God, the special Buhl CA-6, in flight.

Refueling the *Spokane Sun God* over New York, Aug. 18, 1929.

A young Nick Mamer, bundled against the cold & snow, stands by aircraft.

Mamer in his flight gear at Kelly Field, Texas, 1919.

Young Mamer in the open cockpit of his airplane.

A 21-year-old Mamer, recently discharged, grins from the cockpit in 1919.

Mamer in Lincoln-Standard's cockpit while E. E. Tattersfield prepares for an aerial stunt, probably 1920 -- the rectangular object above the motor is the radiator.

Smiling barnstormer Mamer enters Lincoln-Standard's cockpit, ca. 1920.

Mamer captioned this photograph of him with Faye Carey, "Faye and Nick at Newman Lake 1921."

Mamer in jodhpurs and high boots with wings on left pocket flap stands by Lincoln-Standard, ca. 1920.

Mamer captioned this photograph "Eddie Stinson receiving films of Japanese earthquake at Great Falls, Mont. delivered by me with plane from Seattle, Sept. 1923, Off for New York".

Mamer shakes hand of Chief Garry of the Spokane Tribe prior to the 1929 flight of the *Spokane Sun God*.

Pilot Mamer with copilot and mechanic Art Walker before the 1929
flight of the *Spokane Sun God*.

Mamer with unidentified photographer next to Buhl CA-6 Airsedan with
Mamer Air Transport insignia on snowfield, early 1930s.

Frank — I know — I have'nt
said much on this flight
simply because I have'nt
time honestly we have'nt
had a minute to spare —
I told you about the wobble
Pump taking all our time —

I believe I will load up to
the top with gas here — and
go straight to St. Paul
without refueling, I can
make it O.K. — without bad
head winds, If I
cannot I will drop
message to Cleveland

The first page of one of Nick's handwritten messages to Frank Hawks. It was dropped from the *Spokane Sun God* at Roosevelt Field, New York, August 18, 1929. Transcribed wording is in Chapter 9.

Mamer, standing next to his Ford Tri-motor with its
Mamer Air Transport insignia partly visible, ca. 1933.

Mamer smiles in his Northwest Airlines Captain's uniform, ca. 1935.
(damaged photograph)

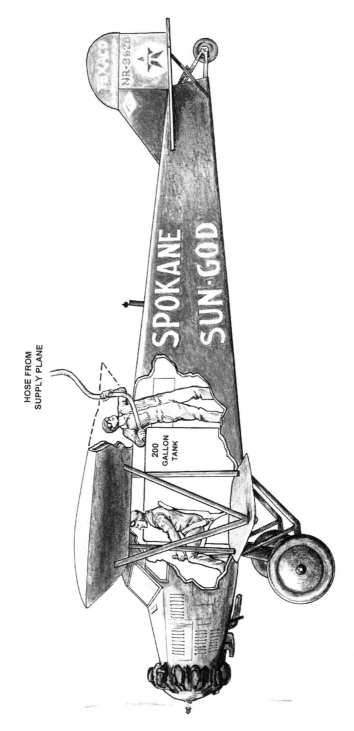

Cutaway of *Spokane Sun God* showing setup for aerial refueling.

HOSE FROM
SUPPLY PLANE

200
GALLON
TANK

PART IV

A LIFE ALOFT

17. THE URGE TO FLY

The airplane dives toward the ground, the fabric of its wings fluttering like a wind-tautened flag. Seeming only feet from crashing, it pulls up and whooshes over a field of sorghum. After gaining a few tens of feet, Nick Mamer pulls back the stick, then tilts the craft to the left. It rolls into a side somersault that he completes with a grin.

The watching farm families whistle, shout and wave. "Too much cannot be said of...Lieutenant Mamer," pipes the *Bemidji Sentinel* in 1919, "...he is a wonder in the air."

To the rural folks around Bemidji, Minnesota, this is the thrill of a lifetime. To barnstormer Nick Mamer, just released from the Army Signal Corps, this is a boy on a bicycle, veering and wheeling, colored streamers whipping from his handlebars on a devil-may-care dash.

When Nick was barely a teen, he sold himself as a mechanic to the Duesenberg Motor Company. On weekends, he churned the dirt trying to win motorcycle races. And around Minnesota county fairs in July he jumps out of open-cockpit airplanes and jolts to the turf in a parachute. But all along it seems—his urge is to fly.

Born in Hastings, Minnesota, January 28, 1898, Nick is the son of Jacob H. and Mary Weber Mamer. But before he's born, his father is dead from a horse runaway accident. Almost nothing is known of Nick's early life or schooling. But like his older brother James, Nick slips the restraints of Hastings early and enlists at age 18. *The Hastings Gazette* reports on July 1, 1916, that Nick "passed the federal examination at Minneapolis on Monday [June 26]" and "left for San Diego yesterday [June 30], where he will go into training." A few days later, on July 6, *The Hastings Democrat* notes that Nick had been studying "aviation and mechanics" prior to his enlistment, and that he left for the Aviation Section of the Signal Corps, San Diego, California, "where he will receive instructions in the art of flying an aeroplane. After a number of months of training he will...be examined and if he passes he will be advanced to a position...similar to that of second lieutenant in the army with the same pay." The *Gazette's* description of the benefits of enlistment in the Aviation Section, which are reminiscent of recruiting literature, may have contributed to young Mamer's eagerness to become an aviator.

In its July 17 edition, *Aerial Age Weekly* reports "Minnesota's first recruit in the army aviation corps is Nicholas B. Mamer, of Hastings, Minn." Commenting July 1 on Nick's enlistment, *The Minneapolis Star Tribune* said he "is well known to visitors to the various county fairs, where he has performed many daring feats in motorcycle races and parachute jumps."

At the time of his enlistment, Nick was eighteen, a blue-eyed daredevil with dark brown hair. At five-feet-nine-inches, he was tall for his age. Perhaps this encouraged him to claim to be born in 1895 rather than in 1898 as is shown consistently in the available military records. He may have thought adding three years to his age would lend him advantage in the competitive environment of the military.

Certificates and other documents in the Mamer Family Archives yielded Mamer's service number, 348467, and significant events and dates during his military career. To complete the record of his military service for *Low on Gas – High on Sky*, we petitioned the official custodian of United States' military records, the National Personnel Records Center, National Archives, in St. Louis, Missouri. Our request was assigned the number 2-21657788780.

The Records Center's response recognized Mamer's Army service, but provided only substitute "reconstructed" information that duplicated information already in our files. In a letter dated July 26, 2018, Archives Technician Derek Springmeyer explained the lack of data. "The Official Military Personnel File for [Nicholas B. Mamer, 348467] is not in our files. If the record were here on July 12, 1973, it would have been in the area that suffered the most damage in the fire on that date and may have been destroyed." Springmeyer further explains that the fire destroyed the "major portion of records of Army...personnel who separated...between 1912 through 1959..." Thus, of necessity, Nick Mamer's military activities during his enlistment have been deduced and/or assembled from unofficial sources. This limits both the extent of information in this Chapter, and, potentially, its accuracy.

The year of Mamer's enlistment (1916) is barely a dozen years after the Wright brothers' first powered flight at Kitty Hawk, North Carolina, December 17, 1903. The airplanes of the time were largely wood and fabric affairs with motors that provided enough power for flight, but little extra power for emergencies. Flight instruments were almost nonexistent. Flying these crude machines required superior 'seat-of-the-pants' sense and control, and accidents were common.

The application of flying machines in wartime was in that era thought to be restricted to reconnaissance, a Signal Corps' primary function. This categorization applied to both powered and lighter-than-air vehicles. Called the "Aviation Section," it thus became a small and needy branch assigned to the U.S. Army's Signal Corps. The Section's pilots were young men from various other organizations commanded mostly by non-flying Signal Corps officers, an unworkable arrangement. It is not surprising this military unit of 1916 was barely functional.

About a month after his enlistment, on a July 31, 1916 roster at the Army's "School Detachment of the Aviation Section" in San Diego, Nicholas B. Mamer is named among sixteen other enlisted men as a recruit "Private." The group is described as having "Joined from Recruit Depot on July 19." An excerpt from an article appearing in the May 9, 1919 *The Hastings Democrat* (after Mamer's discharge on May 1, 1919) summarizes this early part of his military career:

> "...Nicholas B. Mamer...left Hastings in June, 1916,
> enlisting in...the aviation section, signal corps [*sic*], San
> Diego, Cal., and attached there to 1st aero squadron [*sic*],
> and in September of that year transferred to New Mexico,
> remaining on the Mexico border until January, 1917..."

The combination of these two references appears to place Private Mamer in training at San Diego for about two months before being sent to New Mexico the following September.

In March of 1916, Mexican revolutionary Pancho Villa had raided Columbus, New Mexico, killing nineteen Americans. Following this attack, President Woodrow Wilson ordered Brigadier General John Pershing to assemble a force to capture Villa. Part of Pershing's 6,000-men army included the First Aero Squadron. The new and inexperienced First Aero Squadron arrived at Camp Furlong in Columbus, New Mexico, March 15, 1916. Pershing sought to use the squadron primarily for reconnaissance, although its aircraft were mechanically undependable, unsuited for mountain flying and in other respects poorly-adapted to the task.

Although no reference has been located which supports Private Mamer's transfer from San Diego to New Mexico as reported (above) in *The Hastings*

Democrat, it is presumed he was sent to the First Aero Squadron at Camp Furlong as a reinforcement. He would have served there for about three or four months during the final phase of Pershing's pursuit, which wound down early in 1917 without the capture of Pancho Villa. Nothing is known of his duties during this deployment.

At this time—early in 1917—the United States was close to entering the World War raging in Europe. As part of its preparation, the military planned defensive measures. The Panama Canal, vital to the U.S. in peacetime as well as in wartime, was considered to be a potential target for German attack, so the Washington administration took steps to bolster its defenses. The *Washington Post* on February 25, 1917, just over a month before the United States entered the war on April sixth, reported the appointment of Capt. Henry H. Arnold to command of the 7th Aero Squadron. This Squadron, said the report, "...will be organized in the Canal Zone and equipped with hydroaeroplanes" for the "air defense of the Panama Canal."

Capt. Arnold was at the time in Washington seeing to "equipments and supplies," and was scheduled to proceed to the Canal Zone, accompanied by First Lieut. Clinton Russell, "who had been on duty with the first aero squadron [sic] at Columbus, N. Mex." The inclusion of Lt. Russell is notable and perhaps an indication that future transfers of personnel from the First Aero Squadron in New Mexico to the 7th Aero Squadron in the Canal Zone were contemplated at the time of the initial organization of the Seventh Aero Squadron.

Capt. Arnold, nicknamed "Hap," is the man who later went on to become a general during World War II. He is today considered the architect of the U.S. Air Force, having directed the fledgling air service from one of about 1,200 men and 55 inadequate airplanes to one of 2.5 million personnel and 75,000 high-tech aircraft, the largest and most potent air arm in history.

As of March, 1917, the initial complement of the 7th Aero Squadron at the canal was 51 men. It's possible that Private Mamer was part of that small detachment. The above summary from the *The Hastings Democrat* of May 9, suggests this: "...and then sent to the Panama Canal zone where he served as aerial patrol engineer...".

However, a San Diego, California, newspaper on March 8 reported, "fifty mechanicians from the army aeronautical academy [sic] here will leave Friday for the Panama canal zone. The men will form the nucleus of the Seventh aero squadron, [sic] which will be commanded by Capt. Henry H. Arnold." This may suggest Mamer returned to San Diego from New Mexico before being ordered to the Canal Zone. Either way, it seems that Private Nick Mamer, in early 1917, became a member of the 7th Aero Squadron stationed in the Canal Zone.

Prior to August, 1917, the 7th Aero Squadron had been deployed on the Pacific Ocean side of the canal, despite the German threat existing on the Atlantic Ocean side. During the latter half of August, however, the Squadron moved from Empire, to Ft. Sherman, on the Atlantic side. At the time of the move, it still had no airplanes. Shortly, two staggered-wing Curtiss R-4 airplanes were reported to have been the first delivered to the squadron.

Early in October 1917, Maj. W. W. Wynne was named new commander of the 7th Aero Squadron, and on October 13, Nick Mamer was promoted to Corporal. Later, on the twenty-second, he flew in the observer's seat with Maj. Wynne at the controls during a 32-minute practice flight. They probably flew the Curtiss R-4, a 2-place, open cockpit, biplane. Two of these, powered by a 200 h.p. Curtiss motor, were available. Two R-3 floatplanes were later delivered in December, 1917, and augmented in February of 1918 by Navy-supplied R-6s. The floatplanes were equipped with wider wingspan of 57 feet to help lift the increased weight of twin floats.

All of these R-series airplanes were underpowered, rudimentary flying machines without radios. For navigation, they included nothing more than a compass. Despite this, the aviators were expected to regularly fly offshore in search of the enemy, either surface ships or submarines. Becoming disoriented during the changing weather conditions of the tropics was common, and men and planes were often lost.

On March 1, 1918 Mamer received a promotion from Corporal to Sergeant. A short time later, on March 14, he was promoted again, to Master Signal Electrician (a rank perhaps equivalent to Master Sergeant). These promotions in quick succession signal his superb grasp of the mechanical and electrical aspects of the aircraft in his charge, his adaptation to military life, and his leadership capabilities.

Beginning March 14, M.S.E. Mamer flew a series of short flights as observer with Maj. Wynne during which he apparently learned the skills of reconnaissance and directing artillery fire. This training was designed to develop the observer's ability not only to find and visualize targets, but to accurately signal the target's position to shore batteries.

Emboldened by his successes and promotions, Nick composed a letter to the Chief Signal Officer, Air Personnel Division, in Washington, D. C. It is dated March 30:

"I respectfully request that I be put on flying status and instructed in the art of flying...I believe that familiarity with the actual handling of an airplane in the air under flying conditions, would greatly assist an aviation mechanic in increased efficiency in their repair and upkeep, besides fitting him for the regular duties of a pilot.

"Out of a class of eleven men instructed in aerial reconnaissance, observation, artillery directing and kindred subjects...I was one of the two men selected to direct artillery fire on the recent maneuvers...

"I have studied Aeronautics and the Theory of Flight for the past three years. I was employed by the Duesenberg Motor Company...as racing mechanician...I am 23 years old, have attended high school for three years, and know of nothing wrong with my physical condition."

Major Wynne, his commander, wrote a covering memo recommending approval.

In March through June of 1918, M.S.E. Mamer flew as observer with other officer pilots, not only directing artillery fire, but on "coast patrol" and cross-country flights (a flight over the length of the canal was about 45 miles). These flights generally lasted from forty minutes to more than two hours. Between March 14 and June 17, he logged 28 flights as observer.

A cablegram sent from Adjutant-General Henry McCain's office in Washington arrived at the Panama Canal Department headquarters in Ancon June 14. It directed that M.S.E. Mamer be sent to the School of Military Aeronautics, Princeton, N. J. Apparently, Mamer's March 30 request to Washington for placement in flying status was considered valid.

On June 18, with Lt. Malloway as observer, M.S.E. Mamer took the airplane's controls for the first time. The flight, on Coast Patrol, lasted an hour. The same day, Mamer again piloted the plane for more than two hours. Later on June 21, again with Lt. Malloway as observer, Mamer flew for 80 minutes. Mamer lacked formal pilot training, and it is unknown if these flights, with Mamer at the controls, were within normal protocols for the 7th Aero Squadron. They were nevertheless recorded on Mamer's "War Department Weekly Airplane Report," and demonstrate Mamer's remarkable intuitional grasp of flying.

The Panama Canal Department transmitted the Adjutant-General's order on M.S.E. Mamer to Major Wynne, Commander of the 7th Aero Squadron. It reduced Mamer's grade to private first class and sent him, via Panama Railroad Steamer, back to the U.S.

The reduction in grade was necessary for Mamer to qualify as a flying cadet eligible for eventual elevation to a flying officer and receipt of an appointment as a 2nd Lieutenant. Mamer knew this and was jubilant at attaining his quest to become a pilot. He immediately began preparing to leave the 7th Aero Squadron.

On June 21, Lt. Winslow wrote a recommendation:

"To Whom it may concern:

"Five months association with Nicholas B. Mamer and I have no hesitancy in saying that he has proven himself by far the most valuable man in the Flying Department.

"His ability to command men and his methods of handling them are two of his most valuable attributes...

"Enlisting as a private he attained in a comparatively short time the rank of Master Sergt. Electrician – the highest rank attained by any man in this squadron...

"His character, as his service record shows, is "EXCELLENT" and it gives me considerable pleasure to recommend him.

"Kenelm Winslow Jr., 1st Lieut. R.M.A., O.I.C. of Flying."

This was followed by a letter from the Squadron Commander, also addressed "to whom it may concern:"

"While a member of the 7th Aero Squadron, Nicholas B. Mamer, passed from Private 1st Class through the grades of Corporal and Sergeant...[h]e discharged the duties of each grade in a thorough and efficient manner. During that time he acted as First Sergeant, and Non-Commissioned Officer in charge of flying and operation of hangars.

"He has had considerable experience as an observer in an airplane, has had some instructions as a pilot and showed unusual aptness for both.

"He is a man of excellent bearing and other soldierly traits. His character and habits have been irreproachable during the time he has been under my observation.

"I earnestly recommend every consideration be given him for any position requiring good judgement, responsibility or trust.

"Walter W. Wynne, Major, N. A., J.M.A., Signal Corps. Commanding 7th Aero Squadron."

Within a short time, Private First Class Mamer was aboard the S.S. Panama, sailing under military orders. The steamer left Cristobal, Canal Zone, on June 25, 1918 bound for New York City. "Adventurous," is how Nick described the journey, a slow and lazy trip through the Caribbean Sea, then up the Atlantic coast, with numerous calls at tropical ports along the way. Eighteen days later on July 13 the small, two-stack, 15-knot ship arrived at the Port of New York. Mamer immediately crossed Staten Island on his way to Princeton, New Jersey, where he signed in at Princeton University's dormitories. He explained he was there under orders from the U.S. Army Signal Corps to attend the U.S. School of Military Aeronautics.

During the height of World War I, the U.S. Army had asked Princeton University to host a School of Military Aeronautics to educate cadets in aeronautical and engineering subjects prior to their training as pilots. The full-time curriculum, which ran for twelve weeks, covered the topics of Aeronautical Motors, Theory of Flight, Cross-Country and General Flying, Aerial Observation, Gunnery, Signaling and Radio, Infantry Drill and Calisthenics. Cadets wore military dress to classes, which were held in Guyot Hall and Palmer Physical Laboratory.

Mamer completed the course on October 5, 1918. His certificate of graduation is signed by the Commandant (signature indecipherable). A photograph of his graduating class in high-collar Army tunics and knee breeches shows him on the back row. A key, typed on paper and dated October 9, identifies each of the 48 graduates of his class by name.

The May 9, 1919 summary in *The Hastings Democrat* (above) purports to describe Mamer's Princeton training and his subsequent activities:

"[he] was sent to the officers' training camp at Princeton, N. J., and from thence assigned to Camp Dix, Dallas Tex., being commissioned second lieutenant,

November, 6th, 1918, and since November 28, of last year, has been engaged as flying instructor at Kelley [*sic*] Field, Tex."

Although this item in *The Hastings Democrat* places Camp Dix, New Jersey erroneously in Texas, Camp Dix (later Fort Dix) is less than 30 miles south of Princeton, so Mamer may have been ordered there following his graduation from the School of Military Aeronautics and before his official transfer to Kelly Field.

However, no other document in our sources places Mamer at Camp Dix. It seems doubtful that Mamer was stationed there, especially as the *Democrat* article associates his presence there with an incorrect date of his commissioning as second lieutenant.

Mamer was transferred to Kelly Field, although the date is not known. Located near San Antonio, Texas, Kelly field was begun by Capt. Benjamin Foulois in November 1916 to expand Aviation Section training. Originally called Aviation Camp, it was renamed for Lt. George E. Kelly, killed in a crash in 1911.

Mamer's commissioning as a second lieutenant occurred in April of 1919 rather than in November 1918 as reported in *The Hastings Democrat* (above). The formal certificate of promotion issued by the Adjutant General's Office— the original is in the Mamer Family Archives—appoints Nicholas Bernard Mamer as "Second Lieutenant, Aviation Section (flying status) Signal Officers' Reserve Corps of the Army of the United States" as of April 19, 1919. The appointment occurred at Kelly Field, and is confirmed by a letter from Lieut. Colonel B. B. Buttler, Commanding Officer, Kelly Field, dated April 22, 1919.

Most importantly, Special Order 112, dated April 22 of 1919, issued from Headquarters, Air Service Flying School at Kelly Field, names Nicholas Bernard Mamer as "having successfully passed the tests required of Reserve Military Aviator...is announced as a Reserve Military Aviator [R.M.A.]..." effective April 19, by order of Lt. Colonel Buttler.

In the aviation parlance of the time, receiving the R.M.A. was the equivalent of being awarded "aviator's wings," the highly valued endorsement of a pilot's flying skills.

Other documentation illustrates Mamer's service at Kelly Field, including the "Roster of Detachment of Flying Cadets," in *Kelly Field in the Great World War* by Harry David Kroll, which includes "Nicholas B. Mamer." Whether he was there from November 28, 1918 forward, as *The Hastings Democrat* reports, is uncertain. It's also quite uncertain that he, from that time "has been engaged as flying instructor," as stated in *The Hastings Democrat*.

Another Kelly field document illustrates his presence at Kelly Field during 1919. A letter from Kelly's Air Service Flying School, dated April 23, 1919, certifies

> "...that N. B. Mamer has had a total of sixty-three (63) hours and ten (10) minutes flying time *at this field.* [emphasis added]. He has completed the course required by a Reserve Military Aviator and is classified as a Pursuit Pilot. (signed) L. A. Walton, Major J.M.A.S.C., Officer in Charge of Flying."

This amount of flight time might have been accrued during the period November 23, 1918- April 23, 1919, or during some shorter period.

Nick Mamer's Army discharge certificate is annotated. The annotation states that he is Honorably Discharged, "...by reason of completion of primary flying training per auth [*sic*] letter Nov. 30, 1918 fr. [*sic*]A.G.O. to D.M.A." This annotation suggests that Mamer underwent primary flying training for almost two months from his graduation from Princeton's School of Military Aeronautics until November 30, 1918.

The Honorable Discharge from The United States Army, signed by "J.M. White, Major, A.S.A., Executive Officer" states that "Nicholas B. Mamer, #348467" A.S.A., Det. Flying Cadets Kelly Field, Texas, The United States Army, as a Testimonial of Honest and Faithful Service, is hereby Honorably Discharged..." It is issued at "Kelly Field, So. San Antonio, Texas," and is effective "...this 1st day of May, one thousand nine hundred and nineteen."

The certificate awards him $60.00 Bonus and five cents per mile travel pay (to Minneapolis, Minnesota), and also awards him "back pay as Cadet at S.M.A. (School of Military Aeronautics) and as Aerial Flyer, $172.72."

However, it is likely that the best award of all was earning the R.M.A.— Nick's "wings."

18. The Stormer

In the spring of 1919, Nick Mamer fingered his discharge paper. "Honest and Faithful Service," it said. But the document felt thin, maybe too thin. He'd spent nearly a month visiting his mother on East Seventh Street in Hastings, and now the itch was back. He wanted to fly, and the word around the Minneapolis Aero Club was that an outfit called Federated Fliers was forming a thrill show. An aerial thrill show.

Clarence W. Hinck, along with Colby Dodge, and former military pilot Dick Grace, thought staging outdoor shows with speedy cars, motorcycles, and airplanes was a great idea. It might even make money. They formed Federated Fliers, Inc. and bought eighteen surplus JN-4 Jenny airplanes, in crates, cheap. On a plot of land northeast of Minneapolis in what is now Fridley, they created a flying field and built a hangar.

Hinck, as manager, made a pitch to the Minnesota State Fair to stage a show. He was turned down. But Clarence was not a man easily discouraged. As "Promotors of Open Air Events" and "Greatest Novelty Exhibitions," Federated Fliers advertised "Flying Circus, Parachute Jumps, Aerial Acrobatics, Motorcycle and Auto Races"—not to mention flying news photographers over the city, transiting mail between towns, and dropping flyers and business cards all over the place.

Nick joined Federated in June of 1919. Clarence quickly saw that Mamer was a skilled pilot who also knew how to fix airplanes. Taking advantage of Nick's enthusiasm and leadership abilities, Hinck kept Mamer busy flying as well as supervising the multi-faceted activities of Federated Fliers. Others hired included Al and Clarence "Nippy" Opsal, Elmer Hinck (Clarence's brother), Pete Rask, Charles Holman, E. E. "Ernie" Tattersfield and Harold G. Peterson.

Peterson, ex-Army Air Service Lieutenant, had become famous as star, together with Lt. Paul H. Davis, of a border drama during General Pershing's 1916-17 pursuit of Pancho Villa. He and Davis had been "captured by bandits, held for ransom, and finally rescued by a daring United States Officer in spite of plots by [their] captors to kill [them] and keep the ransom...”

In this post-war era, the United States' economy boomed. “New” seemed to be the word of the day, as technical advances like telephones, radios, motion pictures and luxury motorcars astonished an eager, accepting public. Jazz flourished, writers rose to celebrity, flappers frolicked. Within weeks, Clarence Hinck was accepting large fees for outdoor events at county fairs, carnivals, and multifarious celebrations. Federated Fliers oversaw dog races, auto “push-ball” and polo, and motorcycle competitions. These preceded the headline events of stunt flying, parachute jumps, balloon ascensions and aerial acrobatics.

With the other pilots, Nick took passengers for short $5 joyrides in a Jenny before each show, then turned to his skill as an aerobatic flier. He completed midair loops at a low height so crowds could easily view the intricacy. Coming out of a loop, he'd execute an Immelman turn (swooping up, turning over and descending while turning the plane upright). He often flew more than a half-mile upside down, then righted the Jenny while climbing to a height sufficient to begin a tailspin. He became famous for halting the spin and pulling out at such a low height that spectators screamed in fear he'd smash dead into the ground.

The JN-4, or “Jenny” biplane was manufactured in the thousands during WWI. It served as a slow, low-powered trainer. It had two open, tandem seats with controls for instructor (rear) and student (front). It was constructed of wood with small additions of metal. Its fuselage was formed of slim pieces of ash bent and trussed into a skeleton, held together by small metal connectors. Separated by rigid struts, the two wings had spars of spruce that spaced the multitude of thin ribs (airfoil shapes) that, in turn, produced the wing's lift. Wires strung from posts on top of the upper wing helped support the wing's span.

Metal wire was, in fact, a major element of the Jenny's construction. Tightened wires laced the wood elements into tight frames. Other wires drew the frames and longitudinals into rigid structures. A multitude of external wires spanning between the fabric-covered fuselage, wings and empennage completed the assembly. As might be guessed, this wood-and-wire structure afforded no protection to its occupants during a crash.

Two wheels and a metal tail skid sufficed for ground travel. Two more metal skids below the lower wing tips prevented contact with the turf during takeoff and landing.

The wood propeller was driven by a single V8 gasoline motor of 90 horsepower (later by other, somewhat more powerful motors). Empty, it weighed less than a ton, about 1,400 lb, such that when loaded, the heft of its motor, gas and two aviators made up about half its total weight. It landed at about 40 miles-per-hour, had a top speed of 75, and cruised at 60.

Thousands of WWI aviators, including Mamer, were trained in Jennys. Many piloted them later as utility aircraft or in barnstorming operations. Charles Lindbergh first soloed in a JN-4 in 1923.

Nick performed the twists, turns and tumbles with such consummate skill that crowds roared their approval. Judges, if there were a competition, often awarded Mamer top prize. At September's Minnesota State Fair, he so outclassed his competitors the judges named him "King of Flyers" and agreed to award him first prize ($600 and a silver cup) before he had actually finished his aerobatic routine.

More demonstrations of Mamer's art occurred throughout Minnesota that season. In August, he gave Hastings, his hometown, some thrills with what were described as "fancy dips." With his stunts finished, and before returning to Brown's field, he flew under the city's High Bridge, swooping to within a couple of feet of the river's surface. These events usually took place without mishap, although in September, Federated's Pete Rask lost control of his plane. It crashed into Mamer's airborne Jenny. Neither pilot was injured, but Rask's craft was badly damaged.

Seeking advancement for the 1920 season, Nick signed on with C. H. Messer of the United States Air Craft Corp. of Spokane, Washington as "expert pilot and instructor in Aviation." The guaranteed salary was $250 per month. In addition, the contract said he would earn ten percent of the gross receipts from all passenger and exhibition work. In return, he agreed "to put forth his best efforts" on the company's behalf, and "not hold the company responsible for any personal injuries sustained" while working for the company. This caveat suggests Mamer's high level of self-confidence.

Clarence Hinck understood Nick's move to the Spokane company. In a letter of recommendation penned at Mamer's departure, he said, "his purpose in leaving our company is to accept a better position and to broaden his experience by extending his activities to new fields." Hinck went on to praise Nick: "I have found him to be a man of high character, unquestionable integrity, and splendid ability...[a]s an aviator of experience, judgement and skill, Mamer stands in a class by himself. He is a thorough expert in every phase of the aviation industry, and understands perfectly every mechanical feature of planes and engines...his record is clean, being entirely free from accidents. His flying record as confirmed by numerous newspaper reports is the best evidence of his ability." Hinck went on to tabulate his flying time with Federated at "nearly four-hundred hours," including "instruction, cross-country, exhibition and passenger flights."

One of the benefits of Nick's new employ was the opportunity to fly a brand new airplane, the "Vamp," a craft somewhat similar to the Jenny. When the Chief of Police of Kalispell, Montana, arranged a flight with Mamer in the Vamp, the community at Flathead Lake took notice. Alerted to its upcoming arrival, spectators gathered in downtown that evening to watch the Vamp, with Chief Sanford aboard, land on Main Street.

But first, Nick circled and performed a few expert turns and wingovers, fascinating the crowd. Beginning near Filsen's Garage, Mamer glided down to within a few feet above the street, touched down and came to rest between St. Matthew's school and the Court House.

Once the Chief of Police had alighted and the crowd was cleared, Nick turned Vamp around and drove it up the street to Filsen's, from where he then roared off in the direction of the Court House. Airborne, now, he circled. The crowd gasped as the Vamp headed down again, appearing as if to land. Instead, the airplane did a nose-dive under the telegraph wires, nearly touching the ground, then rose quickly and sailed away into the evening sky. It's not difficult to visualize Mamer grinning "from ear to ear."

Messer believed outstanding stunt work on behalf of United States Air Craft would enhance its reputation. "The Lincoln-Standard plane, the most powerful stunt ship in the city," he said, "is especially adapted for stunt work. It is our claim that we can put on exhibitions which can not [sic] be duplicated in the west, and [we] are willing to post a forfeit, to be given to any firm who can duplicate our work."

New stunts included those by E. E. Tattersfield, who'd also signed up with Messer. He walked out on the wing of Mamer's airplane and hung by his toes from the landing gear beneath the machine. Another stunt called for Tattersfield to stand on top of the upper wing while Mamer executed a "loop-the-loop."

An incident in August of 1922 demonstrated both the high risks and the rewards of skill in those days of barnstorming. Nick, at the controls of a Standard J-1 with a Curtiss motor, flew low over Spokane's downtown. Observers on the streets could not help but stare upward, fascinated. Barely skimming over the flagpole atop the tallest building in town, Mamer swung the craft in a large circle. In the other seat, mechanic Bob Henderson scattered handbills over the side of the airplane. As they edged out of downtown, Henderson ceased tossing handbills—throwing them now would waste their handbill supply. He watched as the last of the bills fluttered behind them.

Nick banked the craft and they headed west. As they crossed the O.W.R. & N. railroad shops in the Latah (Hangman) Creek valley, the motor quit. Mamer immediately hollered, "Did you shut the motor?" Henderson replied that he did not.

Nick switched tanks, but nothing happened—there was plenty of gas.

The two men quickly assayed their gauges to find what was wrong. Everything looked okay. Nick glanced—the tachometer needle was dropping toward zero. He tried a restart, but nothing happened.

The propeller stopped dead. The plane began a slow, silent slide down. Scanning side to side, Nick searched. Nothing but buildings, roads, houses... then a square of green.

Nick banked the plane in a tight turn. They headed east, over the Spokane River that curved beneath. In the aftermath of spring runoff, the river was low and slow, but still—a river. He signaled to Henderson where they would land. Henderson recognized it: Glover field.

The wind whistled. The altimeter needle spun, showing only a few hundred feet of height remaining. Nick aimed for the green. But he saw movement—children playing on the field! Nearby adults switched their attention—from the children to the gliding airplane.

Nick turned slightly left. As the banks of the river closed in, he kept the wings level, nose slightly up. The J-1 settled and slowed. Directly ahead were the abutments of the Monroe Street bridge.

The Jenny's landing gear dug into the water. That resistance caused Nick intense struggle keeping the craft from nosing over. The plane settled onto the water, its fuselage and lower wing churning a wave. It halted, half submerged near the north bank. The men threw off their seatbelts and scrambled out. The water felt cold, but within a few strokes, their feet hit bottom. They slogged to the bank, soaked and sloppy, but unhurt.

Nick dragged his goggles from his eyes and looked back. Slowly, the J-1 nosed over and its tail rose. Within moments, the plane stood with its fuselage vertical, tail straight up. Nick squeezed his jacket to shed some of the water. Spectators on the riverbank applauded and cheered. City firemen arrived. They, with the aid of men and boys in the crowd, dragged the airplane across the rocks onto the bank. The propeller and the lower wing were damaged, but the rest was simply wet.

Later that day, now in dry clothing, Nick Mamer was summoned to the city police station. He appeared and was informed he'd be booked for illegally distributing handbills over the city. Following the booking he was released without bail.

We don't know how the illegal distributing case worked out. But it seems risking death while crashing one's airplane into a river is not the only aviation hazard pilots should work to avoid.

Despite his busy (and risky) schedule, Mamer was not always in the air. On his time off he'd begun to date a young lady from Coeur d'Alene, Idaho— the lake city close to Spokane. Her name was Faye Carey. This led to certain aviation-related courting procedures, one of which was described in the local newspaper:

"A mysterious aviator, a possible modern Lochinvar, has startled and entertained campers and residents of Newman Lake for the last week by making daily stunt flights over the lake, dropping letters and flowers to a young woman staying at Sutton's Bay, and leaving without letting his identity be known.

"Each afternoon, the purr of a heavy aerial motor is heard at the lake. The residents and campers gather to watch. From high in the air, the plane begins to turn over and over, stunting until it gets to within a few feet of the water. Each day the flyer drops, in a tiny parachute, a letter and some flowers tagged with the name of the girl for whom they are intended. A rowboat or two are always waiting the coming of the plane to pick up the parachuted message.

"Residents at the lake are anxiously waiting to see if the mysterious flyer will not finally land at some convenient field near the lake, lift the lady into the machine and fly away with her. They hope to learn his identity then.

"Local flyers profess ignorance as to who the modern young Lochinvar may be."

On the 7th of July, 1923, in Yakima, Washington, Nick married Faye, the daughter of Mr. and Mrs. Joshua M. Carey. Mr. Carey worked as a logging contractor. The ceremony was performed by clergyman F. C. Whitney. Immediately after, the couple—she accoutered in flight jacket, helmet and goggles—returned to their airplane and took off.

Newspaper reporters, upon learning of the Yakima flight by the well-known aviator, termed it a "Honeymoon in the Clouds." The couple actually flew to Portland, Oregon, followed by visits to other cities on the west coast.

19. Earthquake, Wildfires, a Prizefight

The great earthquake struck on September 1, 1923. Centered south of Tokyo (then spelled Tokio), it was not immediately thought to be catastrophic. The giant jolt, lasting minutes, transfixed its victims with the sound of "unearthly thunder." A huge tsunami swept thousands to their death, followed by fires that roared through the cities of Tokyo and Yokohama, burning everything. The death toll eventually reached an estimated 140,000.

The "radiotelegraph" of the day transmitted the first photographs, but the process was limited and exceedingly slow, and the resulting pictures were crude and lacked detail. Other means were needed to meet newsreels' and newspapers' needs for massive visual coverage, by photographs, still and moving. Transport by aircraft was a solution offering the speed demanded by editors and producers across the country.

Nick Mamer quickly found himself at the controls of the Standard with urgent requests for fast delivery. In one instance, photographic negatives of the earthquake destined for *The New York Times* arrived by sea and air from Japan aboard a steamship. A chartered seaplane flew from Seattle to the steamship, where it received the negatives and returned them to Seattle. After overnight processing, the receiving studio packed the pictures and placed an emergency telephone call to Mamer. With Nick piloting and A. A. Bennett, his partner for this operation aboard, they were quickly aloft.

Arriving over Easton, a foothills town on the east side of the Cascade Mountains northwest of Ellensburg, Washington, pilot Mamer assessed the weather. He saw that his airplane might be trapped on the Seattle side of the Cascades by fog, so he and Bennett left the airplane in Easton, and drove by car to the Georgetown quarantine station, where they received the eagerly-awaited cargo. They then returned to Easton. Nick relates the next part of the journey:

"I left Easton before daylight with the pictures and rushed [by air] through to Walla Walla, where the first stop was made...I filled my big 65-gallon gasoline tank, took on oil, and left. The next stop was Boise, Idaho, where I refueled. The next stop was Salt Lake City.

"It was just steady, straight flying all day long. I left before daylight and landed after dark. My plane and motor functioned perfectly and I did not even have to change a spark plug on the entire trip."

Nick's rush flight met the Air Mail airplane in Salt Lake City. From there the pack of pictures was sped over the Transcontinental Airway to New York. The chartered flights enabled *The New York Times* to publish photographs of the Japan earthquake 24 to 36 hours ahead of any other newspaper. For Mamer and Bennett, it was a whirlwind 36 hour trip, Seattle to Salt Lake and return to Yakima, flying 1800 miles in less than 24 hours actual air time.

Even three weeks after the quake, fierce competition between news organizations continued. Several competed to be first with moving pictures of the Japanese disaster. Of the firms battling to be first to deliver, one had shipped its reels from Japan to San Francisco, the other from Japan to Seattle. Chartered by the second firm, Mamer and his airplane waited in Seattle. Arrival of the films, followed by customs inspection, preceded their consignment.

Although the coverage seems overblown, commentators reported at the time that $50,000 (more than $700,000 in today's dollars) would be spent by rival teams attempting to be first to New York City with the films. Regardless of whether the dollar figure was true, Eddie Stinson, flying a big, all-metal Larsen with A. C. Gray, had been sent from the east to meet Nick Mamer and return films to New York. He landed at Great Falls, Montana, eleven-and-a-half hours after leaving Minneapolis.

With the canister of film loaded aboard his plane in Seattle, Mamer took off at 5:30 a.m. on the first leg of a relay—an all-out race against the clock. Climbing east to nearly 10,000 feet to clear the Cascade Mountains, he met headwinds that caused him to be behind Stinson in landing at Great Falls, Montana. After landing at about 3:40 p.m. Mamer tossed the canister of film to the waiting hands of Stinson's crew. Stinson swung the big Larsen onto the runway and took off for Chicago. He told reporters he hoped to make it to Chicago for breakfast. His New York partners, on the other hand, were only interested in seeing the films in their possession within the next 24 hours.

Not every one of Mamer's commercial assignments during the early 1920s required cross-country flying. When a young Spokane girl attempting to cross the Spokane River fell from her horse and was drowned, authorities tried diligently but unsuccessfully to locate the body.

According to Spokane's Motorcycle Officer Hudson, who was detailed to the case, the incident had occurred above the Mission Street bridge, but every effort to locate the body downstream from there had failed. Officer Hudson requested Mamer's help. Within a short time after taking to the air, Mamer and Hudson sighted the body and carefully noted the location. "From the plane, we could see the bottom of the river everywhere," Mamer said. "It is the third body I have located in this manner since flying in the Northwest." Subsequently located at a depth of fifteen feet, the body was brought up by a local lifeguard and returned to the family.

Earlier, in March of 1923, what is believed to be the first contract for forest patrol from the air was signed. Nick Mamer signed the contract to fly about 500 miles a day between June 15 and September 15 on behalf of the Potlatch Timber Protective Association. "Speedier and more accurate information relative to fires is possible by airplane," C. S. Chapman, of the Western Forestry and Conservation Association said. "Where the [ground-based] lookout has to look almost horizontally through 10 or 15 miles of smoke, an airplane observer, looking down, has perhaps only a few thousand feet, and at most not over a few miles diagonally, to peer through the smoke."

Two new Standard aircraft with 150 horsepower Hispano Suiza motors were employed to patrol the Association's 900,000 acres in Idaho. "Only one ship will be in the air at a time," Mamer said, "but to keep flying every day, two machines [are] necessary. One can be gone over every other day while the other is in the air." Thorough inspection of the airplanes between flights was required to assure safety in the air. "Five hours a day will be required to make the patrol..." Nick explained. "In addition to the pilot, an observer will be carried."

Temporarily absent from his forest patrol duties for Independence Day, Nick Mamer that year spent the 4th of July at an outdoor arena in Shelby, Montana, thirty miles south of the Canadian border. There, in the center of the arena, was an elevated boxing ring. Professional-looking though it appeared, its odor of pinewood revealed its construction as days-fresh. Two men whom Nick had partnered with had set up their speed graphic camera in one corner, well back from the ring, but with a wide view of the proceedings.

The front rows of the grandstands around the ring were crowded with noisy boxing fans, but behind them were plenty of empty seats. The absence of a capacity crowd at this nationally-touted prizefight was not the fault of the town: Shelby's population was less than six-hundred. Except for the Great Northern Railroad, which passed through the town, Shelby was connected with the rest of the United States by two so-called highways, parts of which were rough and unpaved.

Although accusations and recriminations abounded, most folks blamed the railroad for the skimpy attendance by out-of-towners. It seems the Great Northern had initially agreed to run special passenger trains from Chicago on the east and Seattle on the west to ferry fans to the boxing extravaganza—and then they'd changed their mind.

It was about three in the afternoon before Tommy Gibbons entered the ring to wild applause from a contingent of special fans. Jack Dempsey's entry was more elaborate. As he came down the gangway, the heavyweight champion was surrounded by handlers, police and other escorts.

Despite all the national ballyhoo before the match, the fifteen rounds of the prizefight were pretty dull. Dempsey, in white trunks, was declared the winner on points. Gibbons, in dark trunks, took pride in hanging on for the fifteen.

Nick Mamer, who was there on business, accepted the package of film from the two men from the N. E. A. Syndicate and took off for Spokane. Flying west across the Rockies, he encountered tremendous headwinds. As it grew late, he finally had to land at Kalispell, Montana for gas, where he spent the night. At daybreak the next day he got a good start from the Kalispell runway, but again fought high winds over the Bitterroot Range before finally arriving in Spokane. Even so, his time was better than others, and *The Spokane Press* was able to publish photos of the prizefight in its forenoon editions, ahead of competition. Mamer left early the next morning delivering other photographs to *The Seattle Star*.

On June 25, 1925, *The Spokane Daily Chronicle* reported, "Lieutenant Nick B. Mamer of Spokane today received appointment as forest fire patrol pilot for eastern Washington, northern Idaho and western Montana. He will leave Spokane tomorrow night for Rockwell Field, San Diego, to get his Liberty-motored De Havilland Airplane which will be used on the patrol..." This area was designated Region 1; the other pilot named to the Region 1 patrol was R. T. Freng.

The DH-4B biplane was powered by a twelve-cylinder, water-cooled Liberty motor driving a two-blade propeller. The fuselage held two open cockpits; the observer rode in front, the pilot in the rear. A USFS photograph shows one of these with "U.S. FOREST FIRE PATROL" in large letters on the side of the fuselage. The patrol airmen wear parachutes during flight, and the aircraft carry emergency supplies as well as precise topological maps of Region 1 forests in township and section sizes.

Upon returning from patrol, the crews' work continues. To assure reports on succeeding days are not duplicated, they mark on maps the locations of the known fires and those being fought. New fires, depending on number and conditions, may result in differing responses. Observers are responsible for noting whether surrounding timber is merchantable, cut over, or second growth. Pilot and observer also try to assess possible spreading of fires resulting from changes in wind direction and/or speed. The most important aspect, Mamer explained, "...is to know each minute the exact position of the plane and the exact location of the ground over which one is flying." In most cases, he said, "we can bring it [the location] down...right to the quarter section." Because each patrol may cover as many as five-hundred miles, intense concentration by the fliers over the full duration of the flight is required.

Another feature, aerial photography, was now employed in documenting the results of fires. This was done in the Kaniksu national forest, for example, using a Fairchild aerial and mapping camera loaned to the forest service. In-stalled in the aircraft to permit focus directly below the flightpath, it housed 150 feet of eleven-inch wide film and weighed 75 pounds. The film is advanced as pictures are taken, resulting in about 240 separate exposures over a three-hour period. These may later be assembled into a mosaic from which damage can be determined more accurately than by ground survey.

Although still in his twenties, Mamer was accumulating more hours in the air than many competitors. Well-known for his aerial stunting and adventurous flying, he during these years acquired an enviable reputation piloting patrol, commercial and charitable flights. To this time he had not experienced an accident in which he or a passenger had been injured.

As a result of his many successes in widely varying activities during this period in the early 1920s, Mamer adopted a revised attitude about flying. He said that in the future, he intends to avoid stunt flying, and will instead favor full engagement in these newer, more pertinent and useful phases of aviation.

20. Races, Crashes and an Air Circus

They'd just gotten married, but to Faye Mamer, Nick Mamer sometimes seemed like a stranger. He wasn't ignoring her, he was just, well—flying. The wire she received at their Spokane home from San Francisco concerned Nick's flight north from Rockwell Field, San Diego, in 1923. It said, "BIG DH WITH 400-HORSEPOWER LIBERTY MOTOR WORKING PERFECTLY." It beat the ten-word limit and may have cost fifty cents, or about $8.00 in today's money.

Nick and Captain A. E. Easterbrook had landed without incident at Crissey field, San Francisco and Nick didn't want Faye to worry. The pair had left about a week before on orders received by Captain Easterbrook, commandant of the National Guard's 116th Observation Squadron. At Rockwell, they were to pick up the Army's De Havilland airplane, the first of several new DH-4Bs destined for the Guard's hangar at Parkwater field in Spokane.

The flying went well out of San Francisco with Easterbrook piloting. But from Redding to Portland, the going became tenuous. They'd surmounted the dangerous Siskiyou Range only to find themselves facing increasing fog. As Easterbrook hugged the ground, the men hung their heads over the sides of the open cockpits, swiping moisture from their goggles. They sought landmarks that could identify their location. Soon there was so little visibility, Easterbrook was forced to set the craft down on a field near Hubbard, Oregon. The big plane was not damaged, but the fliers were now stranded some thirty miles outside Portland, Oregon.

A short time later a passing motorist stopped and learning of their plight, drove them into Portland. When the weather cleared, the pilots returned and flew across the Columbia River to Vancouver, Washington, where they filled up with gasoline. About four hours later, the big airplane settled to the turf at Parkwater and Nick was able to hurry home and embrace Faye, whereupon he may have told her 'nothing much happened.'

At this time, Nick, an army reserve lieutenant, cooperated with the Observation Squadron. Easterbrook, a regular Army Captain, had served in France in WWI and remained on in the Army Air Service until being assigned commander of the Spokane Guard unit. He was relieved of command in 1924 by Major John "Jack" Fancher.

Fancher, his second-in-command Captain Lawrence Albert, and Nick Mamer are shown in a news photograph as he assumed command of the squadron. Major Fancher and Captain Albert stand stiffly in front of a De Havilland in their Sam Browne belted, high-collar uniforms. Nick, with his sheepskin tucked under his left arm, relaxes to the left of them in shirt, tie and an unbuttoned jacket. The caption under the photo reads: "Captain Jack Fancher, who will command the national guard [sic] unit, took his first airplane trip in six years yesterday when he soared into the clouds with Pilot Nick B. Mamer. This is the first time Major Fancher has hopped off since he flew over the German lines in 1918...Fancher said he was 'rusty' but would pick up flying again quickly with practice. ...Reserve Lieutenant Nick Mamer... will have charge of mechanical work on the planes..." On April 19, 1924, Nick received another appointment as a Second Lieutenant, Army Air Service Reserve.

Besides running the Mamer Flying Service at Parkwater, Lt. Nick was busy keeping the fledgling 116th Observation Squadron DH-4 and JN-6 'Jenny' trainers flying. Part of the squadron's activities was performing in air shows or air circuses. On Sunday, September 20, 1925, the squadron, together with others from Portland and Seattle, put on a military show at Parkwater that included speed and skill competitions. About thirty-thousand spectators watched as Lt. Nick Mamer, Lt. Pring and Lt. Schuyler Priestley completed the DH-4 race won by Priestley.

Other planes took off, demonstrating. Meanwhile, 2-man teams from three squadrons went aloft to compete in a contest called balloon-busting. This time, Lt. Priestley flew a Jenny, with Private John A. Avey Jr. as observer. As these members of the 116th Squadron flew at a slow speed and only 400 feet above the field awaiting their turn to compete, the Jenny went into a spin and crashed. It's possible that because Priestley, winner in the previous race, had just stepped from the powerful Liberty-powered DH-4 into the underpowered Jenny, he failed to sense the Jenny's impending stall. At such a low height, there was not time or space in which to recover. The plane crashed near the west end of the field, killing both men. The other fliers continued their demonstrations in what was described by the *Seattle Morning Star* as "a vain effort" to distract the crowd from the accident.

Death from flying accidents was fairly common in these years, but Nick and two others managed to escape unscathed in a seemingly impossible way from a crash, less than a year later, on June 22, 1926. The adventure, as related by Nick, started a few days earlier when pilot Paul C. Vernier landed a new plane at Parkwater.

Manufacturer J. Don Alexander climbed from the craft and introduced it to pilots at the field as the "Alexander Eaglerock," the second of a type he had first introduced in 1925. It was an open-cockpit, three-place biplane with a Curtiss OX-5 motor of 90 horsepower. At the invitation of owner Alexander, Major Fancher and Lt. Mamer put the plane through "all of the stunts it was capable of except spinning" and declared that it "apparently possessed a good combination of flying qualities." The plane was also tried out by other pilots, who rated it similarly. One pilot put the Eaglerock in a spin and after three rotations recovered from the spin and landed safely.

Later, Mamer introduced a couple of students he was training to Mr. Alexander. The manufacturer, sensing potential sales, invited Mamer to take the trainees for a ride. After flying them around for a quarter of an hour, Mamer asked what they thought of the airplane. They said they were pleased and requested that he perform a spin. At a "good safe altitude of 2000 feet", Mamer later recalled, "I pulled the nose up, kicked on rudder and pulled back my stick and throttle," and the plane began to spin.

After the plane had gone around twice, "I applied full opposite rudder, stick forward and away from the spin and gunned the motor. To my surprise, the nose gradually worked its way up until [the plane] was almost horizontal and the ship continued spinning faster and faster." Again he applied full power and corrective rudder, but the plane did not come out of the spin.

The aircraft was now in a flat spin—the fuselage approximately horizontal—rotating in a very tight, rather than a wide, circle. Nick complained that, "Every combination of control was tried but without results. It was estimated the ship made twenty turns in 2000 ft."

"Before we had dropped to the 1200-foot mark, I knew we would hit the ground," he said, noting that the men were without parachutes. "The ship was spinning fast, but falling comparatively slowly... I had hope that we would hit slow enough so the metal frame of the [fuselage's] body would take the shock and save us," he said.

Now, he recalled, "...being only two to three hundred feet from the ground, there was nothing left to do but cut the [motor's] switch and hold the ship in the spin..." keeping its rotation as flat as possible to reduce its downward speed at impact.

Nick's description of the impact follows:

> "Looking to see what was below I observed we were directly in line with the high tension wires running parallel to the interurban line. Anticipating fire or electrocution if we survived the crash I planned on jumping clear after the first interruption of the fall. When this happened I slid my hand across my safety belt, called to my companions to jump and cleared the ship in what seemed an instant, landing on the ground 20 feet below I turned in time to see my companions hurtling through the air with the ship completely enveloped in flames. All three of us made good landings and escaped without a scratch."

Apparently, a wing of the aircraft hit the wires and the other swept downward and contacted the track. An electric arc of current shot from wires to rail. But by this time, all three men had cleared the plane. The plane burned and was a complete loss.

This extraordinary tale of survival was picked up by the Associated Press in breathless exposition:

> "SPOKANE, Wash., June 22.—Lieutenant Nick Mamer, reserve officer and forest patrol flier, and two student fliers fell 900 feet near here today and escaped with their lives when their airplane alighted on high-power electrical transmission lines. They jumped to the ground as the machine hit the wires and it burst into flames and was destroyed."

Although the AP error of "900 feet" is not explained, the writer may have mistaken the 2,000-foot altitude as height above mean sea level and reduced it to account for the elevation of Spokane, although the difference of 1100 feet is an incorrect elevation.

The crash was also the subject of a July 12 paragraph by E. Harve Partridge in the pages of *Aviation* magazine:

"The plane started to spin and he [Mamer] pushed the stick forward and kicked on reverse rudder. Nothing happened but the spin continued at full speed, the machine almost on a level keel. At 300 feet, Mamer saw striking the wires was inevitable but there was nothing to do but wait. The plane hit the wires and one wing hung while the other dropped to the rails, short circuiting the current and setting fire to the wreck. Mamer and his companions dropped to the ground from a height of 10 ft. and all escaped without a scratch."

Mamer credited the slow descent of the craft for the fliers' survival: "the vertical speed was estimated to be about equivalent to parachute speed," meaning about the same speed as that of a parachutist in a round, 1926-style parachute at the moment of impact. However, there is a lack of careful reasoning explaining how the three men escaped "without a scratch."

Mr. Alexander and pilot Vernier later caught a train back to Denver, perhaps to reconsider the Eaglerock's airworthiness. Mamer is quoted in one newspaper as saying the 2000-foot fall was "rather exciting."

In February, 1927, Nick became a father. Patricia Ann was born at Spokane's St. Luke's hospital on February 13. The Mamers declared her to be Spokane's newest air pilot, and Nick assured the newspaper that "thirteen doesn't mean any bad luck to a good aviator."

In May, another squadron-member death occurred when Lt. James Buell Felts crashed his Jenny near the field and died. Not long after, the NAA, the National Aeronautics Association designated Spokane, Washington as host for the 1927 National Air Derby and Air Races. This event would make its headquarters at the Parkwater field, newly-renamed as Felts Field in honor of Lieutenant Felts' death.

National Air Derby and Air Races in Cleveland and Los Angeles had in prior years been less than successful, and Spokane aviation enthusiasts were determined to reverse the trend. Major Jack Fancher, commander of the National Guard, powered the effort, gaining support from local businessmen, contacting influential friends in the east, and meeting with U. S. President Coolidge at the summer Whitehouse. In the six months leading to the event, Spokane lumber magnate Milton McGoldrick, investment tycoon Harlan Peyton, newspaper owner William H. Cowles, and twenty six other business leaders formed the master organization, while an Executive Committee headed by Walter Evans, Victor Dessert and Harlan Peyton managed the overall approach and approved numerous subcommittees to implement the project. In addition to the two big air races, these committees planned air stunts, bombing demonstrations, skywriting and parachute jumps. More than $60,000 was raised in support (almost $900,000 in 2018 dollars).

Nick had the sides of his new Swallow open-cockpit biplane painted with large letters: "NATIONAL AIR DERBY – $50,000 in Prizes – NATIONAL AIR RACES – Sept. 19th – 24th – SPOKANE, WASH." Major Fancher and Sergeant Raymond Carroll flew the Swallow to New York and back in July, drumming up interest and making arrangements along the route of the upcoming Class A race.

At the September opening of National Air Derby and Air Races in Spokane, Lieutenant James "Jimmy" Doolittle flew upside-down over downtown at a low altitude, attracting everyone's attention by the wild roar of his specially-equipped 600-horsepower Hawk airplane. Gaining altitude, he performed his original stunt, the outside loop, in which the open cockpit of the powerful Curtiss Hawk remained on the outside of the loop throughout the maneuver.

Doolittle later became famous in the early phase of WWII for the daring flight of B-25 bombers he led all the way from the deck of an aircraft carrier to Tokyo, Japan, where they dropped bombs on the surprised Japanese. As part of the U.S. tour celebrating his May crossing of the Atlantic, Charles Lindbergh also contributed to the buildup of the Spokane Derby by flying his *Spirit of St. Louis* airplane in to Felts Field on September 12 and giving speeches.

In addition to stunts, military exhibitions and air races around the local area, the 1927 Spokane Derby included long-distance races, with significant prizes. Cross-country air races originating in both New York and San Francisco, with short "5-minute," intermediate fueling stops, ended at Spokane.

A nonstop race from New York was also included. These long-distance races were begun on differing days and times for different classes of racers and differing starting points. For aircraft with high or low horsepower and speed the staggered starts were designed with the intent that the contestants would arrive in Spokane within a relatively short span of time, adding to the general excitement. Cash prizes for the races aggregated to $63,250 (about $950,000 in 2018 dollars), not including several valuable trophies.

Racing planes arrived at Spokane at all hours, drawing crowds each day to Felts Field—a time of dreams, competition and aviation innovation—and a time to view the daring people and the great winged machines that represented the age.

Major attention focused on the New York to Spokane races, both Class A (powerful), Class B (less powerful) and the nonstop airplanes. The nonstop race from New York to Los Angeles drew five entrants, but only two of them were able to depart New York on schedule. Both planes were forced to land in Montana, disqualifying them from the competition.

The Class A racers left New York's Curtiss field at staggered intervals starting at 6:00 a.m. on September 20. Weather conditions were more favorable than they had been for the Class B group takeoff the day before. Brief fueling stops for the Class A group were scheduled at Cleveland and Chicago, with an overnight stay at St. Paul, Minnesota. This was followed the next day by stops at Aberdeen, South Dakota, Miles City and Butte, Montana, and landing in Spokane for a total of about 2,300 miles.

Nick Mamer, in a new Buhl Airster with the Wright J-5 motor, was entered in the Class A race. The first airplane off from Roosevelt Field on Long Island was a Buhl Airster with R.E. Hudson piloting and J. P. Radike as passenger. A short time later, it crashed in New Jersey and they were killed. Nick Mamer, with passenger Bruce McDonald in the open-cockpit Airster, took off and climbed out safely to the west. The next stop, a nominal "five minute" landing for gas, was to take place in Cleveland. Photographs in the Mamer family archives show Mamer's plane approaching to land at Cleveland and also on the ground at Cleveland receiving gasoline (with its motor running and the propeller spinning!).

An even more telling portrait of the frenzy of the Class A race took place at Butte, Montana. A scant seven and a half minutes after landing, C. W. "Speed" Holman's Laird taxied toward the hangar and turned south to take off. As the plane rose from the field its left tire flew off. Holman and his mechanic appeared to have realized what happened, but the plane continued to climb and disappeared to the west. Race officials immediately wired Spokane on the theory race officials in the host city might be able to warn Holman of the absence of a tire before he attempted to land.

Twenty minutes later, a white biplane with blue wings and a red tail approached the Butte airfield from the east. Nick Mamer's Airster circled, landed with precision, and halted squarely at the fueling station. He stayed in the cockpit while McDonald assisted in fueling the plane. He gulped a cup of soup and studied his maps while some friends from Butte came over to shake his hand. When the official timer called out "four minutes," Mamer shouted to the refueling crew, "Let's go, boys, with that gas!" McDonald climbed aboard and Nick taxied out and was airborne after about six minutes on the ground.

Somewhat later, the Butte crowd cheered as E. E. Ballough in his gold-colored biplane sped down the field on a takeoff run. For the previous hour and 26 minutes he had frantically overseen the repair of his Laird aircraft. Ballough had led the race until landing at Butte, when, on touchdown, the landing gear buckled. The plane nosed over, bending the propeller. Now, however, he was off, but trailing behind Speed Holman's Laird.

In Spokane, a roar from the packed grandstand greeted the arrival of every contestant. As they touched down and halted, the crew was taken by car to the reviewing stand where they were urged to speak a few words into the microphone.

Speed Holman had the shortest time for the transit from New York to Spokane of 19 hours, 42 minutes, 47 seconds. He made a precise landing at Felts Field during which his Laird stayed on the good wheel until the plane had almost stopped. He was awarded the first prize of $10,000. Second prize of $5,000 went to E. E. Ballough. His time was 20 hours and 18 minutes, despite the time lost in repairing his Laird at Butte. Nick Mamer, who arrived forty-one minutes after Ballough, won third place and $2,000. Fifteen Class A airplanes had started the race from New York, but only seven finished in Spokane.

The 1927 Air Derby and National Air Races were a complete success. Thanks to its name appearing in newsprint throughout the U.S. in reporting the event, Spokane was now considered a leading aviation center. Lt. Nick Mamer's name also became well-known, and he was increasingly involved in many other aspects of the aviation business.

Less than seven months later, Felts Field and Spokane aviation lost its most ardent booster. Major John "Jack" Fancher was killed in a freak accident in East Wenatchee, Washington. He and members of the National Guard unit produced an air show there as part of the Apple Blossom Festival. Following a demonstration of the Army's aerial bombing technique, he unloaded several of the small "grenade-type" bombs from his airplane. Similar bombs had failed to explode when tossed from his airplane during the demonstration, and he was determined to see why they were defective. As he checked them, one of the bombs exploded in his hand. He died of his injuries a few hours later, on April 29th, 1928.

The next Air Derby and National Air Races were held in Los Angeles in September of 1928. The nonstop race now increased its distance to that from New York to Los Angeles—about 2,500 miles—and offered prizes totaling $22,500. This daunting distance would require aircraft to launch from New York's Roosevelt Field with heavy loads of gasoline.

For this Derby, Nick Mamer signed as a competitor in the nonstop race, rather than in the Class A or B races. He would fly a special, enclosed cabin Airsedan from the Buhl factory equipped with a Wright Whirlwind motor. In addition to its two wing tanks of fifty-gallons (each) capacity, it featured a large 300-gallon gas tank situated in the forward part of the cabin, ahead of the pilot's control station. The design was based on the idea that 400 gallons of gasoline would be sufficient to propel the aircraft across the continent.

Locating the tank forward in this craft had the advantage that its weight when full of 300 gallons, 1,900 pounds, was supported by the wings without changing the balance of the aircraft. Had the weight of such a full tank been placed behind the pilot, it would have negatively influenced the balance. This could cause the plane, when fully loaded, to be difficult—perhaps impossible—to fly.

The forward placement of the 300-gallon tank forced the pilot's control station well back in the fuselage. Seeing forward through the front windshield is not possible from this position. The pilot must lean out the large window on the left side of the cabin to maintain his view forward, for example during takeoff or landing.

The Mamer family archives contain black & white photographs of this airplane, NX6874. One of them shows Nick seated inside at the controls. The plane was painted a darker color, with white or lighter lettering. A large "25" near the tail, a Buhl insignia in a large circle, "MAMER FLYING SERVICE, SPOKANE WASH." underneath the rearmost window and the name "Miss Spokane," painted on the cowling, completed its identification. Mamer's passenger, seated to his right, was to be his business associate, Clarence "C.I.P." Paulsen.

According to George Kivel's report in the *New York Daily News*, September 13, 1928, only five of the nine contestants for the Derby's nonstop prize actually flew on toward Los Angeles from Roosevelt field.

Mamer had difficulties of his own. As the second pilot scheduled for takeoff, he drew the fully loaded No. 25 to the starting line. Giving the Airsedan full throttle he dashed between a phalanx of spectators and parked automobiles on one side and a roped-off viewing area on the opposite side. A huge cloud of dust stirred behind the Airsedan, but quickly dissipated. Mamer had cut the switch and braked, fearing he would not become airborne before reaching the gulley at the end of the field.

Kivel wrote that Mamer was "mindful of the disaster which met Rene Fonck when he failed to get off...," a reference to a deathly crash of two years before, when Fonck, piloting the 4,000-lb overweight Sikorsky S-35 down the field on an attempt to cross the Atlantic to Paris, failed to become airborne soon enough. The three-motored craft plunged down the slope at the end of the field and burst into flames. Although Fonck and his co-pilot escaped, two other crewmen perished in the crash.

Mamer returned the Buhl aircraft, with C.I.P. Paulsen aboard, to the starting line and again began a takeoff run. Halfway, certain it was unsafe, he shut down the motor, stopped and returned to the starting area again. Nick, in light colored coveralls, alighted. He and Paulsen talked over the situation, and quickly began removing extra clothing, packages, and other materials from the airplane, leaving only two sandwiches and a quart of water on board. Paulsen and Nick parted, with Paulsen heading for the viewing area. Nick climbed behind the controls of the Airsedan, wheeled to the starting line, and, with goggles protecting his eyes and with his body partway out the left side window, roared down the strip and, fortunately, into the air.

The favorite to win, Art Goebel of Chicago, was almost last to get into the air from Roosevelt Field. He lifted his Lockheed-Vega named *Yankee Doodle* off the field in fine fashion with passenger Harry Tucker. Twenty-three hours and 50 minutes later, he flew over Mines Field, the only nonstop race contestant to reach Los Angeles. He swooped low to the cheers of the assembled crowd of 4,500.

The enthusiasm was soon quelled, however, when it was announced that Goebel had landed at Prescott, Arizona on his way to Los Angeles, disqualifying him for the nonstop Derby trophy and the prize money. When interviewed, Goebel said he had fought fierce headwinds, rain and sleet, and had carburetor trouble. He'd added 75 gallons of gas during his stay of 70 minutes in Prescott. He added he did not see how any plane and pilot could battle the storm conditions he met and have enough fuel to continue to Los Angeles.

Earlier, at 3:45 a.m., Nick Mamer's Airsedan was sighted over Cheyenne, Wyoming. But fog, snow and a forceful headwind caused his speed over the ground to nearly vanish. At about 9:30 that morning he set Miss Spokane down at the airfield at Rawlins, Wyoming, after spending most of two hours searching through fog trying to find the field. He said he had experienced carburetor icing at altitude, and that this led to engine problems and the need to land. He wired the Los Angeles Derby officials: "Carburetor iced up, fouling plugs forcing me down after 23 [hours]. Sorry I couldn't come in. (Signed) MAMER."

Interviewed later, he said,

"I lost my earth inductor [compass] after taking off from
Roosevelt Field. Although I had a magnetic compass and
an emergency compass, I was determined not to continue
the flight without knowing where I was, so I followed the
transcontinental air mail route for some distance. About 50
miles east of North Platte, Nebraska, I encountered a fog
bank, but came out of it all right...over Cheyenne, I was
about 65 miles north of my course. I thought everything
was set for a successful journey to Los Angeles and [sat]
back in the cockpit for the rest of the grind..."

But a storm was ahead. "...lightning was striking all around me...It was
terribly cold [at 14,000-feet]...storms forced me to turn back, and I sought a
landing at Rawlins."

Informed that there were no finishers in the nonstop cross-country Derby
race, Nick Mamer slept for the first time in more than 24 hours. Afterwards,
he flew to Casper, took on gasoline, and returned beaten, but not bowed, to
Spokane.

Although Mamer had dropped from the nonstop-transcontinental 1928
Los Angeles National Air Race, he had developed great confidence in the Buhl
Airsedan. He vowed to continue to prove his and the aircraft's mettle by setting
records for long-distance flying.

21. TIN GEESE TO SKY FUTURE

The loneliness was unequaled. The speed, the howl of the wind, the roar of the J-6 radial motor barreling through the night, it all came with the risk. Yet to Nick, wedged into the open-cockpit of the low-winged airplane, it was somehow exhilarating.

Almost a year had passed since he and Art Walker had completed the record flight of the *Spokane Sun God*, coast-to-coast and back without stopping. When on the ground, he was now greeted everywhere as the Spokane flier who'd made refueling a kitchen-table word across America. Though fame rested easily on his shoulders, he found the escape from it soothing.

Headed west, he'd had to detour north, dodging lightning squalls. "Not a light on the ground for miles and miles," he later said. "[E]ach time I turned, a flash of lightning would greet me."

From sleek cowling to faired tailfin, the CA-1 racer was the slickest airplane Nick had ever flown. Designed by Etienne Dormoy and built at the Buhl factory near Detroit, it even sported wheel 'spats,' slim covers fabricated to reduce the air resistance of the landing gear's wheels.

Now, on this night of July 17, 1930, Mamer left St. Paul, Minnesota, intent on setting a record. But the absence of landmarks across the windswept, wild land of South Dakota made navigation almost impossible. He wouldn't know if his course was correct until he glimpsed the Yellowstone River and Miles City, Montana, another forty minutes from now.

Earlier this year, a restricted group of leaders from the aviation industry met with the Postmaster General of the United States. General Walter Folger Brown had summoned them to Washington, D.C. for what later became known as the Spoils Conference. Congress had replaced the flawed Kelly Act that had allowed abuse of the airmail system by commercial carriers. The new act, among other provisions, gave the postmaster general the authority to extend or consolidate airmail routes "when in his judgement the public interest will be promoted thereby."

It was well-understood at the time that the budding airline industry could not survive without the government cash subsidies that accompanied carrying airmail. Postmaster Brown interpreted the new act of congress as allowing him to award airmail routes to "solidly-financed carriers" with the most aviation experience that he saw as essential to passenger safety. He therefore arranged that most of the airmail route contracts were awarded to just the three largest carriers, United Aircraft, Aviation Corporation and the North American-General Motors group. This action became known as the Spoils Conference and led to the significant and disastrous Air Mail Scandal. It later influenced the fate and fortunes of Nick Mamer.

The twinkle of lights in Miles City, Montana, in the distance to the west, welcomed Nick. Although his estimate of forty minutes to the field was inaccurate, he was happy to warm his hands and stretch his legs after landing the racer there for gas. Once the gasoline was topped off, he was back in the air, heading for Butte, Montana, the mountain passes, Missoula, and Spokane.

A roar out of the eastern darkness at 3:24 a.m. alerted the mechanics and fuelers of Mamer's arrival at Spokane. As he clambered from the open cockpit and the gas truck pulled up, a smiling cluster of welcomers closed around him. He complained of the cold and asked for hot coffee. Dressed in a flying suit over his business suit with his parachute hanging low, he said, "A sealskin suit and a bearskin coat would have helped..." Shortly, a fur-lined coat and two cups of coffee arrived. Fifteen minutes later he was back in the cockpit, and the sleek monoplane was buzzing off Felts Field and turning west.

At 5:44 a.m., an hour and 57 minutes later, he touched down at Seattle. Ten minutes later, after refueling, he slipped cleanly into the predawn sky, retracing his path eastward.

Although he was expected back at Spokane between 8 and 9 a.m., he landed at 7:42 a.m. As he landed he saw that the parking area now held almost a dozen cars. Among those greeting him during the brief stop for gas was Washington State's U.S. Senator, Clarence Cleveland Dill. But he was most revitalized by the presence in the office of his wife, Faye, and his young daughter, Patti. These cheering events consumed a bit more ground time than he'd expected, but after less than a half-hour he was airborne again.

He arrived at his starting point of St. Paul after dark on July 18, 1930. He'd faced headwinds on the eastward trek, but still maintained a round trip from St. Paul to Seattle and return in 24 hours and 25 minutes, with just two stops, at Miles City and Spokane. Although somewhat haggard for all the continuous piloting in an open cockpit, he was elated.

As he'd often done before, he mentioned to the crowd that regular ten-hour passenger and mail service could be developed in either direction between St. Paul and Seattle, especially with the addition of lighted beacons and other airway aids to navigation.

About a month later Mamer finished second in the Class A Pacific Derby race from Seattle to Chicago.

A previous record attempt two years earlier had also shown advances in speed and duration. In October of 1928, Mamer set a *nonstop* record: eleven hours and twelve minutes flying from Spokane to St. Paul. The aircraft flown was the same Airsedan that had almost finished the 1928 National Air Race's nonstop competition from New York to Los Angeles. Nick left Spokane at dawn and arrived at St. Paul at 6:50 p.m. on October 24. "The ship landed after dark and averaged 140 miles an hour in the last 600 miles," he said.

What made this 1928 flight newsworthy, besides the record set, was the person next to him during the trip—the young Mary Genevieve Paulsen—the wife of Clarence I. Paulsen, Spokane businessman and sportsman. "Cip" as he was known, had almost flown off with Mamer on that September race day, only to be left behind to lighten the load at Roosevelt Field, Long Island. Strangely, the press of 1928 failed to note the irony of Mrs. Paulsen's passage a month later on the same airplane.

As usual, Mamer's flight served more than one purpose. He wanted to advertise that this Buhl aircraft, especially equipped with its 300-gallon tank and rear pilot's station, was a durable, high speed airplane despite having been forced to land in stormy weather before reaching the conclusion of the race in Los Angeles. This record also drew attention once more to Nick's advocacy of an airmail and passenger route connecting St. Paul with the Pacific Northwest.

Thanks to diligent handling of his personal and company finances during these years, Mamer was able by March of 1929 to purchase a new Ford Tri-Motor airplane on behalf of Mamer Flying Services. The craft, powered by three J-6 300 horsepower motors, was sheathed in corrugated metal, earning it the popular nickname of Tin Goose. Its corrugations also led to it being dubbed 'The Flying Washboard.'

News reports labeled the Ford a "giant," the biggest aircraft most people had ever seen, and its price of $50,000 (about $700,000 in today's dollars) made it something people wanted to see. A March 21, 1929 news photograph shows Mamer and the president of Universal Auto Company holding a $44,100 check that completed the plane's purchase.

The Ford Tri-Motor was one of the first airplanes designed specifically for airline service. By today's standard, it's difficult to imagine how unusual and daring it was considered to be in 1929. Carrying twelve passengers and two pilots at a cruising speed of 115 miles an hour, it was advertised to be as comfortable as 'a passenger train's Pullman car.'

Tri-motor pilots accessed dual yokes and controls, though the instruments and controls, compared with those of a modern jet, were minimal. Passengers were seated in wicker chairs, and at the rear was a lavatory and storage for luggage. Thanks to two of its three motors being positioned outside and below the wing and its metal construction, "You hardly notice [the noise]," Nick said. "Our passengers converse all the time they are flying and never seem to realize that the motors are operating."

The airplane was named the *West Wind*. It inaugurated the Mamer-Ford Tour of sixty U.S. cities across the northern tier, all coordinated by and with Ford auto dealers. Nick, excited by the planned tour, purchased a linen-bound ledger with 150 blank pages. The cover of the ledger to this day retains his printed-in-pencil notation, "Press Book." Onto the pages of the ledger he pasted newspaper and magazine clippings from the tour. At first he noted beside each clip, in pencil, the source and date, but by page 51 and hundreds of clippings later, he had abandoned that; there were simply too few hours and too many clippings.

Aiding in the Tri-motor endeavor was Nick's experienced co-pilot and mechanic, Art Walker. Along the way, hundreds of passengers undertook their very first flight. Nick met the press, gave after-dinner speeches and conversed with local leaders and businessmen. Most were impressed to learn he'd accumulated more than 6,500 hours in the air. At La Grande, Oregon, more than 200 attended a banquet honoring him at the Sacajawea Inn. Congressmen and Senators pledged their support for his effort. The tour earned him honors of varying quality, including a ten-gallon cowboy hat and being named "Chief Silver Eagle" by the Yellowstone Tribe.

As Nick had explained before leaving the Ford Tri-Motor factory with the plane: "Our flight has a dual purpose...to stimulate aviation interest in the northern states...[and] to create a greater public demand for early establishment of the proposed northern airway...[which] compares more than favorably with the transcontinental route, over which the mail is being flown daily with great success."

By the middle of 1929, however, the Tour was winding down. Mamer had purchased a second Ford Tri-motor, the *West Wind II*, which he placed into passenger service to Portland, Oregon. At about the same time, the first rough plans were being formulated for a nonstop coast-to-coast flight by Mamer. Within a month, most of the details of what was to become the flight of the *Spokane Sun God* had been worked out.

The Sun God flight, the best-known of Mamer's records, was nevertheless only one of his achievements over the decade ending in 1929. The twelve-page brochure for the Mamer Flying School, for example, notes that it "is the only flying school in the Northwest approved by the United States Department of Commerce." Four courses for trainees were described: Airplane and Engine Mechanics Ground Course; Private Pilots Course; Limited Commercial Course; and Transport Pilots Course.

The school's staff consisted of Mamer; Newton Wakefield, pilot and M.I.T. graduate in aeronautical engineering; George Hallet, pilot with four years instructing in California and eight years flying; Art Walker, pilot, engine expert and co-pilot on the Sun God flight; Ralph Daniels, transport pilot on Mamer Air Transport; and Al Connick, field manager in charge of operations. According to a year-end summary, 42 of 75 registered students successfully graduated from the school.

Aircraft flown by Mamer or under his direct supervision covered nearly 1.5 million miles. More than 75,000 passengers had been transported without injury. Nick's energy, vision, and dedication to aviation over the period easily matched that of better-known flying personalities such as Lindbergh, Rickenbacker, Doolittle and Earhart. But 1929 ended on a sour note. An unexpected collapse of the economy followed the stock market crash in October. Nick, like many Americans, lost money in the crash.

The Great Depression that followed 1930 dealt the budding air transport industry a crushing blow. During the depression years, the need for rapid transport and the pool of potential passengers contracted.

During the summer of 1930, however, Mamer Air Transport planned trips in the Ford Tri-motors over the South Fork country to Glacier park. Mamer still held hopes his Air Transport would be awarded an airmail contract. In June, tri-weekly passenger service from Spokane to St. Paul was inaugurated using the Buhl CA-6 airplane with a capacity of six.

In the fall of 1930, Mamer was instrumental in securing a government appropriation of $20,000 (about $280,000 in today's dollars) for a survey of a proposed airmail route through the Northwest.

But by 1933, citizens of the U.S. had seen their income almost halved, and 40 percent of home mortgages were in default. Although Mamer persisted on the course he had laid out for Mamer Air Transport, the contraction of the market curtailed his progress.

As if to emphasize the downturn of the Great Depression, on September 11, with Newton Wakefield at the controls, a Mamer Air Transport Buhl Airsedan was forced down at Mullan, Idaho, a few miles west of Lookout Pass.

On his run out of Missoula, Wakefield had struck so much fog and rain, he decided flying further was dangerous. He set the aircraft down on the Mullan ball field, a designated emergency landing area. The plane hit a wire, turned on its side and ended in a ditch. The four passengers were shaken, and suffered superficial cuts and bruises. The pilot also suffered cuts and bruises. All received first-aid and were transported to Spokane by automobile. The landing gear and wings of the aircraft were heavily damaged.

Details of the Spoils Conference became available later that year, making clear the big three of the airlines were to control most of the airmail contracts to be awarded by the U.S. Postal Service in the future. Although it is uncertain Mamer Air Transport's action was a direct response to this news, operations through Montana ceased in the fall of 1930.

Frank Wiley wrote that Mamer's company was "blocked in their hope of acquiring valuable mail contracts through lobbying in Washington by Northwest Airlines and United Airlines."

Early in 1931, Mamer Air Transport announced a doubling of its Seattle-Spokane service. At the same time, a resumption of the discontinued St. Paul-Spokane service was said to depend on completion of a government "survey of a proposed mail route between the two cities."

In May, the U.S. Forest Service announced Mamer Air Transport was the low bidder on forest patrol work for the season. The last week of July saw Mamer flying a Stinson cabin monoplane over fires raging in the forests of western Montana. Jack Jost, from regional headquarters in Missoula, was his observer. "We are not called upon to make regular trips..." Mamer said. "We are brought into service following electrical storms that might set a number of fires at one time or when existing blazes have created such a haze of smoke that the regular lookouts cannot work efficiently." Whether this was a thoughtful reassessment of priorities or a cover story for reduced government outlays is difficult to know.

In early September, Nick was in Eugene, Oregon, with the Buhl CA-6, meeting heavyweight boxer Jack Dempsey there after Dempsey had arrived by train. Mamer was to fly Dempsey in the Buhl to Reno, Nevada. Apparently, Mamer was making himself available to Dempsey for the week, during which Dempsey was scheduled for a Labor Day boxing match.

The years 1932-33 witnessed continuation of the economic downturn. The bonus march of disgruntled war veterans on Washington, D. C., the agricultural disaster known as the dust bowl, and the failure of thousands of banks were dire examples. Franklin Roosevelt, elected overwhelmingly in 1932, took office in early 1933. But by that time, the life of nearly every American had already been disrupted, and demoralization was rampant.

Little more is known of Mamer's activities during this period. The frequent press coverage of his aerial exploits and his companies that was common during the 1920s diminished to almost nil. In one of the few newspaper articles, Mamer proposes an optimistic plan for the future: "N. B. Mamer, vice president of the Mamer Air Transport company said...development of the northern airway is the next logical move of the United States postal department." Mamer had returned from a trip viewing the latest models of aircraft in California factories. "Speed is the most important consideration in the designing of the 1933 model passenger planes," he said. "Speed is the big advantage of air travel...[t]he faster the schedule the more passengers the line will obtain...The new planes will cruise at 200 miles an hour or more."

In November of 1933 the traffic manager for Northwest Airways was quoted on extending that airlines' mail route between Billings, Montana and Spokane. "Today we started the handling of express and within a short time will be carrying passengers," K. R. Ferguson said. He went on to explain that the Airways had secured the services of Nick Mamer of Spokane to negotiate leases for lands for emergency landing fields. "We will be using planes of 200 miles an hour speed and upwards," he said, "and naturally must have the emergency fields laid out before the fast ships are placed in service."

After discussing fields at Big Timber, Livingston, Townsend, Helena, Superior, and Dixon, Mamer was quoted as saying each of these fields must measure up to rigid requirements of both Northwest Airways and the Department of Commerce. No field, he said, will have a runway of less than one-half mile, while several will have runways longer. These press notices constitute the first mentions of Nick's formal association with Northwest Airways, evidence his Mamer Air Transport was being supplanted as the northern route carrier by the larger, better financed, St. Paul-based Northwest Airways.

Croil Hunter, vice-president and general manager of Northwest Airways, in a formal announcement, said passengers on the Spokane-St. Paul line would be carried by Orions, five passenger, low-wing monoplanes built by Lockheed that cruised at 206 miles per hour. Among their new features were retractable landing gear, metal wing flaps, and controllable pitch propellers.

Shortly thereafter, on December 3, Mamer was at the controls of a Northwest Airways airplane—probably a Hamilton cabin monoplane—completing the airline's inaugural flight into Seattle. According to a dispatch dated four days later, vice-president Croil Hunter announced, "N. B. 'Nick' Mamer, a pioneer in developing the northwestern air route, has been employed by Northwest Airways, and at present is a pilot on the Spokane-Seattle line. Later, Mamer will assist in managing operation of the Billings-Seattle division." He went on to say that a public works appropriation of $650,445 (or about $9 million in today's dollars) would provide lighting of the airway.

During 1933, airmail was transported by airlines on 26 air routes covering about 25,000 miles. The mail was carried on more than 60 flights each day, 38 of them night flights. However, with Executive Order 6591, President Roosevelt, in office less than a year, cancelled all airmail contracts with civilian airline companies effective February 19, 1934. Henceforth, it was announced, the U.S. Army would be charged with transporting airmail. Roosevelt's action was in response to the previous administration's award of contracts by Postmaster Brown to the three largest air transport firms at the 1930 Spoils Conference (above).

Those knowledgeable of the Army's Air Corps and the rigors of airmail piloting condemned the President's abrupt action on grounds the Army air service lacked pilots trained in the all-weather and nighttime flying required for airmail service. In ensuing weeks, sixty-six Army flights crashed and ten Army pilots were killed while delivering the mail. This sequence, which became known as the Airmail Scandal, provoked such a public outcry Roosevelt was forced to reverse himself and cancel his cancellation.

While this scandal ruled the news, Northwest Airways pilot Nick Mamer was flying a newly delivered Lockheed Orion, originating its operation from Spokane, where it would be headquartered. Again, vice-president Croil Hunter spoke of the operation: "The extension of operations...across half a continent...made a wide change in our...operating plans. It became necessary to build new radio stations, locate many intermediate fields, order new equipment...and generally broaden the entire operation[al] scope of the company. The [airline's] first [Lockheed] Electra will be test flown in a few days."

Although Mamer sold both Ford Tri-Motors in late 1934, he retained his interests in Mamer Flying Service and his flying school at Felts Field. At the same time, he enjoyed test-flying the new Douglas airliner out of Los Angeles and attending a dinner honoring Sir Charles Kingsford-Smith and Captain P. G. Taylor upon completion of their record trans-Pacific flight from Australia.

By 1936, *Northwest Airliner*, a magazine published for its passengers by the now slightly re-named Northwest Airlines, described its planes "that travel three times as fast [as those of 1926] and carry 10 passengers and two pilots snugly enclosed in a rigid, streamlined fuselage." This was its description of the Lockheed Electra, newly in service at Northwest. The *Northwest Airliner*, on page 13, profiled three Northwest Airlines pilots, "Veterans Over the Mountains," they were called, active in the newest, western, part of the line. Mamer's profile was one of the three.

Indeed, in 1936, Nick Mamer celebrated 10,000 hours in the air, or a distance of about a million miles. This record was assembled in flights crisscrossing the continent, and included his Isthmus of Panama service, even though during the past two years he'd restricted his flying to the western leg of the St. Paul-Seattle route as first pilot for Northwest Airlines.

Mamer tried to explain what had changed over the years:

> "The pilot of a decade ago," Nick said, "was a colorful if sometimes irresponsible individual concerned chiefly in keeping the airplane in the novelty field. As long as he could awe the public with his hair-raising gyrations and challenge its nerve by inviting it to share his danger at so much a hop, he was happy.
>
> "Today, airline pilots are highly skilled, self-disciplined, the world's finest airmen. They can have no physical or mental handicaps. They must be versed in radio, meteorology, navigation, instrument flying, and must keep abreast of technical developments. Passenger comfort and safety is the pilot's first thought.
>
> "As to the future, the sky is boundless, and we have just begun to explore it."

A search for another pilot with Nick's knowledge and expertise on flying the mountains of the Northwest was almost certain to come up empty. The profile in the *Northwest Airliner* referred to above named him, simply, "The most experienced mountain flier in the world."

22. THE FINAL FLIGHT

On January 10, 1938, Flight 2 of Northwest Airlines, with Nick Mamer at the controls, crashed into a canyon fourteen miles northeast of Bozeman, Montana, killing Mamer, copilot Fred W. West, and the eight passengers on board (see Notes for names).

The flight, from Seattle to Chicago, left Seattle at 10:15 a.m. It had been delayed briefly on the ground in Butte by bad weather. At about 3:00 p.m., minutes before the crash, pilot Mamer reported by radio "Cruising at 9,000 feet with everything okay."

Witnesses on the ground said the airplane stalled, fell in a spin or tight spiral, crashed and burned on the east side of the Bridger mountains. The weather report read, "Ceiling 4500 feet, sky overcast, visibility 20 miles, 47 degrees, wind southwest at 34 m.p.h., heavy gusts, storming all mountains, occasional sprinkling, few small breaks in clouds, sky conditions rapidly changing."

The airplane was a new 14-H Super Electra from the Lockheed factory, with which Northwest Airlines was replacing its fleet. A low-wing monoplane, it was powered by two wing-mounted Pratt & Whitney R-1690 Hornet motors driving 3-bladed propellers. The plane was of conventional layout except for twin vertical tail fins which were mounted near the tips of the horizontal tail fin. Its top speed was about 230 miles-per-hour.

This metal skinned airliner seated twelve or fourteen passengers in rows of two. Luggage was stowed in the nose and under the elevated crew deck. The airline called it the Sky Zephyr, or sometimes, simply Zephyr.

Photographs of the crash site show a snow-filled, shallow canyon with clear-cut stumps bordered by heavy-growth forest. The wreckage is a charred, flattened jumble. Two workers, C. A. Larson and Glen White, who were cutting wood in the rugged area at the time, watched as the airliner struck about 200 feet from them and burst into flames. Although they could not approach because of the fire, they said a single body was thrown clear of the plane. They immediately left to summon help.

Word of the disaster was issued by Elmer Johnson, a rancher living in the sparsely-inhabited area, who also saw the plane fall. A search party including him, Sheriff Lovitt Westlake, Alfred Nikles, J. A. Nee, and J. T. Trowbridge, set out for the crash site. They met the two woodcutters on the way. It was obvious from first view there were no survivors. A blizzard began after their arrival, which forced them to post guards and retreat. The word in Bozeman was that they would return to town around midnight.

The next day, January 11, Gallatin County officials and others, as well as post-office inspectors and newsmen, struck out. They abandoned automobiles and used skis, sleds and snowshoes to traverse the final miles to the scene. The wreck was still smoldering. Aviation inspector A. D. Niemeyer from the Department of Commerce probed the crumpled, charred airframe, searching for a cause. County Coroner Howard Nelson of Bozeman picked carefully through the twisted wreckage, exposing human remains. Upon brushing snow from the uniform sleeve of the body thrown clear of the plane, Coroner Nelson identified it as belonging to Nick Mamer.

On January 12, Northwest Airlines grounded all ten of its new Lockheed Zephyrs, pending "a final report of the qualified investigators" regarding the cause of the crash. The announcement only slightly preceded a similar grounding order issued by Fred D. Fagg, director of the aviation bureau of the Department of Commerce, the cognizant governing organization of the time.

Croil Hunter, president of Northwest Airlines, issued this statement: "An investigation into the circumstances surrounding the crash near Bozeman indicates to us that the accident was not due to weather conditions, visibility, nor to human error, either of the ground crew or of the pilots."

Lockheed officials also arrived in Bozeman to conduct an inquiry.

At an inquest held late that day (the 11th) in Bozeman, Coroner Nelson testified that the eight passengers and two pilots met instant death when the airplane struck the ground. "All the safety belts were snapped, apparently by the terrific impact when the plane struck, and in my opinion every one of the ten was dead before the plane burst into flames," he said. "The clothing was burned from all [nine] of them...the condition of the bodies was such that extreme care was necessary in handling them..." Although the bodies within the wreck were burned beyond recognition, Nelson was able with the help of relatives to identify each through personal effects such as jewelry or watches.

A watch on the body of D. McKay of Canada was stopped thirty seconds past 3:07, which confirmed the time of the crash found on a loose wrist watch, which also stopped at seven minutes past three. In Washington, D.

C., Secretary of Commerce Daniel Roper announced that a formal board of inquiry would meet in Bozeman on Tuesday, January 18, to investigate the crash.

On January 13, a certificate of death for Nicholas Bernard Mamer was signed by Howard Nelson, coroner, based on his observation and affirmed by Ellis Marshall of Northwest Airlines.

The tragedy unfolded differently for Nick's wife, Faye. She had been taken to the hospital in Seattle on December 21, 1937, seriously ill from peritonitis. She received four blood transfusions and remained hospitalized for about two weeks. Upon returning home the week of January 2, 1938, Faye continued to be bedridden. Friends, such as Mr. and Mrs. D. C. Jensen, were helping her through her convalescence when notification of the crash arrived. The friends took 12-year-old Patricia into their home, and Faye's parents, Mr. & Mrs. John Carey from Coeur d'Alene, Idaho, stayed with Faye.

Nick's body arrived at Seattle from Montana by train and was held at Butterworth & Sons Mortuary pending burial. Although the funeral for Nick was scheduled for Saturday, January 15 in Seattle, Faye was quoted as saying, "Spokane made Nick and that is where he always wanted to be. It is where he would want his funeral and it is where his funeral would be if it were only possible for me to be present."

The day after the accident, Faye dictated a telegram to Nick's older brother, James Mamer and family in Hastings, Minnesota:

> "Awaiting word about getting bodies. Have only been out of hospital a week myself. Am trying to be brave although know sometime would have to expect this. Have satisfaction of knowing was through no fault or misjudgment of Nick's, but due to mechanical trouble of new ship. Have prayed Nick will be intact without mar or burn but will not know definitely until this p.m. Wish to have funeral and burial here near me. Hope it will be possible, if not all the family, that you can come. Will wire definite details later. Give my sincerest sympathy to mother, sisters, and yourself and family. Thank you for your thoughtfulness at this time. Lovingly, Fay C Mamer and Patty."

It is apparent from this communication that Faye Mamer was aware that the accident was caused by some "trouble" with the Lockheed Super Electra, and not the fault of Nick's piloting. Perhaps she had received some notice of this from aviation inspector A. D. Niemeyer, who had already discovered alarming evidence at the crash site.

A day or so after the accident, Faye suffered "a serious setback, and was given stimulants." Her three doctors forbid her to travel.

Tribute telegrams tumbled in to the home on Mount Rainier Drive from the U.S. Forest Service, the Airline Pilots Association, the 116th Observation Squadron of the National Guard. Washington Governor Clarence D. Martin said he was "very anxious" to have a memorial erected at Felts Field in Spokane to honor Nick. "The Governor looks on Mamer as the pioneer of aviation in the Northwest. He believes it would be unfortunate to let the services of such a fine pilot and citizen go without proper recognition," a spokesman said.

The funeral mass for Nick Mamer went forward as planned. It was held January 15 at 10:00 a.m. at St. James' cathedral in Seattle. The funeral cortege was four blocks long leaving the church. Burial was at Veterans Memorial Cemetery, also known as Evergreen-Washelli, in Seattle.

On Tuesday January 18, the formal board of inquiry met in Bozeman, Montana. Chairman Miller C. Foster said its charter was to "determine probable causes" of the accident, and that the board was interested in any light that might be shed that would help prevent a recurrence.

Mr. A. D. Niemeyer, the inspector who'd been at the site the day after the crash, said the airplane's two vertical fins and the attached rudders were missing from the wreckage. "I soon found evidence that satisfied me that the surfaces missing [the fins] had not been carried off by impact with the ground, but came off while the plane was in flight." He described the vertical fins as being large, about four and one-half feet high and four feet across. Searchers, several on skis, had spent the day previous scouring the vicinity of the crash, but had found no trace of the missing parts.

An airline maintenance inspector from Oakland, California testified that he found nothing within the engines "which would indicate a failure." In other testimony, the radio equipment was said to be in satisfactory condition, and the Department of Commerce's "radio beam" was in operation at the time of the accident.

James Gerschler, assistant chief engineer of Lockheed, described in detail the tests and materials of the plane's manufacture. He concluded by saying, "the Lockheed Company and the Bureau of Air Commerce spent more time in flight testing this new model (the 14-H) than any other airplane I have knowledge of." He said he'd ought to "sleep on" the cause because "so many things might have happened I hesitate to express an opinion."

Chairman Foster asked Fred W. Whittemore, vice-president of Northwest Airlines, how he regarded pilot Mamer. "He was rated at the top of his profession. [He] was known by all of us as the outstanding pilot of the Pacific northwest. Airport officials and private flyers certainly held him in high esteem, probably more so than any other pilot of the Pacific northwest. He was better acquainted with the terrain than any other pilot." Asked if anyone else would be better in handling an emergency in the air, Whittemore replied, " No."

Northwest Airlines pilot R. L. Smith, the first company representative to reach the crash scene, was asked "Is it your opinion that the vertical fins left the plane in flight?" "It is," he replied.

Mr. Niemeyer expanded upon his earlier testimony by saying he had recently made a trip in a plane of the same type, a Lockheed 14-H, near Butte, Montana, when "the air became exceedingly rough. My attention was called to considerable buffeting in the tail sections," he said. "[I]t was easy to notice a twisting motion in tail surfaces that was visible to the eye." He added that this motion was different from that in other types of planes flown by Northwest Airlines.

Pressed for his opinion, Lockheed's assistant chief engineer James Gerschler later said, "I am quite sure [the vertical fins] left in the air, but until they are found I wouldn't be one-hundred percent sure." Mr. K. O. Larson, chief engineer for Northwest Airlines, agreed, and described the cause as "flutter" set up by vibration.

Gerschler soon admitted he had telephoned the Lockheed factory that "it would be desirable to redesign the surface so as to alter the vibration period [frequency]."

Niemeyer told the board,

> "There were holes in portions remaining [parts of the
> wreck at the scene] and pointed fragments of metal around
> the holes from which rivets had been pulled. [They were]
> pointed toward the rear of the plane. I also found the
> [rudder] tab control cables had been torn through pulleys at
> high speed. The guard bolt which holds the pulley had been
> ripped almost in two, and the cable, apparently being jerked
> out of the ship at high speed, had burned or cut notches in
> the sides of the…holes [through which the cables pass to the

rudders]. Evidence of the loss of the surfaces [vertical fins] indicated they had gone off to the left and rear of the ship."

On January 19 following the hearing, Northwest Airlines offered a reward of $50 for the recovery of any of the missing tail pieces of the crashed plane. (A news account of February 7 reported Fred Ham, Bridger Canyon rancher, found a rudder from the plane half to three-quarters of a mile from the crash site. And on February 20 "a second piece" of a vertical fin was found "upright in the snow" by Evans Forsythe about one-half mile west of the crash site.)

This airframe was unique, with right and left vertical fins placed far apart on its tail. The stabilizers, each with its own rudder and tab, were located twenty-two feet apart at the outboard ends of the horizontal stabilizer. Damage shy of destruction, such as the enlargement of rivet holes in the attachments, might have been present from previous flights, and gone unnoticed during inspection of the craft's airworthiness.

Whether or not earlier damage was present, it is highly improbable that both vertical fins detached from the horizontal member at exactly the same instant. Flight 2 had just crossed the Bridger peaks at about 9,000 feet. Strong turbulence from roiling air near the mountaintops probably excited flutter of the tail fins—Niemeyer had called it a "twisting motion." When one stabilizer broke away, it would tend to generate yaw. A yaw deviation from the path of forward progress, and the pilot's attempt to correct, might have caused detachment of the remaining, weakened fin.

Regardless of the sequence of detachment, the pilots would have abruptly become aware. Absence of resistance to pressure on the rudder pedals would alert them to the missing rudders. If they glanced to the rear, they could probably also see that the vertical fins were gone.

Despite the failures, the momentum of the aircraft would briefly propel it forward along its flight path. But loss of the fins would immediately induce a rotational (yaw) instability in the horizontal plane. The craft would most likely veer either right or left, resulting in loss of lift (a stall) and abrupt descent into a spin.

The description by W. R. Diteman, a rancher within a half-mile of the crash site, seems apt: "I first saw the plane flying overhead near my ranch. It seemed to be in some difficulty. I saw it circling in the sky—it fell, nose downward."

The wreckage was located in a canyon below timberline at an elevation of perhaps 5,000-6,000 feet. This suggests the aircraft, prior to the incident, was three or four thousand feet above ground. As the incident began, Captain Mamer would have ascertained the loss of the stabilizers as well as the rudders, and begun desperate actions in the available minutes prior to impact. He would have coordinated his actions with co-pilot West in an attempt to counter the stall, spin and descent.

It is impossible to know the steps taken during their descent (no "black box" recordings existed in 1938), but it is likely the pilots exercised their training and experience. They would have employed elevator, aileron and engine controls in an attempt to manage the accelerating instability. For example, if the plane was spinning leftward, they might have given full throttle to the left engine while retarding the right engine, and activated opposite ailerons to counter the spin. They might have applied elevators in an attempt to increase lift. These actions may have slowed, or even reversed the spinning, but were bound to fail in restoring the airplane's stability. Because of piloting instincts and training, however, the pilots would likely have continued these actions all the way to impact with the ground.

Sometime after Nick's funeral, Faye Mamer received a handwritten letter from Bozeman, Montana, dated January 14:

"Dear Mrs. Mamer:

"True we have never met—and how unimportant that is.

"I know you are very ill, and I would like to extend to you the consolation that I felt, for all the loved ones of those in the crash, as we unintentionally were witnesses at the time of the removal of the men.

"The crash was so sudden and complete that all present knew that those men only momentarily had to suffer the pains of humanity.

"All present were very quiet and respectful, and worked with the knowledge that they had a sad duty to perform.

"Your husband remained the great Pilot that he was, to the end.

"As the plane came to rest in one of the very few clearings in a heavily forested area of pine, above which is a high and very rugged mountain range.

"'May the quiet of the white snow and green pines comfort you.'

"Sincerely, Mrs. C. E. Vogel, R.3, Bozeman Mont."

Faye also received a handwritten letter on a Seattle Trust and Savings Bank letterhead from Kenelm Winslow, Jr.:

> "Dear Mrs. Mamer:
> "The sudden and tragic death of your husband came as a great shock to all who knew him and I want you to know of my deep sympathy for you. Nick and I were in the Seventh Aero Squadron together and I have followed his career with a great deal of interest as a result of this early association. He was undoubtedly one of the most able pilots in this country and I had the highest respect for his abilities. It may be of some small comfort to know from one who knew him over a long period of years that the accident was a matter beyond human control and unquestionably is no reflection on his fine record.
> "I hope that if in any way I can be of assistance to you at this time you will let me hear from you.
> "Very Sincerely, K. Winslow, Jr."

In February, the Bureau of Air Commerce announced that it would authorize Northwest Airlines to resume passenger service using the Lockheed 14-H Super Electra airplanes as soon as they completed "proving runs," which began February 7. Each of its six aircraft was to undergo fifty hours of flight time without passengers to qualify.

Sixty-one years later in 1999, Mary Lou Williams, Nick Mamer's eldest niece, published a long letter about the aviator's family. In it, she explained her relationship with Patricia, the Mamer's daughter:

> "In late 1942, my mother Rose Mamer and I visited Patti [sic] and her widowed mother in Seattle. Patti was a beautiful tall slender girl with the high cheekbones and the blue eyes of her father. I recall a graceful elegance about both Patti and her mother."

Mary Lou's letter says later, during the 1980s, she and Patti began corresponding and exchanging visits. Mary Lou relates some of what she learned from Patricia:

"There was no [Northwest Airlines'] insurance on pilots, no pension plan, no aid to the widow of a pilot who had given his life to fly a plane with its faulty rudder. Faye filed suit against Lockheed, the manufacturer of...the plane in which Nick crashed. Nick had told his wife of his misgivings about the feel of that plane...Faye Mamer and her attorney were up against a team of Lockheed attorneys. She had no help from Northwest Airlines. She received nothing."

Although our research located a September 12, 1938 lawsuit against Northwest Airlines by heirs of Walter Borgenheimer, one of the passengers killed in the crash, our search of newspapers and other resources of the period failed to uncover any reference to a lawsuit filed by Faye Mamer.

On Memorial day, May 30, 1939, a huge memorial to Nick Mamer was dedicated at Felts Field, Spokane. Located near the administration building, it is a square tower of poured concrete 24 feet high, with nine-foot-diameter clocks high on each of its four 14-ft-wide faces. It was constructed by the Works Projects Administration (W.P.A.), with funds contributed by citizens of Spokane through the Mamer Memorial Association.

Embedded below each of the clock faces on all but the north side is a large bronze plaque. On each plaque, below a raised image of a winged propeller, is the following inscription:

IN MEMORY OF
LIEUTENANT N. B. 'NICK' MAMER
VETERAN FLYER OF THE WORLD WAR
FOUNDER OF THE
NORTHWEST TRANSCONTINENTAL AIRWAY
BORN JAN. 28, 1898 DIED JAN. 10, 1938

The "founder of" refers to Nick's years of flying and advocacy for the establishment of an official northern airway from New York to Minneapolis/ St. Paul and across the Rockies to Seattle.

Nick's widow Faye and 13-year-old Patricia attended the dedication at which Major H. R. Wallace, commander of the 116th Observation Squadron eulogized Mamer. Governor Clarence Martin said, "I never felt safer on the ground than I did with Nick Mamer in the air." Addressing the widow and daughter, he said, "To you Mrs. Mamer, and to you, Patricia, and in behalf of the Mamer Memorial association, we present this memorial as a symbol of the high esteem in which we held your husband and your father." He then unveiled the tower before the thousands attending the ceremony.

Following the Airmail Scandal of 1934 and the resulting deaths of so many Army pilots, Nick Mamer delivered some words on his philosophy:

"It is experience that counts; a man may know all there is to know about aviation and ships, but he must learn some things only by experience. Hundreds of commercial pilots were killed and equipment lost before commercial flying was developed to the point it has attained. We have passed through the same ordeal. We know what it means to pay the price."

And so he did.

23. Seeking The Sun God

Spectacular aerial stunts, air races and record attempts by pilots in early airplanes thrilled the American public in the 1920s. They flocked to displays and exhibitions of aircraft and eagerly sought stories of these events as they filled the front pages of newspapers and periodicals throughout the nation. It was hardly unusual that Spokane's newspapers featured the heroes and aftermath of the flight of the Sun God.

In its August 21 edition following the famous flight, *The Spokesman-Review* reported "the [Spokane Sun God] will be flown back to the Buhl factory by Mr. Wilson, and will there undergo observation. The motor will be shipped to the Wright works for tests."

Only a few days later the 1929 National Air Races and Aeronautical Exposition opened in Cleveland, Ohio. The Exposition featured displays of new and famous aircraft inside and outside the new $10 million Public Hall, including the *Spokane Sun God*. Thousands attended the nationally-advertised and featured events in this midwest facility.

The Sun God was afterwards returned to the Buhl Aircraft Factory in Marysville, Michigan. On September 19, Buhl factory pilot Robert Wilson flew it into the Kellogg airport at Battle Creek, Michigan on a brief "test hop." It was to be on view in the Municipal hangar at Kellogg until the next day. During an interview, Wilson said the only change made to the special aircraft was the removal of the 200-gallon tank from the cabin. It is thus doubtful the motor was removed as was planned according to *The Spokesman-Review* article of August 21.

Wilson again flew the Sun God into Battle Creek on February 10, 1930. He arrived at the Kellogg airport and left about a week later for St. Louis, where the Sun God was to be exhibited at the International Aircraft Show.

During the five months between Battle Creek trips, the Sun God was repainted. Now having no allegiance to either Texaco or Spokane, sponsors with Buhl of the record flight, the Buhl factory painted out the large white letters on top of the upper wing that spelled "SPOKANE." A black and white photograph of the display area inside the St. Louis Arena during the International Aircraft Show also clearly shows the number NC9628 on the starboard wing, dark against a lighter body color. The original NR9628 of the *Spokane Sun God* was white on a red body color, showing as light against a dark body color in black-and-white photographs. (The change from NR to NC was not a registration change because the second letter is not part of the aircraft registration number: N9628. In the early days of aviation, NC suggested commercial/private use; NR suggested a more specialized application.) It's likely that the Texaco Star emblems that originally distinguished the Sun God's wings and fuselage were also painted out, though we can't be sure.

In 1931, the Sun God was the featured airplane on exhibit during the dedication of the Buhl Airport near St. Clair, Michigan. This dedication on June 13 was marked by an attendance of more than 4,000 people, including leaders in aviation, industry and finance. An air circus, including flights of an autogiro, performed. A highlight of the celebration was Mrs. May Haizlip's attempt to set an altitude record for light planes. In a Buhl Bull Pup airplane she reached an unofficial altitude of 22,000 feet.

Despite the optimism on display during the Buhl dedication ceremonies, most of the participants were well aware that the storm clouds of the Great Depression were darkening. Every industry in the country was feeling the pinch, many closing their doors and declaring bankruptcy, and the aviation industry was hard hit.

On Independence Day, July 4, 1931, the Seventh Annual National Air Tour for the Edsel B. Ford Reliability Trophy began in Detroit, Michigan, but attracted only fourteen entrants. In what may have seemed a desperate grasp at the glory handle, the Buhl factory entered the *Spokane Sun God*. The Sun God was flown in the Tour by Jack Story, a Buhl pilot and by some accounts a garrulous sport when on the ground. On the official Tour scorecard issued July 25, Story finished fifth, which was worth $1,250, half the amount paid the winner, Harry Russell. (Russell flew the reliable Ford Tri-Motor, though the Tri-Motor era was nearing its end.) Once the post-race coffee shop bluster quieted, Jack Story ferried the Sun God back to its hangar at St. Clair.

The airplane industry continued its decline. The stock of Curtiss-Wright slipped from $30 to less than a dollar.

Buhl Aircraft had been ably managed by the young and industrious Herbert Hughes on behalf of the mostly-absent, Detroit-based Buhls. In an effort to remain viable in a contracting economy, the company made what was described as "an intensive and exhaustive market analysis." The study prompted a decision to design and build a line of low-priced airplanes. The first, the Bull Pup, was a light, mid-wing wire-braced monoplane with an open cockpit. It was spirited in performance and priced low. But in the depression days of 1932 it failed to attract buyers. During 1932, as well, Herbert Hughes became ill and resigned his position as general manager. The inventory of Bull Pups was later sold off at about half its original advertised price.

In mid-June of 1932, six majority stockholders filed a petition in Circuit Court for dissolution of the Buhl Aircraft Company. The six stockholders were Arthur H. Buhl, Lawrence D. Buhl, Arthur H. Buhl, Jr., Theodore D. Buhl, Christian H. Hecker, and Phelps Newberry, all residents of Detroit. Judge Fred W. George appointed Fred Clark, of Marysville, Michigan, secretary of the Company, as temporary receiver.

On the last day of August, Herbert Hughes died in Oxford, a suburb of Detroit. He was only 43 years old.

In a lengthy legal notice dated October 6, 1932, Judge George ordered the sale of all of the Buhl Aircraft Company's assets to the highest bidder, exclusive of "cash, corporate books and records." The sale was ordered to take place at the company's premises at Buhl Field, Monday, October 31, 1932. To be included in the sale were land and buildings, various patents on airplane construction, raw materials, work in process, machinery and equipment, office furniture and fixtures, and finished airplanes—presumably including the Sun God.

On the Saturday before the sale, *The Times Herald* of Port Huron reported that the scheduled auction would be held at 10 a.m. Monday. The newspaper quoted Fred Clark, former secretary of the company and receiver, as saying the Buhl Aircraft company's goods would be sold "in parcels," and that "a few airplanes of various types" were to be sold. The implications of this announcement at this time prior to the sale are uncertain.

On the date of the sale, about fifty people attended the auction near St. Clair, Michigan. It was conducted by auctioneer James R. Turnbull. The entire Buhl Aircraft Company site, "hangar, airplanes and all material on the premises, including furnishings" were sold to the high bidder. The high bid was made by an agent of Arthur H. Buhl and Lawrence D. Buhl of Detroit. In effect, the Corporation headed by the Buhls was dissolved and by virtue of the bid at auction, all its assets became the personal property of brothers Arthur and Lawrence Buhl.

To the author's knowledge, nothing further on the whereabouts of the

Spokane Sun God airplane following this date of October 31, 1932, appears in print.

The foundation of the Buhl family's wealth was the Buhl Sons Company, a hardware firm inherited in 1916 by Arthur H., as president, and Lawrence D., as vice-president.

Thirteen years later, in 1929, the fourth generation of Buhls, C. (for Christian) Henry Buhl and Arthur H. Buhl, Jr., sons of Arthur H., took over the backbone hardware firm as president and vice-president. Upon the dissolution of the Buhl Aircraft Company in 1932, the Buhls continued their other interests besides the hardware company, including Detroit's Buhl Stamping Co. and the Buhl Land Co.

Shortly before Christmas of 1932, the Buhl family dynasty was shaken by a sensation. Arthur Kugeman, 32, a New Yorker who'd married Julia Buhl, Arthur H. Buhl's daughter, was found dead of a gunshot wound in a bathroom of the Grosse Pointe Farms home. Police seemed baffled by a lack of motive for the apparent suicide. A dispute soon developed over whether Kugeman had shot himself, or been murdered.

As expected, the tabloids nearly ran out of ink covering the ensuing investigation. A short time later, the matter was resolved when Mr. Kugeman's handwritten suicide note, which had been withheld by a family member, was handed over to authorities and verified, upholding the verdict of suicide.

The senior Arthur H. Buhl died in 1935; the senior Lawrence D. Buhl died in 1956.

Between 1929 and 1931 four CA-6 Airsedans, the same basic model as the Sun God, were imported by Ontario Provincial Air Service (OPAS) for aerial fire-fighting. What subsequently happened to them is not known.

In 1934, George Ponsford was appointed Director of OPAS. Ponsford had earned his wings with the Royal Flying Corps during World War I. He became interested in obtaining additional CA-6 airplanes for the OPAS, but Buhl Aircraft was by then out of business. Aware that brothers Arthur H. and Lawrence D. Buhl controlled the Buhl Aircraft assets, Ponsford negotiated a sale of CA-6 plans and jigs to OPAS. Although nothing is known of the Buhl Aircraft inventory under control of the Buhls at the time of this sale (1934), it appears doubtful it included CA-6 airplanes.

Following receipt of the CA-6 plans and jigs, OPAS mechanics, craftsmen and engineers built four replicas of the CA-6 in their hangar at Sault Ste. Marie. They attached Vickers floats to the planes for seaplane service. Unfortunately, initial trials showed that the aircraft with its 300 horsepower motor was unable to take off from water because of the added weight of the Vickers floats. Replacing the 300 horsepower motor with a 400 horsepower Pratt & Whitney motor, rendered the seaplanes flyable. The four served OPAS usefully from 1937 into the 1940s, although additional modifications were made to increase lift and reduce weight. None of these four airplanes are now flying.

In 1960, the Buhl Sons Co., wholesale hardware firm, was sold to an Illinois company operating the Tru-Value chain of retail stores. Arthur H. Buhl, Jr., vice-chairman, Arthur Buhl Hudson, nephew of the board chairman and vice-president, Allan Shelden III, J. H. Wiles, Sherman Mitchell, Robert M. Surdam, Lawrence D. Buhl, Jr., and T. D. Buhl, all resigned.

Board chairman and great-great grandson of the founder, C. Henry Buhl, announced the sale of the 105-year-old company, which netted the Buhl family over $3.5 million. "The buyer gave us an offer that was so attractive that we simply could not turn it down," he said.

About 2007, Addison Pemberton, Washington state businessman, well-known pilot and avid restorer of vintage airplanes, heard of a possible sighting of the Sun God. He remembers it like this:

> "Larry Howard and I had been told rumors of Buhl CA-6
> Sun God remains being stored at the Flabob airport in
> Riverside, California. I went to Flabob on a business trip
> in my Cessna 185 in or around 2007 to ask around the
> airport…I was led to the Marquart hangar with the remains
> of several historical aircraft hanging from the rafters.
> Among the aircraft was indeed a Buhl Air Sedan but not a
> CA-6 and it was determined that it could not have been the
> Sun God based on interviews with local pilots in the know."

In 2018, during research for this book, our researcher was able to arrange retrieval of digital copies of a few of the original blueprints of the CA-6 which had become part of the Buhl exhibit at the Bushplane Heritage Center Museum in Sault Ste. Marie.

Somewhere, the 90-year-old remains of a famous airplane sit in solitude. The once-red fabric of the *Spokane Sun God* rots, perhaps revealing its space frame of welded tubing. Etienne Dormoy, famed designer, was proud of that chrome-moly structure. Sheet aluminum on its cabin is probably white with corrosion, its nine-cylinder Wright engine up front rusted into silence.

The 001 Concorde is displayed at Le Bourget, France, and the B-29 *Enola Gay* at the Steven F. Udvar-Hazy Center in Washington. The *Spirit of St. Louis,* Wright Flyer, and Wiley Post's *Winnie Mae* are at the National Air and Space Museum, and the B-17 *Memphis Belle* is at the National Museum of the Air Force in Dayton, Ohio.

An unsolved mystery remains: Where is the Buhl special CA-6 Airsedan, registration number NC9628, Buhl No. 42, the *Spokane Sun God,* and why is it not restored and on display?

EPILOGUE

Over centuries, celebrated for bold exploits and favored by the gods, the central characters of myth and legend came to be known as heroes. In the brief history of powered flight—not yet a dozen decades in length—Nick Mamer has earned the status of hero. We may well ask: what defines such a man? Is it simply acts of courage and strength, or is there more to say?

Nick Mamer lost his father before he was born. Though we know little of his early life, his boyhood during the era of gas streetlights and horse-drawn buggies informed him of the strains of poverty, the strictures of parochial school, and the smallness of Hastings, Minnesota. Perhaps these inspired in him assertive actions and reactions, but we cannot know.

We do know he abandoned high school before graduation and while not yet eighteen, raced motorcycles, parachuted from airplanes and worked as a mechanic for the famous Duesenberg Motors. Yet these ventures left him searching; his vision fastened on the sky.

Nick lied about his age, passed the tough preliminary exams, and became Minnesota's first recruit into the Aviation Section of the Army's Signal Corps. Perhaps he joined the Army as an echo of his older brother's Army service. More likely he was drawn to it as his opportunity to learn, in the phrase of the time, "the art of flying an aeroplane."

The year was 1916. World War I had been underway in Europe for two years. When the US entered the war in April of 1917, Nick was with the 7th Aero Squadron at the Panama Canal. His performance there as an enlistee was so outstanding he gained the unanimous high regard of all his commanding officers. Within a span of five months he was promoted from Private to Corporal, from Corporal to Sergeant, and from Sergeant to Master Signal Electrician.

Had he so desired, Nick could have remained with the 7th Squadron on the Isthmus and enjoyed a Master Sergeant's perquisites and pay. Instead, he was willingly demoted to Private so that he might qualify for training as a pilot. Five weeks following his graduation from ground school at Princeton, the war ended. Shortly thereafter, he completed his primary flight training at Kelly Field and about six months later, was honorably discharged as a 2nd Lieutenant R.M.A., with 63 hours, 10 minutes of flight time.

Free of the restraints of the military, Nick responded to the dance-crazy and gin-swayed postwar decade with daredevil flying. Fearless performances of ground-skimming loops, tail spins and inverted flight in aerial circuses across Minnesota earned him titles like "King of Fliers." To thrill his home-towners in the summer of 1919, he sped a few feet off the water underneath Hastings' spiral river bridge.

But throughout the barnstorming, Nick sensed that the future of aviation lay in its less-spectacular aspects. By the early Twenties, he'd moved deliberately from the bold and risky to private transport and public service. He flew fans to fights, businessmen to meetings, and families to vacations. He searched for bodies from the air, delivered disaster films for news outlets and emergency supplies to stranded citizens. His summer months were often spent in the air, spotting forest fires and marking their location. Passengers felt safe when he was at the controls.

"Fly with Nick" became a byword.

Later in the decade, aircraft builders and oil companies sought him out. They saw the benefits that flowed from his successes in races, marathons, and record attempts. His name was now recognized and his advocacy for the Northern transcontinental route earned him friends, sponsors and honors. Nick's record attempts and finishes in the National Air Races of 1927 and 1928 provided the impetus for the famous nonstop transcontinental round trip that is the subject of this book.

Throughout his career, during a life of less than forty years, Nick Mamer proved his mettle, his daring, his skill and his superb knowledge of the sky. Only when the airplane that he depended upon failed him did the life of this American hero end.

END

NOTES[1]

1. A New, Blue Home

The reference to a gravel base and a "fast field" for Felts Field is from "Airplanes Race to Spokane!", *Nostalgia Magazine*, Sep.-Oct. 2010, Brian Shute (ref#42). Nick Mamer's dropped message about the magneto is from *One Man's Opinion of The Spokane Aviation Story*, J. P. McGoldrick II, Ye Galleon Press, 1982, p.172 (ref#114).

On Thursday, August 15, 1929, after a ten-minute final test flight, the *Spokane Sun God*, topped off with 320 gallons of gasoline and with Lieutenant Nicholas B. Mamer at the controls, was readied for flight.

"Nick" Mamer was 31 years old, and had been flying since 1916 (*The New York Times*, Aug. 15, 1929, although the article misstates his age as 30, ref#5). Mamer served in the Signal Corps Air Service during World War I, and among other aviation activities, was one of the first forest fire patrol pilots ("Nick Mamer, Early Aerial Fire Patrol Pilot," *The Static Line*, Vol. 3, Quarterly, July 1998, Ed. 5, ref #68). He had also started the Mamer Flying Service at Felts Field in 1927 (*Aero Digest*, September & November, 1927, ref#45)

The Sun God airplane was a 1929 Buhl CA-6 with a fully-enclosed cabin and fixed landing gear. It was supplied by the Buhl Aircraft Company to pilot Mamer and his sponsors, The Texaco Company, and the businessmen and citizens of Spokane through the National Air Derby association ("Mamer Flying Across Continent And Back", *Aero Digest*, Sept., 1929, p. 218, ref#69).

The airplane was equipped with an opening in top of the cabin through which a crew member could accept and handle air-to-air transfers of fuel, supplies and communications. A distinctive external feature of this biplane was the lower wing, narrower and much shorter in span than the upper wing ("The Flight of the Spokane Sun God," Richard L. Meister, Jr., in www.aerofiles.com, ref#25; also "Introducing An Advanced Phase of Endurance Flying" by Nick B. Mamer, in *Aero Digest*, October 1929, p.53, ref#328).

The airplane was powered by a Wright "Whirlwind" engine of 300 horsepower, with two wing tanks with a capacity of 60 gallons each. Factory modifications included a 200-gallon tank in the fuselage (ref#5).

---

1 Abbreviations used in Notes: SDC – *Spokane Daily Chronicle*; SR – *Spokesman-Review* (Spokane); MFA – Mamer Family Archives, the collection of clippings, documents and photographs preserved by the descendants of Nicholas B. Mamer, and accessed in 2018-19 by the author of this book.

The August 12 newspaper clipping (ref#335) from the MFA describing the modifications, states, "The special 200-gallon tank has been installed on the right side of the ship just 10-inches off the center of balance." In the photograph of Nick Mamer with local jeweler Oscar Levitch standing in front of the *Sun God* (*Libby '29*, #40127), this tank is clearly visible through the right-hand windshield section and the angle-shaped side window. The photo reveals that the top of this rectangular tank is very close to the top of the cabin interior.

Measurements taken from a second photograph of the *Sun God* displaying the right-hand side of the airplane (*Libby '29*, #40145) allow the fore-and-aft length of the tank to be estimated at about five feet. Additional measurements taken from the aircraft drawings of the Buhl CA-6 in the *Aircraft Year Book for 1930*, Vol. 12, Aeronautical Chamber of Commerce of America, Inc., & D. Van Nostrand Company, Inc. New York, yield an interior cabin height of about four feet and a cabin width of about three and one-half feet.

Combining the above measurements with the volume of 26.7 cubic feet required for a capacity of 200 gallons yields a tank width of about 16-inches. Thus the passageway remaining on the left side of the cabin is only slightly over two feet wide. This arrangement is illustrated in the rear-facing *Libby* photograph (#3850) with the crew's striped mattress, a radio headset, and—on the left in the photo—the tank.

With Nick at the controls, the airplane taxied across Felts Field, "trailing a cloud of dirt." The SDC of August 16, 1929, (ref#330) states, "...hundreds of people were caught in the backwash of wind and dirt. Many hats went sailing down the field..." The crowd was estimated at 6,000. The takeoff began from the far eastern end of the field (ref#330).

According to the *The Spokesman-Review* article by Nick Mamer on August 16 (possibly August 17), 1929, (ref#314) the run for takeoff took 4000-feet. Also according to ref#330, Art Walker was standing up, with his head and shoulders visible outside through the refueling opening, during takeoff.

One clipping in the MFA reported Nick "in the center of the field placed a mark... [such that, if] the wheels of his plane [had] not left the ground by the time he reached that mark his intention was to have shut off his motor, used his brakes and stopped." This was to insure that the *Sun God* would clear obstructions at the west end of the field. If his wheels were still on the ground, he could safely abandon the takeoff.

The placement of 200-gallons of gasoline—about 1,300 pounds—ten inches to the right of center produces a turning force of more than a thousand foot-pounds. This turning force acts in a clockwise manner when an observer faces the direction of travel.

Although partly offset by the weights of the pilot and co-pilot on the left side, this heavy load of gas causes the plane to tend to veer to the right when on the ground. When the plane's speed increases enough for aerodynamic effects to become effective, the turning force must be countered by the pilot's rudder and stick (aileron) actions.

Complicating the pilot's attempts at countering the turning force is the fact that the air-pressure forces on the control surfaces (rudder and ailerons) are negligible at low speed, yet accelerate markedly at higher speeds. This latter phenomenon is caused by the so-called "velocity-squared" effect. This means that the pilot, trying to keep the airplane straight and level during takeoff, can unwittingly overcorrect, resulting in a loss of control and a subsequent crash.

It is a tribute to Mamer's piloting skill that he carried out the difficult balancing actions this aspect of the Sun God's initial takeoff required. Despite Nick's later comment that the "Sun-God was perfectly balanced," (ref#314), his comment probably applies only after sufficient fuel had been used and the gasoline loadings distributed to offset the imbalance. (A hand-operated, so-called wobble pump was incorporated in the Sun God fuel plumbing to propel gasoline from the 200-gallon tank up to one of either of the two 60-gallon tanks in the upper wings.)

The Sun God was equipped with an Earth Inductor Compass as well as a magnetic compass (refs#328,335). This device, invented by Pioneer Instrument Company, was a distinct advance over the magnetic compass for navigating, (refs#98, 100, "The Pioneer Earth Inductor Compass," *Aviation*, June 20, 1927). Its generator was driven by a small, cupped windmill tower on top of the fuselage that connects to its generator. This is seen located part-way back on the Sun God's fuselage (visible in the *Libby* photo, '29, #40145).

The five practice flights on Tuesday, August 13 followed the delivery of the special Buhl airplane the day before. This was reported in the Mamer archive clipping (ref#335). News of the other activities of Tuesday, are from the MFA's newspaper clipping with the headline "Spokane Sun God Passes Its Test," subheaded "Aides Hop Today," (ref#349).

Films shot by *Pathe News* and *Movietone News* August 18, 1929 above Roosevelt Field on Long Island, NY show the Sun God and a supply plane during aerial refueling. The supply plane, a Curtiss Robin flown by R. W. Wassall, with hoseman "Shorty" Chaffee, was the same plane and crew assisting the record flight of the *St. Louis Robin*, July 13-30, 1929, (ref#328). These films vividly demonstrate the intricate flying and fuel handling required to successfully and safely transfer gasoline while airborne. Video versions of these films were viewed on the Internet (refs#1A, 1B, and 347).

The British *Pathe News* video appeared on YouTube, and is titled "Petrol Stations in the Sky Soon?"(ref#1A). The *Fox Movietone News* video consists of outtakes from the news film. Titled "Sun God aerial refueling—outtakes", it is preserved by the Moving Image Research Collections at the University of South Carolina (ref#1B). A third video, taken from the *Pathe News* footage, is from the Sherman Grinberg Library, Getty Clip #841821404, (ref#347). The latter video is slightly longer than the British *Pathe News* clip and of higher quality than either of the others.

The special Sun God aircraft had a single set of flight controls. The pilot's seat is on the left, directly behind the left section of the two-piece windshield. Nick Mamer is clearly visible behind the windshield of the Sun God in the Grinberg clip. He smiles at the cameraman, and later waves. The *Movietone News* clip, at about 1-min-58 sec, reveals the pilot's left hand and arm extending outside from behind the windshield. The arm curls around and the hand (perhaps with a rag) wipes the front of the windshield.

The motor installed in the Sun God is the new 300 horsepower J-6 Wright Whirlwind. The oil capacity was increased to ten gallons. An oiling system (called an Alemite system) was installed by Mamer's mechanics (ref#335).

The horizontal stabilizer (on the aircraft's tail structure) is adjustable in flight, to trim for load imbalance (ref#307). This, together with adjustment of the gasoline loads, allows the flight controls to be vacated long enough for the men to switch piloting duties (refs#16, 29, 307, 335).

The various pieces of equipment carried aboard the Sun God come from *Marathon Flyers*, Russell Plehinger, Harlo Press, Detroit, p.48, (ref#116).

The *Tri-City Herald* article of April 5, 2016 by Kristin M. Kraemer (ref#323) on the first commercial airmail run out of Pasco, Washington, is the source for Pasco's place in U.S. Airmail history. A photograph shows townspeople watching as the airplane arrives in Pasco on April 6, 1926. This airfield no longer exists.

Mamer describes "...our motor, which up to this time had been running sweetly, got a fit of coughing" in "Texaco Across the Sky, The Flight of the Spokane Sun God" published in *The Texaco Star*, Vol. 16, August 1929 (ref#179). In a different reference (#314) he says, "that gave us an unpleasant thrill." Fortunately, after a few minutes, "the coughing ceased and we flew easily on." The cause was either never discovered, or not revealed.

As darkness came, the men strapped on their parachutes (ref#314), and stared into the brown clouds from forest fires (ref#324). Several times during this leg, the men change off piloting (ref#314). Occasionally, and for brief periods, they fly blind (ref#179), although they are able to spot Mt. Rainier in the dim distance (ref#314).

The arrival time at Portland (around 9:00 p.m.) was calculated using the "Estimated Distance Flown Between Refueling Points" in the Appendix of 341 miles from Spokane to Portland. The speed over the ground was taken as somewhat over 100 miles per hour, based on a cruising airspeed with modest or little headwind.

2. The First Refueling

Two photographs of the inside rear of the *Spokane Sun God* were taken by *Libby* (refs#372, 373). Both show the radio receiver, headphones, and the mattress in the compartment.

Headlined "Wonderful Start For Mamer Plane," *The Spokesman-Review* article (probably of August 16) from the MFA (ref#374) reports that "Ed Jackson" supervised the installation of the Atwater Kent radio in the Sun God. The hourly broadcast bulletins were also a product of E. F. Jackson's effort, as reported in the August 12 newspaper clipping (ref#335) from the MFA. Portland's station KGW is one of the broadcasters recommended (ref#374).

An early broadcast receiver, this radio was probably an Atwater Kent Model 20, or similar, powered by dry-cell batteries. In describing Walker's struggles with the radio, I drew liberally from the rebuilding efforts and operating notes of Clint Turner in "Restoring my Atwater Kent Model 20," (ref#370). Its operational difficulties are real: "This receiver is a 'Tuned Radio Frequency' type. The most obvious difference is the presence of *three* tuning knobs (Turner's emphasis). Operating this receiver is decidedly more complicated...than one made since the 1930s," he says. Good results depend on "fairly large antennas." This is why an external antenna system (visible in photographs taken before the flight) swung well below the Sun God's fuselage.

The problem is described by Mamer at San Francisco and published in *The Spokesman-Review*, August 16 (possibly August 17, 1929), (ref#314): "The radio has gone out on us, and I think we'll transfer it to the refueling plane to cut down our weight a little." It seems fairly certain the absence of reception was caused by loss of the pendant antenna, possibly during the takeoff run. By severely limiting the crew's access to weather updates, this loss constituted an unfortunate blow to the operation.

Nick's remark on not seeing Mt. Shasta because of haze comes from the same report (ref#314). Of navigating the Siskiyou Mountains during this period, the AIR COMMERCE BULLETIN, Vol. 2, No. 7, October 1, 1930, pp. 170-174, said: "... between Redding, Calif., and Eugene, Oreg., some of the most difficult flying terrain in the United States must be negotiated. Much of this section is frequently covered by Pacific coast fog, and is flown a good portion of the time above the fog and low-lying clouds, the mountain peaks of the Cascade Range being the only landmarks by which the progress of the flight can be checked. Tracts of ground suitable for landing fields on this part of the airway are extremely few and far between...", quoted from the dreamsmithphotos website (ref#165).

During this phase, the fliers got little rest. "We were busy all the time working with the auxiliary oiling system, and every bit of gasoline was pumped from the auxiliary [200-gallon] tank into the wing tanks with a wabble [sic] pump, which is a hand device," Mamer later writes in the SDC, August 21, 1929 (ref#342). Still, they ate nuts and sipped coffee (ref#314), and said they were pleased with their new home: "We are familiarizing ourselves...I think we are going to like it a lot." (ref#314)

The "jammed" incident comes from Nick's article of August, 1929 in *The Texaco Star*, Vol. 16, pp. 4-5 (ref#179): "At 1:15, when changing controls, we got stuck in the narrow passageway between the gas tanks and the side of the ship and thought we were goners." (The plural "tanks" here is wrong, probably a typo.) The next sentence is: "By removing our parachutes, we found we could navigate more comfortably within the cabin." This suggests the parachutes caused the jamming during the exchange. But the narrow width, about two feet, was limiting even without parachutes. Following the jamming, "Art flew the ship for an hour, and then I took her back," he wrote at San Francisco (ref#314).

In his October article for *Aero Digest*, p.53, (ref#328), Mamer describes the refueler: "The Aviation Accessories Corporation of San Francisco arranged to have a Travel Air J-5 monoplane refuel us over Mills Field, San Francisco, the first scheduled refueling point." This Corporation was apparently paid by Texaco, sponsor of the Sun God flight. According to the *Aero Digest* article, "This crew [Donald Templeman and James M. Warner] had had previous experience with refueling, having made numerous contacts with the *San Franciscan* endurance plane." (ref#328) These experiences are confirmed by Russell Plehinger in *Marathon Flyers*, p. 52, (ref#116).

Nick's recollections of the arrival of the Buhl airplane that became the *Spokane Sun God* is from the SDC, August 12, 1929, clipping headlined "'Miss Spokane' Here For Flight." The newspaper described, "...this morning the drone of a Wright J-6 whirlwind [sic] motor could be heard over Felts field, telling of the arrival...of the huge orange [sic] Buhl six-place airsedan [sic] to be flown in the Spokane-New York-Spokane nonstop flight by Nick Mamer and Art Walker."

This article describes the plane's central tank: "The special 200-gallon tank has been installed on the right side of the ship just 10 inches off the center of balance. The balance is maintained by proper use of gasoline out of the two wing tanks, which hold 120 gallons of gasoline."

It is important to note that the gasoline supplied during refueling always goes into this 200-gallon tank. From there, it is pumped (by hand) into either of the two 60-gallon tanks in the wings.

The second sentence in the newspaper quote above can only refer to the attempt to balance the aircraft when the tanks are no longer full. Keeping the left-hand wing tank full while minimizing the gasoline in the right-hand wing tank will tend to counter the imbalance of weight caused by the placement of the 200-gallon tank offset to the right of the fuselage's centerline. The pilot can, by use of a selector valve, favor the use of gasoline from the right-hand wing tank by the J-6 motor. This is apparently what is meant by "proper use of gasoline" in the quote.

The *The New York Times* of July 26, 1929, in an Associated Press story (ref#3), reveals the origin of the attempt: "In accordance with the suggestion made today by Major Clarence M. Young, aeronautical director of the Department of Commerce, a non-stop round trip endurance flight around the United States to test the practicability of refueling planes carrying full cargoes on long trips is planned by Lieutenant Nick Mamer..." (Young's idea was for a cross-country refueling trip. Mamer apparently suggested it be a round trip.) The SDC, under the headline "Thirty Spokane Business Men in Meeting Today Sponsor Flight..." carried the same message. At this time the plan was tentative, with Mamer initially flying to St. Paul, Minnesota. In an unidentified newspaper from the MFA (ref#357) headlined "Mamer Chooses Plane's Co-Pilot," Victor Dessert is described as stating that a meeting of the committee "will be called immediately for the purpose of sponsoring the coast-to-coast round trip flight."

It is clear the committee backing the flight derives from the success of the National Air Derby & Races held two years earlier in Spokane. Shute describes, "What was then called the 'Spokane Air Port' would witness a gathering of nearly 100,000 people...an additional nine telegraph lines were installed at the field to dispatch sky-breaking news..." in "Airplanes Race to Spokane," by Brian Shute, *Nostalgia Magazine*, Sept.-Oct., 2010, pp. 24-33 (ref#42). The success is also described in a November 8, 2015 article by Dennis Parks in *General Aviation News* (ref#17). Both articles, though broadly correct, contain errors.

More recently, Nick Mamer had been managing the Mamer-Ford Tour featuring the Ford Trimotor named the *West Wind*. Mamer, celebrating 6,500 hours of airtime, had purchased the three-engine, 14-place aircraft for his Mamer Air Service. (This is apparently the same firm as the Mamer Flying Service. According to *Aero Digest*, Sept. & Nov. 1927 (ref#45), "The Mamer Flying Service was recently incorporated at Spokane, Washington, with Clarence Paulsen as president and Nick B. Mamer, veteran Spokane pilot, as vice-president and manager.") Data about the safe miles and landings during the Mamer-Ford tour and Nick's hours is from a Seattle newspaper clipping (date uncertain) from the MFA headlined "Big Mamer Ship Plans Trip Over Mount Rainier,"(ref#368) and from the *Miles City Star* of April 8, 1929 headlined

"Mamer's Record As A Flier Impressive As Results Are Studied" (ref#363).

The message from Herbert Hughes offering the Buhl comes from a MFA news clipping (dateline unknown) headlined "Speed Record Try For Mamer," with a sub-head mentioning "Coast-to-Coast Flight" (ref#356). Nick's statement about the "interest aroused over the country" also comes from this clipping.

The promise of delivery of the Buhl CA-6 in "eight days" comes from a newspaper clipping from the MFA. The unidentified Spokane newspaper (probably July 1929) has a headline "Mamer Flight Aides Organize" and a subhead "New Motor Coming" (ref#359).

The "yeast" story is derived from a news clipping in the MFA (unidentified source and date) headlined "Mamer Flies With Yeast to Village Isolated by Snow" (ref#360).

The "Two hours later..." paragraph refers to *The New York Times* report of August 17 (Associated Press dateline Aug. 16, 1929), headlined "Refuel at San Francisco," (ref#6), which said the plane received about 180 gallons in two contacts—a third is not mentioned. The *Californian* met the Sun God, as prearranged, over the Dumbarton bridge, one of two bridges spanning San Francisco Bay. Farther north, the San Mateo-Hayward bridge has just been completed. The San-Francisco-Oakland Bay bridge did not exist; it opened in 1936.

The details of the refueling here are taken from several references, including Frank Wiley's book (ref#115), the *Aero Digest* article (ref#328), *The Texaco Star* article (ref#179), and *The Spokesman-Review* article of September 15, 1929 with the subhead "Mamer Meets Refueler" (ref#341) in which Carlos Greeley, of Aviation Accessories Corporation explains what happened during the third refueling contact.

3. Climbing the Sierras

The "150-acre cow pasture" comes from the History of the San Francisco International Airport, (ref#142, 143). The weather is from page 44 of the *Oakland Tribune*, Aug. 15, 1929.

The distance of 2,665 miles is from *Wikipedia*, "Transcontinental Airway System," (ref#138), "With a June 1925 deadline, the 2,665 mile lighted airway was completed from New York to San Francisco." The great-circle distance is 2,586 miles.

The information on the airmail route and the lighted airways, including the 83 hour and the 33 hour records, comes from "The 'Highway of Light' That Guided Early Planes Across America," by Matt Novak, Nov. 18, 2013 (ref#138).

Map No. 35, and later, Map No. 34, refer to United States Air Navigation maps downloaded from APA 6th Edition, University of Connecticut Libraries Map and Geographic Information Center – MAGIC. (2012). *United States Air Navigation Maps Index 1923-1935*. Retrieved from http://magic.lib.uconn.edu/_(ref#81).

The gasoline taken on in San Francisco is taken from *The New York Times*, Aug.17, 1929, (ref#6), "Refuel at San Francisco," in which the *Spokane Sun God*, "In the two contacts made the plane received about 180 gallons of gasoline." A smaller figure in the SDC, Aug. 16, 1929, referring to Mamer: "At San Francisco he took on only 175 gallons of gasoline, while press dispatches indicated that he could have had 230 gallons."

The height needed to clear the Sierra Nevada range near Truckee, California, and later, the Rockies, refers to the SDC, Aug 16, 1929 (ref#87): "Between San Francisco and Cheyenne the average flying altitude will be 10,000 feet, and over Salt Lake it will be necessary to send the Sun God to 10,500 feet in order to clear the Rockies."

According to the ship's "List of United States Citizens" obtained from Ancestry. com (ref#63), Mamer sailed aboard the *S. S. Panama* from Cristobal, Canal Zone, June 26, 1918, arriving at the Port of New York July 13, 1918. This source lists his address "in the United States" as "Princeton, N. J."

Mamer attended the School of Aeronautics from July 13, 1918 to October 5, 1918 at Princeton University, Princeton, NJ, and graduated from that program, according to Annalise Berdini, Digital Archivist at the Seeley G. Mudd Manuscript Library of Princeton University (email dated May 08, 2018, ref#117). "Cross Country and General Flying" is included in subjects reportedly taught in the program -- *Princeton Weekly Bulletin*, Vol. 98, (2008-09), No. 28, June 1(ref#118). The list of subjects taught quoted in the Bulletin, together with the list quoted in *Textbook of Military Aeronautics* , Henry Woodhouse, Century Company, 1918, (ref#118) suggests comprehensive instruction was given in visual observation of landscape features during flight.

Mamer instructed flying students at Mamer Flying Service. The Service was "recently incorporated ...with Clarence Paulsen as President and Nick B. Mamer, veteran Spokane pilot, as vice-president and general manager." It afforded "Complete aerial service, including student training..." from *Aero Digest*, Sept. & Nov., 1927 (ref#45). Also, from the *Wikipedia* "Nick Mamer" page: "Mamer served with the United States Army Air Service during World War I ... Mamer was a flight instructor and charter pilot ... Among his flight pupils was Bob Johnson, a well-known aviation pioneer in Missoula, Montana."(ref#24)

Map No. 35 (referenced above) shows almost no landmarks on the river delta between San Francisco Bay and Sacramento, California (sometimes called the California Delta). It is a 1,100 square mile freshwater marsh of channels and sloughs that was partly reclaimed for agriculture during the 20th century. The scarcity of landmarks made differentiating a flier's position over the delta by visual means extremely difficult.

The headwind encountered on the eastbound flight is mentioned several places. *Montana and the Sky*, Frank W. Wiley, Montana Aeronautics Commission, 1966 (ref#115), page 283: "...the plane headed east to Salt Lake and Cheyenne, bucking head winds instead of the anticipated tail wind normal with prevailing westerlies." Also, "Out of San Francisco the Sun-God didn't get the anticipated tail wind; she had instead fought a gusty head wind," from *Airlift/Tanker Quarterly*, Vol.20, No.1, winter 2012, Collin R. Bakse, (ref#2).

The *Movietone News* outtakes of the New York refueling show Art Walker's struggles in the opening, transferring gas from the dangling hose to the Sun God – Moving Image Research Collections (MIRC), Digital Video Repository, *Fox Movietone News* Story 3-434, filmed Aug. 18, 1929, University Libraries, University of South Carolina (ref#1).

Mamer's experience as fire spotter is from "The Northwest Aerial Forest Patrol" by E. Harve Partridge, in *Aviation*, January 17, 1927.

From the SDC, Aug. 16, 1929, under subhead "Send Telegram": "Wilson [in the Buhl], with Vern Bookwalter, pilot of the Ryan refueling plane are now at Cheyenne, where Mamer will refuel before dusk this evening prior to his night flight to Cleveland."

4. Running on Empty

Nick Mamer's performing history with Hinck's Federated Flyers comes from Noel Allard, "Ten Most Important State Aviation Pioneers," in the *Minnesota Flyer* of Feb. 1, 2014 (ref#124). The description of the Elko airfield comes from the "Elko Regional Airport" site, (ref#151), especially the included photo of the hangar with two airplanes parked in front.

Russell Plehinger describes, on page 48, under Equipment Carried [by the] *Spokane Sun God*, 'telegraph blanks (1 pad).' Mamer obviously planned to communicate with the Derby Association committee by telegram.

Under the p.1 subhead "Spokane Sun God Plane Pilots Send Wire to Local Headquarters for Contact at Rock Springs, Wyoming," the SDC, Friday, Aug. 16, ref#87, describes the Wilson-Coppula flight from Cheyenne to Rock Springs.

Air Navigation Map No. 33: Salt Lake City, Utah to Elko, Nev., and Map No. 14: Rock Springs, Wyoming to Salt Lake City, Utah, were downloaded from APA 6th Edition, University of Connecticut Libraries Map and Geographic Information Center – MAGIC. (2012). *United States Air Navigation Maps Index 1923-1935*. Retrieved from http://magic.lib.uconn.edu/, (ref#81). These were sources for the courses, distances, and geographic features described during the two legs from Elko, Nevada to Rock Springs, Wyoming.

A number of sources exist for the cruising speed of the Buhl CA-6 Airsedan (refs#103,20,16). Although there is slight variation, I chose 115 mph as representative.

The fact that a head wind, rather than the expected tailwind—from prevailing westerlies—accompanied the Sun God's flight east from San Francisco is frequently reported (Refs#87, 115, 2). This, together with other factors, caused greater fuel consumption than Mamer estimated, and a resulting need to refuel at Rock Springs, Wyoming rather than at the planned location, Cheyenne, Wyoming.

Geographic details of the Sun God's crossing from Elko to Rock Springs come from Air Navigation maps Nos. 33 and 14, ref#81, and *Wikipedia*, (ref#152).

Since the Sun God apparently did not arrive at Rock Springs until sometime around sunset (ref#121, about 7:15 p. m. local), the initial refueling there was attempted in the dark.

Details about the Rock Springs airfield come from the Southwest Regional Airport site, (ref#153) which locates the airfield "about four miles north of Rock Springs where the current county fairgrounds are." This airfield was abandoned "after a new airport was begun at its present site in the late 1930s."

The hangar description and searchlight detail come from two photos (ref#154A, 154B) included in "Abandoned & Little-Known Airfields, Wyoming" by Paul

Freeman, (ref#155) accessed on the internet. Author Freeman also illustrates that the 1929 Rand McNally Air Trails map of Wyoming places the location of the old Municipal field north of the town.

In Frank Wiley's 1964 interview (in ref#115), he reports Art Walker said they [Sun God] flew at 8,000 feet, "and the refueling airplane [was] unable to get off with very much payload." He's also reported to have said, "The "flashlight taped to the nozzle of the refueling hose was difficult to distinguish from the stars..." and "The refueling pilot had all he could do to hold his plane up at 8,000 feet with the overload condition and the rough, gusty air."

Nick Mamer's report for the North American Newspaper Alliance printed in the Aug. 21 *Montana Standard*, (ref#71), says, "It was at Rock Springs in the heart of the Rocky Mountains that we found it necessary to fly between 10 and 12 thousand feet high to make our flight successful." I interpret this as a general statement applying broadly to the flight over the Rockies, rather than the Sun God's altitude during refueling.

My descriptions of the actions by the participants during refueling rely heavily on videos of films recorded for newsreels, amplified by still photos and texts (Refs#1,114,115,116).

The longest video, consisting of *Fox Movietone News* outtakes of the refueling of the Sun God over New York, is from the University of South Carolina, University Libraries, Moving Image Research Collections (MIRC), Digital Video Repository, for *Fox Movietone News* story 3-434, filmed Aug. 18, 1929. A similar and shorter video appeared on YouTube which derives from film shot by a *Pathe News* photographer. These references clearly demonstrate the risky process and precision flying required of the participant aircrews in decent weather in these early biplanes.

For example, it was necessary to maintain the relative position of the two airplanes in close proximity while flying relatively slowly, perhaps 55-65 mph.

Flying faster (80-90 mph) was necessary at higher altitudes. Elmer Connick, pilot with Mamer Air Transport, claimed in a report published in SR, Aug. 20, p.2, (ref#157), that the refueling over Rock Springs was carried out "at a minimum speed of 85 miles an hour." There is disagreement as to the minimum speeds needed, and what speed was excessive. The SDC of Aug. 17, (ref#88), reporting on a later refueling contact, quoted "airport Officials" as saying "...at such fast speed (number uncertain) the hose was blown out of the Sun God repeatedly."

The breaking of the refueling hose and the inundation of Art Walker by gasoline over Rock Springs is based mainly on Connick's details, (ref#157), and upon Wilson's description in SDC, Aug. 20, (ref#121). Wilson said, "The first contact...we broke the hose. The hose just pulled apart." He also said, "In the first contact we gave Nick 23 gallons of gas but it didn't register on his gauge..."

In the SDC, Aug. 17, Walker said, "Hose broke last night during one contact and gave me a bath. I guess I needed it," (ref#90).

5. Severed Connections

In the SDC of Aug. 20, 1929, ref#121, Buhl factory pilot R. M. Wilson is reported to say, "Nick pulled into Rock Springs just at dusk," referring to Friday, Aug. 16. During the refueling that followed, Wilson added, "...we broke the hose. The hose just pulled apart." Later in the same SDC report, he said that after the addition of three flashlights to the refueling hose, "we succeeded...in five more contacts." However, in the same reference, Al Coppula is reported to have told the crowd gathered for the landing in Spokane, "they [Coppula and Wilson] made seven contacts with the Sun God during the night [at Rock Springs]."

These recollections by the participants formed my basis for the opening and subsequent sequences of refueling events on Friday (and possibly into early Saturday), although different versions of these events, their sequence, and their number exist in other reports.

In particular, in his written SDC article of Aug. 17 entitled "Mamer Tells of Troubles on Trip," [ref#89] Nick Mamer says he was blinded by the searchlight on "our first refueling contact," with the result that the Sun God's propeller sliced through the refueling hose. He also writes, "we...accomplished six refueling contacts since we left Spokane...and four of these were made after dark."

The differences in these (and other's) accounts may be due to varying recollections, inaccurate reporting, or they may result from dissimilar concepts of "refueling contacts," "dusk" versus "after dark," etc.

The failure of the refueling hose, other than its timing and distinct from its severing, is of interest. It seems possible a hose meant for conveying water, rather than gasoline, was employed. If so, some of the materials from which it was constructed may have contained natural, or "gum" rubber. As is well-known, rubber is attacked by gasoline, causing deterioration. This may have weakened the hose, resulting in its failure.

Reports on the National Air Race of 1927 disagree on the horsepower limit for Class "A" entries, the time of day for the start, the number of entries, the number of starters and the winner's time of finish. My account is based partly on the *General Aviation News* article (ref#17) and Wiley's book (ref#115, p. 207), but favors the *Aviation* article of Oct. 3, 1927 as a more comprehensive and seemingly more accurate source. Where conflicts in details arose I chose those details in the *Aviation* article.

Robert Wohl's book (ref#159) contains an extensive section on Lindbergh's flight as well as insights into many other cultural aspects of aviation between 1920 and 1950. There is little disagreement that Lindbergh's feat caused a huge surge in public enthusiasm for aviation, which continued into the time of the Sun God event two years later. It seems likely Lindbergh's flight contributed to Mamer's incentive and diligence in pursuing the Sun God flight.

The participants in the refueling of the Sun God frequently refer to taping things (weights, flashlights, etc.) to the hose. Most likely, this was done using the first "duct" tape launched by Bauer & Black in 1921-22. It was a strong, gray, fabric-backed product called "Tirro." [ref#162]

Ref#121 is unclear which person, but either Wilson or Coppula is reported as saying, "On account of the altitude, we discarded our parachutes over Rawlings, Wyo. on our way to Rock Springs." The quote goes on to report that the Buhl crew flew the entire Rock Springs refueling sequence without their parachutes. The qualifier "on account of the altitude" indicates the Buhl aircraft lacked adequate power to operate successfully at the very high altitudes at Rock Springs, causing the crew to reduce the plane's weight by ditching their parachutes. Although "flying around there all night making these contacts without any parachutes" is called "a funny thing," in the quote, it was obviously quite risky.

The Buhl's insufficient power biased Wilson's approach to refueling by limiting the amount of refueling gas that could be loaded aboard the plane for operations at a safe height above the elevation of Rock Springs (about 6700 feet). This limitation in turn required repeated flights to replenish the Sun God's nearly-empty tanks, contributing enormously to the danger of what was, even singly, highly hazardous flying, especially at night. Only in retrospect can we fully comprehend the determination and bravery of the two crews in accomplishing this pivotal series of refuelings at Rock Springs.

Little mention is made in Sun God references to the almost constant need to pump fuel during the flight. An unattributed quote (presumably from a newspaper account) in McGoldrick, ref#114, p. 168, refers to the "exhausting hours transferring gasoline from the fuselage tank into the wing tanks with the hand device called a wobble pump."

The wobble pump was a popular device for this purpose on airplanes of this era. A double-acting wobble pump conveyed fuel on both the forward and back stroke of its handle. It required vigorous application of arm and shoulder muscles in both directions. As mentioned in ref#113, Mamer initially thought this would be good exercise. However, at about 0.6 lb/hp-hr of fuel consumption typical for aircraft engines of this period, nearly 20 gallons were used each hour of flight at 75% power. At this rate, the Sun God's overhead tanks emptied every six hours, making manning the pump a nearly constant, and tiring, activity.

Mamer's humorous use of hyperbole is in evidence in his description of his note to the searchlight operator, which he wrote in ref#89, in SDC, Saturday August 17 under the headline "Mamer Tells of Troubles on Trip."

The New York Times, in its August 16, 1929 issue, published a preflight schedule for the "Sungod," one of several different schedules that appeared in various publications prior to the flight. Published under an August 15 Spokane dateline, it called for refueling contacts in Cheyenne late Friday, Cleveland Saturday morning, New York Saturday afternoon, Cleveland again (westbound) at dusk Saturday, St. Paul Sunday morning, and arrival in Spokane Sunday night, August 18, a highly optimistic schedule.

The distance to be covered on the aircraft's long flight, the Times explained, is "about 7,200 miles." The source for this number, or how it was determined is not given. The Times' article also gave the following information: "Lieutenant Mamer is 30 years old and has been flying since 1916. Walker is 24 and has been flying for about three years."

The fliers claimed not to have slept much during the flight. Mamer, in the contemporaneous account listed above (ref#89), admitted only to "catnapping by turn now and then," and in a light vein asked "...did you ever try to sleep in a parachute?" He followed with his own answer, "...believe me they don't make the best kind of pajamas."

Most of the information in this chapter regarding applicable research on lack of sleep comes from "Consequences of Sleep Deprivation," by Jolanta Orzel-Gryglewska, a review published in the *International Journal of Occupational Medicine and Environmental Health* in 2010, (ref#111). The information on microsleeps is from an article by Mikel Theobald on the website Everyday Health, (ref#112).

6. Hazards on the High Desert

The Dempsey and chicken thief headlines are from the 1st Edition, SDC, Aug. 17, 1929, (ref#91). Art Walker's comments on sleep and the performance of the motor are from the same edition of the Spokane newspaper, crediting the Associated Press.

Nick Mamer had stated his intention to follow the airmail route east to New York. Our airmail route information comes from "dreamsmithphotos.com," (ref#165). This extensive website includes maps and insights into the Post Office's 1920's establishment of a "lighted and well-equipped airway" allowing night travel, in this section, between San Francisco and Chicago. This Transcontinental Airway constituted a chain of revolving and flashing beacon lights, radio and telegraph-typewriter stations, and lighted intermediate landing fields on a 24-hour basis. In 1927 it was divided into two contract air mail routes, the western part awarded to Boeing Air Transport, Inc., and the eastern part to National Air Transport.

That the establishing of the airmail route was of considerable interest to the public in the 1920s is indicated by an article in the *Philadelphia Daily News* of May 18, 1925. Under a headline proclaiming "Big Beacon Light Seen By People of Region," the article said "A veritable aurora borealis prevailed over the north mountains during Saturday and Sunday nights as the beacon lights, installed by the post-office department for the guidance of the planes that are to participate in the night air-mail service to have its beginning early next month [sic]." "...The long shafts of light from the million candle-power beacons moved in a semi-circle and served to guide the trial planes that were in the air both nights."

The Section Maps included on the ref#165 site show a single line representation of a part of the airway with symbols denoting intermediate airfields and local equipment. For example, the Rock Springs-Medicine Bow map lists fourteen intermediate airfields and beacon numbers 16 through 32, with airfield towns from Reliance, Thayer Junction, Bitter Creek, Tipton and Wamsutter on to Walcott, Dana, Carbon and Medicine Bow. These linear representations facilitated our plotting (and scaling) of the actual paths between Sun God refueling airfields over the intermediate airfields that were followed.

The remark about the cold temperature is based on our estimate that the Sun God flew at an altitude of at least 8,000 feet, or about a thousand feet above the high desert in this part of Wyoming, where the typical elevation of the land (above mean sea level) is near 7,000 feet. A figure of minus 5.4 degrees Fahrenheit for each thousand feet of elevation increase yields a deficit of 43 degrees temperature drop – meaning it would be chilly, even on an August morning.

The items packed on board the Sun God in Spokane is derived from "Equipment Carried, Spokane Sun God/1929," a list of 40 items on p.48 of *Marathon Flyers* by Russell Plehinger, published in 1989 (ref#116).

The path of the Lincoln Highway is taken from the "Midget Map of Best Roads of Wyoming," p. 38 of *Atlas of the Best Roads of The United States* published by The Clason Map Co. (Denver) in 1924. The only significant difference in the Highway's path from the airway is the airway's deviation to Bitter Creek, Wyoming, a distance of less than ten miles which the Highway bypasses.

The information about establishing the Lincoln Highway comes from "The Lincoln Highway" by Richard F. Weingroff, published online by the Federal Highway Administration, (ref#166). In the article, Weingroff writes that by 1921, only 8.66 percent of the 2.2-million miles of roads in the U.S. "had improved surfaces of gravel, stone, sand-clay, brick, shells, oiled earth, bituminous or, as a U.S. Bureau of Public Roads (BPR) bulletin put it, 'etc.'"

Nick Mamer's father, Jacob H. Mamer (1863-1897), died at age 34 before Nick's birth on Jan. 28, 1898 (Nicholas Bernard Mamer on Ancestry.com, ref#61). Mary Lou Williams, the daughter of Nick Mamer's brother James, published a letter on the Internet (ref#167) that includes details of the Mamer family. According to her 1999 letter, Jacob died in an accident involving a "horse drawn carriage in Hastings, Minnesota" when the horses were spooked by tolling church bells. The reference to Hastings' downtown is from the City of Hastings Minnesota website—www.hastingsmn.gov, (ref#55A).

A good treatment of the hazards arising from loss of sleep over periods up to, and including 72 hours, is "What Happens to You When You Don't Sleep for Days," by Mikel Theobald on the everydayhealth.com website (ref#112). Theobald also references the previously cited Orzel-Gryglewska paper (ref#111) on sleep deprivation.

In its August 18, 1929 newspaper, *The New York Times* summarized the situation at Cheyenne: "...Mamer had to circle the airport until 11:30 A. M....and in that time only seventy gallons of gasoline and eight gallons of oil were taken aboard. Vernon Bookwalter, pilot of the supply ship, said the exceedingly thin air prevented him from taking more than fifty gallons aloft at a time."(ref#7) This was echoed in the Associated Press article on the SDC, Aug. 17, (ref#88).

Bookwalter was piloting the Ryan B-1 Brougham equipped with the J5 Wright motor. This 9-cylinder engine was rated at about 200 horsepower at sea level, and was not supercharged. If a 5-percent horsepower loss for each 1,000 feet of added elevation is assumed, the engine would produce only about 160 horsepower at 8,000 feet elevation.

The eight-o'clock reference is back-calculated from the arrival time at Cheyenne (9:11) based on a ground speed of about 72 mph (it's thought the Sun God faced a headwind on this leg).[ref#91]

The quotes from the messages dropped at Cheyenne are from an Associated Press dispatch as reported by *The New York Times*, (ref#7).

The confusion between the Sun God and Bookwalter upon the Sun God's departure from Cheyenne is reported by the Associated Press in the SDC of Aug. 17. It reads, "Mamer flew toward North Platte and out of sight twice as the Ryan refueling ship went up for the second contact. He was endeavoring to get the supply ship to follow him, but a previous message instructed the refueling plane to start for the Nebraska city after the third contact was lost." The first sentence says the Sun God flew out of sight, returned, flew out of sight again, then returned for the second refueling contact (during which 20 gallons of gas and 8 gallons of oil were delivered).

The first part of the second sentence suggests the Sun God's retreats toward Nebraska were a signal for the Ryan to follow it toward Nebraska. But the last part of the second sentence introduces a "previous message" which was either lost, or which instructed the Ryan to head for Nebraska after "the third contact" was lost (aborted?). The content of this "previous message" is uncertain, and what is meant by "the third contact" is also uncertain. Without more information this report from the Associated Press is difficult to understand.

A different Associated Press dispatch with the same dateline (Cheyenne, Wyo. Aug. 17) is reported in *The New York Times* under the banner "Supply Ship Failed to Follow" (ref#7). It said Mamer's message to Bookwalter read, "We are going to North Platte, follow us this time." The report continues: "Twice Mamer tried to lead Bookwalter's plane toward North Platte, Neb., where the Sun God had ordered the refueling transferred. On both occasions the supply plane failed to follow and Mamer was forced to return here [Cheyenne]."

7. "We Made a Beautiful Contact"

The airmail route from Cheyenne, Wyoming to North Platte, Nebraska again followed the Lincoln Highway, per the Airway section maps (ref#165) and the Clason Map Co. highway maps (ref#171). Deviations from a straight, true east bearing are small.

Traveling east, the land forms tilt downward. The distance between Cheyenne, Wyoming and Chappell, Nebraska is 122 miles. Chappell is 2, 360 feet lower than Cheyenne. North Platte, the Sun God's destination during this leg, is more than 3,000 feet lower than Cheyenne.

The Airway maps and information on the beacon stations' markings and positioning is taken from the airmail website, "Arrows Across America," CAM #18, San Francisco-Chicago (ref#165). The number of beacons on the Transcontinental Airway comes from *Aircraft Yearbook of 1928*, cited in ref#165.

Vernon Bookwalter, pilot of the Ryan supply plane, lagged behind the Sun God as Nick Mamer and Art Walker headed east from Cheyenne. Bookwalter, knowing he was flying east to elevations lower than Cheyenne, loaded 100 gallons of gasoline onto the Ryan. Somewhat later, when the Ryan had caught up with the Sun God, the 100 gallons were transferred to the Sun God as both planes flew eastward (ref#88).

The information on Nebraska agriculture is drawn from the Deuel County

History website (ref#186) and the *Encyclopedia of the Great Plains* edited by David Wishart (ref#185).

Bookwalter's note to the Air Derby Association is quoted in SDC of August 17, 1929 under the banner "Refueling Sun God at North Platte" (ref#88). Information and data on the Air Derby Association's activities and personnel are derived from J. P. McGoldrick II's book, *One Man's Opinion Of The Spokane Aviation Story* (ref#114).

The arrival of the Sun God at North Platte was covered by the Associated Press in the August 18 *The New York Times* under the headline "Sun God, Refueled, Off To Cleveland." A subhead referred to "Earlier Difficulties," which reflected another banner claiming "Dissension Shown in Notes." "For God's sake, quit fooling around and bring up that gas," said a quote from one of the notes from the Sun God, apparently meant for Vernon Bookwalter. In another banner, "It Is Expected Here Today," the *Times'* headline writer expressed his prediction of the Sun God's arrival in New York (ref#7).

The incident of the flaming barrels at North Platte's airfield in 1921 is taken from the *Wikipedia* article on the North Platte Airport, (ref#184). The field's lower elevation of 2802-feet affords a faster climb rate for the Ryan following takeoff, even when loaded with a hundred gallons of gasoline (about 650 pounds).

According to the A. P. report in the above-referenced *The New York Times*, the Sun God left North Platte at 8:15 p. m. local time for Cleveland, Ohio. Their dropped note said they expected "to reach Cleveland by daybreak [where they would refuel] flying by way of Omaha and Chicago."

Nick Mamer's quote concerning "a beautiful contact" and the "first time in the flight in taking on a full load," is taken from the his recollections titled "Texaco Across the Sky, The Flight of the Spokane Sun God" that appeared in *The Texaco Star*, Vol. 16, August, 1929, (ref#179).

8. A Night of Hypervigilance

This leg of the Sun God's flight continues along the Transcontinental Air Mail Route, which, according to data from the *1928 Aircraft Year Book* reproduced in ref#165, consisted of 92 Intermediate fields, 185 Rotating beacons and 427 Acetylene beacons. Gothenburg was one of the Department of Commerce's Intermediate fields. A few of those towers and beacons, with sheds and concrete arrows in remote places, still remain as relics of the so-called "highway of light."[ref#165, 138]

According to the sun and moon calculator on www.timeanddate.com, (ref#196), a full moon occurred on Tuesday, August 20, 1929. On the night of the 17th it was at 95.3 percent illumination. I therefore characterized it as "almost-full." At Omaha, according to the same source, the moon rose at 7:22 p.m., and sunset occurred at 8:20 p.m. However, as noted in the region's weather (ref#194), clouds prevented full view of the moon.

A pilot's dependence on an aircraft's instruments at night (as well as when weather conditions obscure) was well-established in 1929, even though Lt. James Doolittle's demonstration of "blind flying"—dependence on instruments alone for successful takeoff, navigation, and landing—first occurred in September of that year. The book

IFR BY THE BOOK: Techniques of Instrument Flying, by J. R. Williams (1980) (ref#197) is a good source for what I learned, and later taught, at the U.S. Navy's Corry Field simulator school at Pensacola, Florida in the course titled "Basic Instruments."

As Williams, an airline Captain with more than 10,000 hours of flight time, says, his book "talk[s] you through the actual 'hands on' flying of an aircraft, on instruments, from the basics through the actual approaches." Because of its date, 1980, his book treats, describes and pictures the basic instruments of the eighties. However, these instruments retain most of the character of their ancestors on the instrument panel in the 1928 Buhl CA-6 Special, as illustrated in the photo of Nick at its controls, ref#29 (not the Sun God, see Appendix). This photo is from McGoldrick's books (ref#114).

Williams is careful to acknowledge how his book may become obsolete: "...we are in a rapidly changing industry...what is in these pages is current only now...and it may be outdated by the time the book is published." (ref#197) Certainly by the current date, most of the individual instruments treated in his book are replaced by computer displays in many modern aircraft, even if the underlying aspects of their function and use remain basic to flying under IFR conditions. (See the *Wikipedia* article on EFIS— "electronic flight instrument system.")

The news report from the *Lincoln Evening Journal* of Saturday, August 17, (ref#198) saying officials at Boeing airfield had stored "two hundred gallons of gasoline" for the possibility of refueling the Sun God, seems odd when considered with their lack of an airplane equipped for aerial refueling. No wonder "local airmen were in a quandary as to what to do should Mamer and Walker wish to take on additional gasoline..."

Omaha, Nebraska and its environs are clearly shown on Airway Bulletin No. 423 dated September 6, 1928, (ref#165), which may have been in the hands of Mamer and Walker during this flight.

Charles Lindbergh's interview, with quotations from it, is taken from the *Des Moines Register* of Saturday Morning, August 17, 1929, (ref#195), which says it occurred on the preceding Thursday (Aug. 15) at the home of his mother, Mrs. Evangeline L. Lindbergh in Detroit. The quotation on the receptions accorded Lindbergh upon his return to the U.S. from his famous flight is taken from *The Spectacle of Flight: Aviation and the Western Imagination, 1920-1950*, by Robert Wohl, (2005), (ref#159), which contains a large and fascinating section on the subject.

The Lindberg interview article is headlined "LINDY SEES ROSY YEARS AHEAD OF AVIATION IN U.S.," with the subhead, "Air Travel is Already Safer Than Rail, He Says." Despite the headline writer's exuberance, Lindbergh seems to have envisioned future aeronautical developments clearly, as when he said, "There will be a development of larger transports [airliners] and faster planes. There will be a development of more efficient airplane motors and the development of planes requiring less skill for safe operation." On the other hand, his call for the marking of towns and cities for visual identification from the air became less necessary with the development of improved aircraft low/medium frequency radios and the advent of four-course radio ("A-N") airway navigation and its radio identification of the source in the early-to-mid 1930s.

There's little doubt that Lindbergh's flight raised the country's aviation fever. In the chapter on "The Spokane Sun God," Frank W. Wiley's 1966 book, (ref#115), Wiley says, "...the Spokane National Air Derby Association furnished the funds and did the planning..." for the flight, and that "Spokane businessmen contributed an additional $10,000 to the project." The chapter also reports, "Mamer was ably supported by the air-minded citizens of Spokane."

The August 24, 1929 edition of *Aviation*, (ref#101) reports the Texas Oil Company supplied all the products and was responsible for the refueling arrangements over both Cleveland and New York. The SDC of August 17 (ref#90) reported the presence of Dan Robertson, James Buchanan and Captain Frank Hawks in Cleveland prior to the arrival of the Sun God. The SDC also quoted Hawks' remarks about leading the Sun God to New York.

According to the Internet's sunrise/sunset calculator on www.timeanddate.com, (ref#196), Cleveland's sunrise occurred at 6:38 a.m. on August 18, 1929.

9. Unheard Cheers

This leg of the Sun God's flight on August 18 continues along the Transcontinental Air Mail Route from Cleveland to the vicinity of New York, where the pilot must deviate to arrive at Roosevelt airfield on Long Island. The original Air Mail Route terminated at Hadley Field, five miles from New Brunswick, New Jersey (Air Mail Pioneers, ref#193).

Dan Robertson, pilot of the Curtiss C-1 Robin, NR82H, and Frank Buchanan, an employee of the Texas Company (ref#201) were directed to Cleveland by Frank Hawks on behalf of the Texas Oil Company, also known as Texaco (ref#101,90). The details on the Jackson-O'Brine record flight is from *Marathon Flyers*, Russell Plehinger, p. 83 (ref#116).

According to the August 17 edition of *The New York Times* (ref#6), Hawks originally flew to Cleveland in his Lockheed Express, discovered that the Sun God was well behind schedule, and returned to New York. The same edition reveals some of the preparations New York made for the Sun God's arrival: "Henry Buchmeyer, parachute jumper, will broadcast the story of the refueling while descending in a parachute ... it will be rebroadcast to the crowd at the field over loudspeakers."

The information about the absence of drinking water comes from the Associated Press release, datelined Roosevelt Field, N.Y., August 18, (ref#234) quoting Mamer's dropped note: "[We] were a little disappointed at not getting any food. However, before we left [Cleveland] the boys sent down some water, and this had a great effect on us ...We had been out of water about four hours."

In his long note to Frank Hawks (ref#200) Nick Mamer complains twice about the lack of visibility out of the Sun God's windshield. He blames this on oil which presumably comes from the Whirlwind motor. Such oil may be transported by high-velocity airflow over the exposed cylinders and valve mechanisms and subsequently deposited onto the windshield behind the motor by direct impact of contaminated air on the glass. Mamer also writes that the visibility might be improved by wipers, "... oil on windshield and no wipers ..."

Regardless of the antidote, there's not much doubt that oil coming from the engine would be darkened by entrained combustion products that would seriously impair visibility when splattered onto the windshield in the manner indicated.

At approximately 2:00-minutes of the *Fox Movietone News* outtakes of the New York refueling operations (ref#1), a hand and arm are clearly seen outside the port side of the Sun God, presumably thrust out a window on that side. The hand, which may hold a rag, is clearly seen wiping the windshield.

A letter from San Francisco Mayor James Rolph, Jr. to James J. Walker, mayor of New York was delivered to the Sun God during the San Francisco refueling and subsequently relayed to New York (ref#234). Quoted in the *The New York Times* of August 19, 1929 (ref#8), it reads as follows:

"Dear Mayor Walker: In these days of marvelous progress in the navigation of the air it is no surprise to be asked to participate in unusual and adventurous events. Hence I am taking it for granted that this note of greeting will be delivered promptly to you by Lieutenant N. B. Mamer and Arthur Walker, who are attempting a coast-to-coast non-stop flight.

"San Francisco sends its good wishes to New York, and I offer my affectionate greetings to you its honored Mayor. Sincerely, JAMES ROLPH Jr., Mayor of San Francisco."

Nick's frustration with lack of time for writing is evident in his notes to Frank Hawks (ref#200). In one note he writes, "I know I hav'nt (sic) said much on this flight simply because I hav'nt (sic) time …"

The telegraphed message from Ellsworth C. French is quoted directly from the Western Union Telegram itself, part of (ref#234) from the MFA. It was sent from Spokane Washington to "Pilot N R Wilson, Refueling Plane, RockSprings Airport RockSprings WYO."

On page 148 of his *One Man's Opinion of the Spokane Aviation Story, 1910-1941* (ref#114B), J. P. McGoldrick II lists French as a member of the National Air Derby Association, which was also known less formally as the Sun God Flight Committee, with Vic Dessert, Chairman.

Nick Mamer is quoted in the Associated Press release, datelined Roosevelt Field, N.Y., August 18, (ref#234) regarding the Cleveland refueling: "We took on 200 gallons of gas at Cleveland, bringing the ship up to capacity load." This article also quotes him on the tail wind experienced on this leg: "Absurd as it may seem, we have not had anything resembling tail wind, except from Cleveland east."

When operating properly, the Pioneer Earth Inductor Compass significantly reduced the piloting burden. After setting the desired course into the "Course Controller' dial, the pilot need only to steer to the desired heading and thereafter observe the "Steering Indicator." As described in the June, 1927 *Aero Digest* by Brice Goldsborough, "A deviation of the needle to the left ["L" on the dial] indicates that the plane is to the left of the course set on the controller and it must be brought back to zero by heading the plane more to the right." Similarly, deviation to the right ["R" on the dial] calls for turning left, always striving to keep the needle centered between the "L" and the "R."

It's not known when, or what part or parts of this Inductor unit, built by the Pioneer Instrument Company, failed. However, the Associated Press release, datelined Roosevelt Field, N.Y., August 18, (ref#234), reports that, at Roosevelt field, "A total of 210 gallons of gasoline ... was put aboard the Sun-God, besides food, water, an altimeter and *parts for an earth inductor compass*," (emphasis added). Presumably, the unit was subsequently repaired, using the supplied parts.

The MFA contain original specimens of Nick Mamer's dropped notes, several of which are signed (ref#200). Those on notebook paper were written in pencil on watermarked Defiance Bond paper, dated 1923. Others were written on odd paper scraps. Where they are reproduced in this book and to the extent possible, we have tried to retain the character of the handwritten originals. Nick Mamer's handwriting is characterized by the looping motions of the Palmer Method, penmanship instruction that was developed by Austin Palmer around 1888 and taught in the U.S. well into the 20th century (ref#241). Accuracy required that we reproduce the punctuation, spelling, capitalization and grammar as found in the originals, although the spacing and dashes are approximate. Short quotes appear inside quotation marks; long quotes are in inset blocks.

The beacon and airfield identifiers (Numidia, for example) correspond to the stations established for the 2,665-mile-long Transcontinental Air Mail Airway (ref#165). Mamer planned to follow this route to Roosevelt Field on Long Island, New York, although the terminus of the Airway was Hadley Field near South Plainfield, New Jersey rather than Roosevelt Field.

According to the Nov. 15, 1928 *Domestic Air News*, Serial No. 40, the Chief Engineer of the Airways Division inspected the Cleveland-New York Section by making landings at the principle intermediate fields of Northhampton, Numidia, Sunbury , Bellefonte, Kylertown and Brookville at the beginning of November, 1929. Plans were made to install a "watch house" for taking care of passengers should airplanes land at these fields due to poor weather or other causes. Two "Airway keepers" at each station would care for the equipment and report weather and landing conditions by teletype each hour. These reports were to be the basis of an improved weather service communicated to enroute pilots by radio-telephone (ref#165).

The heat on this leg became oppressive and the pilots removed their shirts to cool off. The rough air over the Allegheny Mountains also took a toll. "I believe we have just completed the hardest leg of the trip so far," Nick wrote (ref#234). "The rough air over Pennsylvania has worn us both out. I am taking a slight rest to be in shape for refueling," he said upon arrival in New York. "These last four hours have cost us considerably in strength." These expressions comport with the description of the "hell stretch" contained in the 1927 *Aviation* article on the Allegheny weather quoted (ref#240).

The New York Times of August 19, 1929 (ref#8) describes the encounter with Leon Allen at Armonk, New York, and Allen's role in leading the Sun God south to Roosevelt Field. Mamer had apparently strayed north of Long Island and was uncertain of his bearings. The *Fox Movietone News* and *Pathe News* films of the New York refuelings (ref#1) provide evidence of the numerous airplanes that greeted the Sun God over Roosevelt Field.

During the New York contacts, Nick Mamer was clearly concerned about the flight west from New York into Pennsylvania. In his letter to Hawk he asks him to lead them west "as far as possible" with Walker piloting the Sun God so that he might "rest before the dark sets in." Furthermore, he asks, "when you leave us be sure and be on the beacon course" (ref#200) Aware he would be piloting most of the way to Cleveland and in the dark, Mamer by this entreaty sought to ensure he would have the security of the lighted beacons along the Transcontinental Airway during the night.

The description of the refueling sequence with Wassall and Chaffee is derived mostly from my viewing of the filmed *Fox Movietone News* outtakes (ref#1), which represent a significant visual record of the workings of the participants during the contacts.

Mamer's impatience is chronicled in his plea to Hawks: "Will you show us to Cleveland after this refueling," and his parting note after just two hours in New York, "Thanks, fellows. Let's go back to Cleveland," (ref#8).

10. Kylertown Fusillade

As requested by Nick in his dropped notes at New York, Captain Frank Hawks in his own plane led the Sun God from Roosevelt Field on Long Island to Bellefonte, Pennsylvania on Sunday evening, August 18. The bumpy air reference is from Mamer's story datelined Chicago, Aug. 19, for the North American Newspaper Alliance (N.A.N.A.) (ref#229).

Nick, "bending over at the waist," and the squeezing action in the cabin arises from consideration of the dimensions of the airplane's fuselage. At its widest, the cabin is only about 42 inches, so two men exchanging places requires wedging of bodies past one another. The maximum inside height (aft of the windshield) is about 56 inches, but the height where the controls are located is only about 51 inches. Nick's height is about 70 inches, so he must bend low in order to move. These cabin dimensions were derived from a scale drawing of the Buhl CA-6 supplied by Canadian Bushplane Heritage Centre, in Sault Ste. Marie, Ontario, Canada, (ref#257).

Most of the Sun God's battle with the storms near Bellefonte is based on two of Nick Mamer's written reports. In an article written afterwards for *The Texaco Star*, vol.16, "Texaco Across the Sky," (ref#179), he describes the ordeal, "Of course neither one of us slept a wink that night, as we dodged, climbed and spun in an effort to get outside of that storm." And in the dispatch datelined Cleveland, Aug. 19, titled "Pilot Describes Battle With Storm," (ref#229), Mamer gives the result: "We were pretty well used up when morning finally broke..."

The latter article also confirms that Frank Hawks delivered the pilots to Bellefonte on the lighted Airmail route: "We picked up the beacon lights as darkness fell and ran along smoothly as far as Bellefonte" (ref#229). The hangar details are from Bellefonte Historical and Cultural Association, including photos from the Fred D. Smith Collection (ref#244).

The weather conditions for Pennsylvania were taken from the *Pittsburgh Press*, 19 August 1929 edition (ref#243). Information on the route across Pennsylvania and Ohio is based on Airmail route mappings (Ref#165) for the Chicago-New York Airway. The Mercer-Sunbury section, for example, covers a distance of about 180 miles. It lists the following so-called intermediate or commercial airfields equipped with beacons: (listed in westbound order) Sunbury, Hartleton, Bellefonte, Kylertown, Greenwood, Brookville, Emlenton, and Mercer.

Kylertown is nearest the location where Nick encounters the severe electrical storm. He reverses course and returns to Bellefonte, where he "dropped a message to the aviation field requesting signals to indicate the air road to Cleveland," (ref#229). Presumably he seeks guidance around the storms, whereupon, "...there was a great deal of flashing on and off of lights. We hung around Bellefonte for 30 minutes and then the storm became so violent we had to move along." (ref#229)

Wiley (ref#115) and Bakse (ref#2) report this sequence somewhat differently: "By a message system, a pre-arranged signal...whereby the Belfont (sic) airport manager would flash the floodlights on the field—once if the weather was O.K., twice if questionable, and three times if bad," (ref#115, p. 284), the signal indicated bad weather, so "Mamer circled the town, flying a triangular course from the town to an airway beacon to the airport. He had to revise his holding pattern to circle the beacon and the town when the ceiling dropped to 200 feet." (ref#115, p. 284) This is Wiley's last sentence covering the Bellefonte storm sequence.

The airfield, three miles east-southeast of Bellefonte, is listed in Airway Bulletin No. 342, May 2, 1928 as a "sod" field with floodlights for landing. The station is operated 24 hours. It's equipped with a 24-inch rotating beacon in the northwest corner of the field that operates from sunset to sunrise.

The details in the Airway Bulletin, together with Wiley's description, suggest that the "triangular course" flown by Mamer may have connected to a nearby town with an airway beacon, perhaps Hartleton. Hartleton is the closest beacon to the east of the town of Bellefonte. The three apexes of the triangle would thus be the town of Bellefonte, the Bellefonte airfield, and the Hartleton beacon.

With the storm apparently moving eastward causing the ceiling to descend to 200 feet over the Bellefonte airfield, Mamer possibly lost sight of its beacon and decided he couldn't risk flying there. Thus he, as Wiley writes, may have "had to revise his holding pattern" or begin to fly back and forth between the town of Bellefonte and the Hartleton beacon as the storm intensified. The "think quick and act quicker," adage also appears in the same N.A.N.A. article (ref#229).

After a pause trying to wait out the storm, Nick apparently concluded he could not afford to stay in the vicinity of Bellefonte any longer, perhaps for fear of exhausting his supply of gas before reaching Cleveland. But deciding to confront the storm frontally by pushing westward was not easy. Entering the vicinity of such a group of storms is dangerous, and can be deadly. The night's flight, with rain, lightning, and (possibly) hail, must have been, as the pilots' fatigue at dawn suggests, terrifying.

Yet neither danger nor fear seems to deter Mamer. In September of 1919, he won the title "King of Fliers" at the Minnesota State Fair for so outclassing his competitors that it was said they "look[ed] like a bunch of amateurs." According to the *Hastings*

Democrat of Sept. 12, 1919, (ref#247) he accomplished this by "looping the loop, tail spins, nose dives, Immelman turns" (an Immelmann is an ascending half-loop followed by a half-roll, which results in level flight in the opposite direction at a higher altitude) and other risky aerobatics.

When in Hastings, he frequently descended to within feet of the water while flying underneath the high bridge—also known as "the spiral bridge" (ref#248) —over the Mississippi River (ref#247).

The last refueling at Cleveland employs the Robertson-Buchanan duo (ref#96). Both Wiley (ref#115) and Bakse (ref#2) report "the Robbins brothers" as the refueling crew in Cleveland. This mixup is perhaps spawned by the record-breaking aircraft's name, "St. Louis Robin," NC59H, with which the refueling crews hired by Hawks (ref#201-A12) were associated (ref#101,90). According to Mamer's N.A.N.A. dispatch (ref#229-A21), "It was the second refueling these boys have made with our ship, so it shows that a little practice makes a whole lot of difference."

11. Those Are The Brakes

The tail wind and Nick Mamer's remark on the "rough treatment" are from "Texaco Across the Sky," the article he wrote for *The Texaco Star* recalling the incident during the flight of the *Spokane Sun God* (ref#179).

The second remark and conditions at Chicago are from the Mamer Archives newspaper clipping (ref#229).

In the 1920s, Maywood Field was the terminus of the New York-Chicago overnight airmail service, established July 1, 1925, as well as the terminus of the Cheyenne-Chicago Section of the Transcontinental airmail route operated by the U.S. government (ref#165).

From Chicago north and west to St. Paul, Minnesota, the established airway passes through Milwaukee, Oconomowoc, Portage, Mauston, and La Cross, Wisconsin. From there it follows the Mississippi River to St. Paul, Minnesota (ref#165). Although a slightly-shorter bypass exists, Mamer chose to overfly Madison between Oconomowoc and Portage, apparently so he could drop notes there. This slightly increased the mileage between Chicago and St. Paul to about 393 miles (ref#165, also the Appendix).

The origin of the name "Oconomowoc" is from *Wikipedia*.

The quote from, and contents of, the three notes dropped by the Sun God at Madison, Wisconsin are from an Associated Press (AP) dispatch in the SDC of Aug. 19, 1929, under the subhead "Drop Note" with a dateline of Madison, Wis., Aug. 19, 1929 (ref#95). The Bookwalter and Dessert quotations are from the same newspaper article (not credited to the AP, however).

Vic Dessert's family background is from Jesse Tinsley's article in the SR, Monday, Sept. 19, 2016 (ref#265).

Nick Mamer finished closely behind the winner in the cross-country air race during the very successful 1927 Derby and National Air Races in Spokane on Sept. 21-24, 1927. The results and events are reported in numerous publications (ref#17,

182, 183), in the Mamer Archives (ref#268), and in McGoldrick's two books (ref#114, A&B).

Dessert's savvy telegram to Bookwalter demonstrates his grasp of the logistics of the Sun God flight, as well as his relationship with its crew. He wisely defers to Mamer's decision-making, despite Bookwalter's advice, which later turned out to be correct—that the gasoline supply onboard the Sun God would run low before reaching Missoula. Dessert deftly handles the press in his reassuring statement from headquarters (ref#95).

The new 65-foot refueling hose was taken to Wilson by Leslie W. Tuttle of the Northern Pacific Railway. He left Spokane on Saturday night, August 17, with the hose, according to a SR article of Tuesday, Aug. 20, 1929, p.2 (ref#157).

The airway followed north from Chicago through Wisconsin is based on the Chicago-Twin Cities Airway maps covering the lighted airway to Waukegan and Milwaukee, where it turns west through Oconomowoc toward Portage, Wisconsin.

At beacon number 12, this airway splits, with the more western path diverting to Madison. The direct route continues to Portage, bypassing Madison. The Madison airway, taken by Mamer, then rejoins the main airway at Portage, beacon number 17 (Chicago-Mauston Section map). As noted above, Mamer diverted to Madison to drop notes, including the one advising Bookwalter of his needs for the St. Paul refueling.

From Portage, Wisconsin the airway passes near Delton, through Mauston to La Crosse, Wisconsin, and subsequently follows the Mississippi River through Wabasha and Red Wing, Minnesota, into the St. Paul-Minneapolis area.

The irregular path traversed results in an estimated length of 393 miles (Appendix) between Chicago and the Twin Cities.

The welcoming crowd's cheers and waves at St. Paul, and the pilots' reply, is reported in the SDC article of Aug. 19 (ref#95), as coming from J. S. Buck, general agent of the Great Northern Railway in Spokane. He had spoken by telephone to Great Northern officials in St. Paul who quoted these details which he then relayed to the SDC.

The quotations and substance of the Sun God notes and details about the brake failure at St. Paul come from two Minneapolis newspapers of August 20, 1929, the *Minneapolis Star* (ref#266), and the *Minneapolis Star Tribune* (ref#267). The *Star Tribune* article, with the headline "Sun God Gets Gas in St. Paul and Soars On," titled "Break in Refueling Plane's Cable Delays Start From St. Paul," yields details of the refueling contacts, including the favored altitude of 4,000 feet (because of its smoothness), the third plane with its external signage, and the Sun God's departure at 4:00 p. m.

12. On To The Great Plains

Minnesota, known for its underestimated "10,000 lakes," is known also for the headwaters of the Mississippi River. Not so well-known are the rusty rails, windbreaks, or dome-topped grain silos. The Sun God's pilots' writings mention none of these. Still, I felt it essential to add features of the state they traversed during this leg. My sources included the Clason Map Company's wonderful *Paved Roads of the Nation* (ref#171) whose cover with the image of a chieftain in full headdress promises "Road Distances" and "Pole Markings." Its title may be deceptive unless paving includes dirt and gravel.

Another source was the history of the Yellowstone Trail, the first transcontinental automobile road across the northern tier states of the continent as conceived by Joseph W. Parmley in 1912 (ref#275).

Finally, I referred to the map of the Chicago, Milwaukee, St. Paul and Pacific Railroad (trademarked as the "Milwaukee Road"), which closely paralleled the Yellowstone Trail throughout Minnesota and South Dakota (ref#276). These references provide details of the path followed by the Sun God, details lacking in news accounts of the day.

The first element of the Army Air Service arrived at the Isthmus of Panama March 29, 1917—just a week before the U.S. entered the World War. It was commanded by the then Captain Henry H. "Hap" Arnold, who later became General of the Army and General of the Air Force (ref#135). *The Panama Canal: An Army's Enterprise* says, "By the time the United States entered World War I...there was no significant...military threat to the waterway... However, there remained the distinct possibility that a hostile nation might sabotage the canal by blowing up a ship..." (p. 82, ref#134)

Conditions in the Isthmus of Panama were primitive at best, with minimal quarters and no airfield available. The 7th Aero Squadron did not receive their first airplanes (two Curtiss R-4s) until December of 1917. Two Curtiss R-3s arrived later that month. The R-3s were float planes with 57-foot wingspan (to increase the lift, offsetting the weight of the floats). At the end of August, 1917, air operations were moved to Coco Walk (it later became France Field) on Mazanillo Bay near Forts Randolph and DeLesseps, and the Coco Solo submarine base (ref#133, map#139) at the Atlantic side of the Panama Canal (ref#83). A declassified "secret" map (ref#136) shows details of the "Harbor Defense of Cristobal" at Colon Harbor.

In February 1918, the U.S. Navy supplied the Army with Curtiss R-6s. The R-6s were two-seat floatplanes with the R-3 wingspan but with a more powerful Curtiss V-2-3 motor. (ref#283)

In June of 1918, Secretary of War Newton Baker sent a $16 million request to Congress to build aviation stations as "The answer of the war department to Germany's submarine challenge..." As reported on p.3 in the *Pittsburgh Daily Post* on 7 June, the stations "...equipped with bombing and scouting planes, will cover...the Panama canal zone and Hawaii, acting as an aerial patrol against any future surprises." (ref#284)

The recently promoted M.S.E. Mamer flew missions for the 7th Aero Squadron over the Canal Zone, the earliest being in October of 1917, followed by a gap. Then, during the four months beginning in March of 1918 he flew many missions. These flights were generally piloted by Major Wynne, or Lieutenants Winslow, Burnight, Dawson, Evans, or Malloway with Nick as observer.

Mamer itched to be at the controls, which prompted his petition to the Chief Signal Officer of March 30, 1918. Because of its significance to his later life, the carefully-typed letter he wrote is quoted in its entirety below:

FROM: Master Signal Electrician Nicholas B. Mamer, 7th Aero Squadron, Cristobal, Canal Zone.

TO: Office of the Chief Signal Officer, Air Pers. Div., Washington, D.C.

SUBJECT: Flying Status

1. Respectfully request that I be put on flying status and instructed in the art of flying.

2. The reason for this request is that I believe my services would be of more benefit to the Government if I were taught to fly. Since I have been in the aviation services my duties have been associated with the repair and upkeep of aeroplanes and aeronautical motors. I believe that familiarity with the actual handling of an airplane in the air under flying conditions, would greatly assist an aviation mechanic in increased efficiency in their repair and upkeep, besides fitting him for the regular duties of a pilot.

3. Out of a class of eleven men instructed in aerial reconnaiscence [sic], observation, artillery directing and kindred subjects by the Squadron Commander from November 21, 1916 to March 20, 1918, I was one of the two men selected to direct artillery fire on the recent maneuvers held in the Republic of Panama.

4. I have studied Aeronautics and the Theory of Flight for the past three years. I was employed by the Duesenberg Motor Company of Minneapolis, Minnesota, as racing mechanician for two years previous to my entry into the service. I am 23 years old [actual age: 20], have attended high school for three years, and know of nothing wrong with my physical condition.

5. The 7th Aero Squadron, Cristobal, C.Z. is equipped with dual control aeroplanes.

Nicholas B. Mamer (Signed)

7th Aero Squadron (ref#280)

Nick probably had help in writing this letter, designed as it was to impress "the brass" at headquarters in Washington, D. C., on his capabilities and how they might benefit the Air Service. (ref#280) Paragraph 3 seeks to show his competence as a director of artillery fire. In paragraph 4 he reviews his education and work experience at Duesenberg, the Motor Company initially located in the Midway district of the Twin Cities. (Duesenberg, of course, is the famous constructor, prior to WWII, of luxury automobiles and race cars.) He had apparently secured work there while still a teen. His deception about his age simply continues the exaggeration he'd employed when enlisting in the Air Service in 1916.

Mamer's commander, Major Wynne, wrote a covering memo:

"C.O., 7th Aero Squadron, Cristobal, Canal Zone, March 30, 1918 – To Office of the Chief Signal Officer, Air Pers. Div., Washington, D. C.

"1. Forwarded thru channels. Recommending approval.

"2. I have examined Master Signal Electrician Nicholas B. Mamer, and find that he has all the qualifications prescribed by the Chief Signal Officer necessary to become a pilot.

"(Signed) Walter W. Wynne. Major R.M.A., Signal Corps."

While the Office of the Chief Signal Officer considered his petition, Nick continued flying missions over the Canal Zone. They included Artillery Signal Practice, Reconnaissance, Directing Artillery Fire, Cross-country, Aerial Acrobatics, Motor Testing, and Coast Patrol. The flights ranged mostly between 20 minutes to two hours. Usually Mamer was the observer, but on three occasions for flights lasting more than an hour, he was piloting, with Lt. Malloway in the observer's seat. (ref#282)

Mamer flew often with Lieutenant Bob Evans, who was killed in August of 1918 when his airplane fell into Colon Bay. His mother, Mrs. A. M. Evans of Santa Cruz, California, afterwards received a letter of remembrance from Lieutenant Kenelm Winslow (above), a close friend of Evans. In the letter, Winslow writes, in part,

> "Just a word of comfort from Bob's pal. Bob was my best friend and very dear to me...he gave his life in the service of his country... Every effort was made to recover his body, divers from the submarine base, working for several hours locating and lifting the machine from the water...Bob was one of the cleanest and truest friends I ever hope to have... He was admired as well for his ability to handle a flying machine...Only the other night we were talking about our mothers and I remember his speaking very affectionately of you...There aren't many mothers who could make a greater sacrifice unless they lost two like Bob.
>
> Very Sincerely, Kenelm Winslow Jr., 1st Lieut. R.M.A., 7th Aero Squadron, Panama Canal Zone." (ref#279)

(R.M.A. is an abbreviation for Reserve Military Aviator, a designation awarded those who passed the Air Service's so-called "RMA Test" as skilled pilots.)

Nick Mamer's Army service, including his diploma from the Princeton School of Military Aeronautics, dated October 5, 1918, (ref#207) and his official appointment as a 2nd Lieutenant (ref#212) are original documents in the MFA. According to the *Hastings Democrat*, vol 34, no 8, May 9, 1919, (ref#246), Nick subsequently served as flying instructor at Kelly Field, Texas, starting 28 November 1918.

Newspapers across the nation following the progress of the Sun God often were filled with aviation stories, frequently describing failed record attempts, airplane crashes, and deaths of aviators. Stories regarding the loss of the young Swiss fliers, Kaesar and Luescher (ref#278), and the death of 25-year-old Marvel Crosson (ref#277) were contemporaneous with coverage of the flight of the Sun God.

On the other hand, *The New York Times*, in its August 20th edition under the heading "Sun God Reported At Aberdeen, S.D.", accorded three sentences to the plane's arrival.

13. Under a Red Moon

Locations of the numerous forest fires burning widely over the Northwest during the flight of the Sun God come from *The Missoulian* (Missoula, MT) and *The Bismark Tribune* (Bismark, ND) newspapers of August 20, 1929 (ref#301).

Aerial navigation from Aberdeen across South Dakota and over the southwest corner of North Dakota into Montana was accomplished primarily by following the tracks of the Chicago, Milwaukee, St. Paul and Pacific Railroad, known as the 'Milwaukee Road' (ref#276). For most of the distance to Miles City, Montana, the railroad closely follows the route of the automobile road of the time, the Yellowstone Trail (ref#275), as shown in the Clason Map Company's *Paved Roads of the Nation* (ref#171), and the Rand McNally atlas maps (ref#302). In addition to railroad towns, the main landmarks encountered include the Missouri River at Mobridge, South Dakota, the Little Missouri River at Marmarth, North Dakota, and the confluence of the Tongue and Yellowstone Rivers at Miles City in Montana (refs#302, 171).

The Milwaukee Road was a busy railroad in 1929. The movie "Danger Lights," an RKO Radio Pictures b&w release from 1930 affords numerous scenes of steam-train operations recorded on Milwaukee Road tracks in and around Miles City (ref#306). The film's story and acting, dated and awkward, detract somewhat from what otherwise constitutes a near-documentary presentation of 'Road' operations at the time in Montana. Additional details on the Miles City railroads are taken from the Internet article, "Miles City as a Two-Railroad Town," (ref#299).

The "Bridgehunter" site (ref#303) features a photograph of the Yellowstone Trail's 1924 bridge over the Missouri River at Mobridge, SD. This five-span, near-mile-long bridge labeled on the photo "the new wagon bridge," was later replaced by a modern bridge. The railroad's nearby bridge is shorter and less spectacular.

In his dispatch for the North American Newspaper Alliance following the flight, and reported in the *Montana Standard* of August 21, 1929, Nick Mamer wrote, in part, "...we passed over those fires and it was the smoke from these fires that made the visibility so poor...we could not find our way into Spokane..." Thick smoke forced them to linger overnight near Miles City, waiting for daylight (refs#71, 297).

The sun and moon data are from the "time and date" website calculator (ref#196) which yielded sunset at 8:48 p.m. (local) on August 19; moonrise at 7:23 p.m. (local).

The 9:50 p.m. arrival of the Sun God at Miles City is reported in the *Missoulian* newspaper of August 20, 1929. It quotes Mamer, "Visibility is hellish tonight. Smoke or haze. Can not see a thing on ground..." (ref#304)

Descriptions of the Miles City Airport are based partly on the Miles City Chamber of Commerce Airport Master Plan (ref#305). In particular, details were extracted from an included early photograph of the field captioned, "Photo of the original turf runway at Miles City, which is now realigned Runway 12-30..." This photo is credited to the Capt. Robert E. Selff Collection.

Many details of the Miles City Airport actions and interactions with the Sun God are taken from the *Miles City Daily Star* news clipping in the Mamer Archives (ref#297). Included are the time and content of the telegram sent from Aberdeen to E. B. Winter, the runway lighting, Nick's dropped message (content and retrieval), the men at the airfield, the arrangements by Hotaling and Milligan, the crowd of three hundred, the contents of the note from Mamer to Wiley and Mathews, and Nick's message of thanks to Buck Winter, Frank Wiley and Tommy Mathews.

Other details of the actions at the airfield are from Frank W. Wiley, *Montana and the Sky*, 1962, pp. 284-286, (ref#115), including the airport's telephone, the fifty-gallon drum fire, the Wiley flying service and its J-5 Eaglerock, procurement and details for the creamery cans, the Furstnow Saddle Shop contribution, preparation of the Eaglerock and rope actions by Tom Mathews, Wiley's quote on the "oil-streaked" appearance of the Sun God, the timing of the five-gallon can tranfers, the triangular course flown during and following the refueling, as well as the question by the farmer with Wiley's reply and commentary.

Details of the J-5 Eaglerock biplane are taken from *U.S. Civil Aircraft Series, Vol. 1, (ATC 1 – ATC 100)*, Joseph P. Juptner, pp. 149-50, "A.T.C. #57 (8-28) Alexander J5 Eaglerock, A-1," (ref#307). This 1928 airplane, with the Wright Whirlwind motor, was "quite expensive," but "turned out to be very popular...in the western part of the U.S." for its altitude performance.

14. Smoke Gets In Your Eyes

The 600-hours of fire patrol flying comes from E. Harve Partridge's article in *Aviation* magazine, January 17, 1927 entitled "The Northwest Aerial Forest Patrol" (ref#107). This is also the source of Mamer's quote on "...the worst I have experienced..."

The initiation of the Region 1 patrol in 1925 is reported on the Missoula Smokejumpers site under the heading "Early Aerial Recon," (ref#318), which traces the patrol's beginnings back to May of 1919 in California. According to this article, Mamer flew one of the "Liberty-motored" DH-4 deHaviland (spellings vary) airplanes to be used for the patrol from Rockwell Field, San Diego to Spokane. This article also identifies the second fire patrol pilot as R. T. Freng.

The original DH-4 of WWI positioned the pilot forward, under the upper wing, with the gunner in the rear cockpit. Between the two men was the fuel tank. The photograph of a U. S. Forest Service DH-4B, from the *Touch & Go* newsletter (ref#321) shows the revised cockpits, close together behind the wings, with the fuel tank positioned ahead of the two cockpits.

On the Smithsonian National Postal Museum site, "The de Havilland DH-4," by Nancy Pope (ref#319) says day-to-day use of the Army DH-4 in the Airmail Service revealed serious deficiencies which resulted, in early 1919, in decommissioning and renovation. The rebuilt plane was designated the DH-4B model.

According to the *Washington Times* (Washington, D.C.) of May 5, 1919 article "Remodeled Mail Plane Tried Out," (ref#322), the rebuild involved "seventy-six changes." These included a reduction to a single cockpit and a "mail compartment built in." This compartment, ahead of the pilot's seat, was capable of carrying "400 pounds of mail in case of necessity." Twelve of these revised and strengthened airplanes had been finished, and twelve more were being rebuilt "by mail service mechanics."

It seems apparent that the forest service DH-4s were similarly rebuilt, with a second, observer's cockpit installed in the unneeded mail compartment space.

Mamer's description of the observer's actions over a fire is from a Saturday, August 1, 1925 news article from the Mamer Archives (ref#317). This is also the source of the parachute items and his quotes on parachute use.

Additional Mamer quotes are from another news item in the Mamer collection, "Spotting Forest Fires by Air Is Risky Stunt," by "M. B." (ref#316), which Mamer disagreed with. Using a pencil, he crossed out the printed word "Risky," and substituted a handwritten "Thrilling." To this he added, above the printed article title, "you can take the risk out of this story. N. B. M." The intended recipient of his critique is unknown.

Information on navigation, timing and the overflight of Billings comes from the *Billings Gazette* of August 21, 1929, p.3, (ref#310). Information on the Belgrade airfield and refueling is from the *Montana Standard* (Butte, MT) of April 24, 1929, Frank Wiley's book (ref#115), and the extensive local account (of the Sun God progress and arrival) from the Mamer Archives (ref#313).

Finally, news of the fires on the Sun God's route ahead is from page 1 of *The Missoulian* newspaper of Missoula, Montana, August 21, 1929.

15. Almost Home

The listed items aboard the Sun God are from Russell Plehinger in *Marathon Flyers*, p. 48, (ref#116). The "restroom facility" is from Lesley Forden, Chap. VII, The Last Tour, *The Ford Air Tours 1925-1931*, Aviation Foundation of America (ref#15). According to Forden, the arrangement was "mighty cold on the bottom."

Mamer initially planned to refuel at Butte, and locals were surprised by the change, as recounted in the United Press story of August 20, p.2 of the *Billings Gazette* (Montana) of August 21, 1929, (ref#380), and on p. 1 of the August 21 *Montana Standard* (ref#381). The change of plan may have occurred to avoid refueling in the thinner air over the 5,550 feet altitude of Butte (Missoula is more than 2,000 feet lower). Art's piloting, the dropping of messages, Wilson's landing for fuel, and quotes of Mamer's messages are also from these two newspaper stories.

According to *Wikipedia* "Anaconda Smelter Stack," (ref#382), the chimney at Anaconda, visible for many miles from the vicinity of Butte, remains the world's tallest surviving masonry structure. Built in 1918, its overall height is 585 feet (169 m).

The well-flown visual flyway between Butte and Missoula is far from straight. Instead, it follows the Clark Fork River valley. During the 1920s, both the Northern Pacific Railroad, as shown on the rail map (ref#395) and the Yellowstone Trail automobile road (Clason Map Co., *Paved Roads of the Nation*, ref#171) adhered to this narrow river valley. Today, Interstate Highway I-90 and the BNSF Railroad follow essentially the same route.

Local Spokane newspapers were quick to recognize the national coverage of the Sun God drama in articles such as "All North America Learns of Spokane Through

Sun God's Epoch-Making Trip," (ref#294) and in a montage of headings and head-lines from around the country in ref#296 (both from the MFA). Full-page banners, multi-column stories with headings such as "SUN GOD HITS RETURN TRAIL," "Sun God Is Racing West After Reaching New York," and "FLIERS BACK WEST," chronicled the venture. Some also featured speculation, such as "Whether the endurance flight would continue until motor or men are exhausted, or..." etc., as in the page 2 story in the August 21 issue of *The Missoulian* (ref#385).

The basic data on Bob Johnson is from the Missoula International Airport site on the Internet, (ref#284), which also gives the location of the abandoned Missoula Municipal airfield as "near the base of Mount Sentinel...between what is now the University of Montana and South Avenue." The site also mentions that Nick Mamer "is believed to be the first pilot to ever fly over Glacier National Park."

Bob Johnson's Travel Air passenger-sightseeing effort comes from the article in *The Missoulian* (ref#385), as does Mamer's "Hello, Missoula..." quote, the pasteboard, the time, and the first refueling out past the sugar factory.

The factory, a venture of the Amalgamated Sugar Company, was new, having opened in October of 1928 at a cost of three million dollars. It employs three-hundred workers, brags *The Sunday Missoulian* in its "Sugar Beet Section," of October 14, 1928 (ref#379). Its tall smoke stack, however, was inherited from an earlier factory.

The gathered crowd and their disappointment come from the p.1 United Press story in the *Billings Gazette* of August 21 that describes "a curtain of smoke caused by forest fires" that "effectively screened refueling activities from the ground." (ref#386)

The second refueling comes from the Aug. 21, 1929 *The Missoulian* (ref#385) in a column headed "REFUELED TWICE HERE." Despite the conclusion elsewhere that only 50 gallons was delivered at Missoula (see, for example, Wiley, ref#115, p. 286), the delivery of the second 50 gallons is confirmed elsewhere in United Press dispatches that give the total as 100 gallons. This *The Missoulian* (ref#385) article also identifies the delivery of oil and sandwiches with the second refueling, which suggests the Sun God crew made their wishes for food and oil known during the first contact with Wilson and Coppula.

The reported departure time from Missoula of 12:30 p.m., mountain time, comes from *The Missoulian* (ref#385) as well as other sources. Considering the time zone change, the Sun God's arrival in Spokane at 1:43 p.m., Pacific Time, yields a ground speed of about 85 miles per hour, suggesting they faced a headwind of ten or more miles per hour on the trip to Spokane.

16. Wobbly Legs and Fanfare

This chapter relies heavily on the front-page story in the SR of Aug. 21 under the banner headline 10,000 CITIZENS CHEER DARING SUN-GOD AVIATORS' RETURN TO SPOKANE (ref#242). The unsigned article offers extensive coverage, and continues in two columns on page 2. It describes the sack of newspapers and messages dropped from the Sun God as a "letter sack," and includes the quote, "Hello,

Spokane...," the crowd size, the escorts, the timing, the flash of the plane over the crowd, and the downtown whistles of acknowledgement.

Nick Mamer's quotation "Think of it!...," is from Nick's article for the NANA from the *Montana Standard* (Butte) newspaper of Aug. 21, p.2, (ref#71). Details in the aerial view of Spokane are from the Northwest Museum of Arts and Culture (Spokane, WA) photograph captioned "Spokane, 1929" (ref#43).

The time of arrival of the Sun God is reported as 1:43 p.m. in *The New York Times*, (ref#10), SDC, (ref#121), and in other sources. It is reported as 2:00 p.m. in the SR (ref#242), Wiley's book (ref#115) and in others. McGoldrick's books say the Sun God arrived "about noon" on August 20th (ref#114). The time of arrival of Wilson's Buhl at Felts Field is reported in the SR of Aug. 21 (ref#242) as "Wilson and Coppula had arrived at the airport a half hour after Mamer."

Because the time of events is reported differently in the sources, all times must be considered somewhat arbitrary. I selected 2:00 p.m. as the arrival time of the Sun God.

The SDC Edition (ref#121) includes coverage of the actions of the Buhl crew following arrival, posing for photographers as well as interviews on the speaker's stand. The quotations of the interviewer: "the only man who...," Wilson: "Don't let that ten-thousand...," and Coppula, beginning with: "It was a pretty hard job...," are from this source (ref#121). The appearance of the two men is derived from group photographs appearing in McGoldrick's books (ref#114A, p.171)

Two photographs on the front page of the August 21 SR (ref#242) show Leon J. Boyle, in suit and tie, hatless with a pompadour hairstyle, conducting interviews. In one photograph, he's with the Sun God pilots; in the other, with Mrs. J. J. Walker (her dress and appearance are also derived from this photograph). According to a caption under one of the photographs, Boyle is "official announcer at the field."

The appearance of Felts Field from the air (painting on roofs) is derived from the photograph on page 145 in McGoldrick's book (ref#114B).

The actions of the officials of the Air Derby association concerning the messages dropped from the Sun God are from the SDC Edition (ref#121). Boyle's introductions of Faye Mamer and Mrs. Walker, and the quotations of Mrs. Walker, are also from this SDC newspaper. The trimotor sightseeing aircraft and the aerial camera aircraft are covered as well.

The Sun God circled over Felts Field and the surrounding area from the time of its arrival until its 6:00 p.m. landing—approximately four hours. The very brief mention of the transfer of "materials and messages" between the Sun God and supply planes in my chapter is a consequence of vast differences in the reporting of this phase.

The SR of August 21 (ref#242) reports "Repeatedly R. M. Wilson, pilot, and Al Coppula, hoseman, went up to hold aerial converse with Mamer." A long paragraph follows, describing aerial actions between the Sun God and Wilson's airplane. The actions include an exchange during which a bag of "material" ("weighted with rocks") is transferred from the supply plane to Art Walker in the Sun God. Also, a photograph on page 1 showing two other fliers is captioned, "C. E. Mancke and Al Connick, two of the pilots at the field, who made attempts to deliver food and water to the Sun-God pilots."

The SDC Edition (ref#121) reports a different sequence following the arrival of the Wilson-Coppula team: "As the refueling ship continued to circle the field...Newton Wakefield flew up to the east and was followed by Mamer for what was thought to be an attempted refueling contact." Wakefield's goal, however, is reported to be a delivery of provisions to the Sun God. This is followed by descriptions of previous contacts "frustrated by continual hovering about of two photographing planes." Nevertheless, Wakefield is said to report that the Sun God men "are pretty greasy and dirty but they smiled and waved at us." Another attempted contact (third? fourth?) by Wakefield is described as "frustrated by the camera ship." Finally, Wakefield's airplane is said to have "recircled the field and dropped the sack containing provisions hanging from the plane at the end of a long rope." A description of the provisions is not given.

These SDC (ref#121) reports of attempted contacts by Wakefield's airplane are followed by the above-referenced account of the Buhl's initial landing and Boyle's interview of Wilson and Coppula.

In Frank Wiley's summary (ref#115), p. 287, the Sun God simply "circled over the field for four hours..." Also, that "Nick circled Spokane, was twice refueled, and took on food and clean clothes..." (The clean clothes were never taken aloft.)

McGoldrick (ref#114) describes the hours following the Sun God's arrival as a waiting period during which Mamer advised Air Derby officials of mechanical problems (loss of one magneto and failure of a third of the oiling system), and that, although he is okay and Art is "a little tired," he will remain aloft but is opposed to further attempts at record-setting. McGoldrick also presents unsourced messages from Mamer that express frustration over refueling efforts during the wait: "You send that bird up...and he does not realize...I can not (sic) look into the glaring sun and see his ship also." Also, "...when they see you coming for them, they start going like hell, making it all more difficult." The crew(s) causing these alleged problems is/are not identified.

Nick Mamer, in his August article "Texaco Across the Sky," for *The Texaco Star*, a Texaco publication (ref#179), writes that his arrival at the field was at 1:43 p. m. But nothing is included about activities during the four-hour wait until landing at "5:59 p.m.," except "We dropped notes and asked if we might stay aloft to continue the jaunt, but Victor Dessert, vice president of the National Air Derby Association , sponsor of the flight, told us that we had proved our point and might come down to walk as other human beings, with two legs on the ground."

In his summary of the Sun God flight, "Introducing an Advanced Phase of Endurance Flying" in *Aero Digest* of October, 1929, (ref#201), Nick Mamer specifies his return to Spokane as "2 p.m. Pacific Standard Time" and landing "at 6 p.m." "at the urgent request of the backers of the flight." He does not discuss any other activities aloft during the four-hour intervening period.

Many of the activities following the landing of the Sun God are from page 1 of the SR report (ref#242), including the embrace between Nick and Mrs. Mamer, Mamer and Walker's unsteadiness, Walker's embrace by his mother, Nick's arm injury, the fliers' appearance, their trip to the speaker's platform and initial activities thereon.

The security measures by the police are from the caption of the SR photograph titled "Just After Spokane Sun-God Landed," date unknown from the MFA, (ref#399). As previously noted, Mrs. Walker's accoutrements are derived from the SR photograph on p.1.

The fliers' soiled clothing, hearing impairment, their meeting with officials, Art's cigarette, and the politician's formal welcome all are from the SR report, p.1. Nick's complaint of "ringing" ears is also from p.1. The formal welcome by City Commissioner Andrew Fabian is from the SR report, p.2, (ref#242) as is reading the President Hoover's telegram over the microphone. Its message is from Hoover's telegram in the MFA, (ref#402). Description of the interviews of Mamer and Walker conducted on the platform, including quotations, direct and indirect, and their departure, are from the SR report, p.2 (ref#242)

The parade description is from SDC "City Edition" of August 21, (ref#140). The telegram from Mamer and Walker to the Buhl Aircraft Company is from the Company's advertisement in the *Aero Digest* of October, 1929 (ref#401). The two published articles written by Nick Mamer are as identified above.

Activities at the banquet held in the Davenport Hotel are from the SR of August 23, 1929 with the headlines "Sun-God Pilots Presented $1000," and "Air Derby makes Gift to Nick Mamer and Art Walker," (ref#371). This is also the source for the findings by Dr. P. J. Gallagher on his medical examination of the Sun God aviators, although Nick's quotation on the "roar" is from his NANA and SR dispatch entitled, "'Here We Are,' Says Nick Mamer" (ref#343).

The SR report on the banquet is also the source for the tagline quotation from Mamer's remarks there, "Air travel to the northwest…"

17. The Urge to Fly

Because the military records of Nicholas B. Mamer, service number 348467, held in the U.S. government's National Personnel Records Center, National Archives, in St. Louis, MO, were destroyed in the fire of July 12, 1973, almost nothing is officially available from them regarding his military service. Thus, as is noted in the Chapter, Nick's activities from July 3, 1916 until May 1, 1919 have been almost totally reconstructed based on non-governmental sources. In this effort, we acknowledge the significant help rendered through the generosity of the Mamer family. Thanks to them, we were allowed access to a number of original documents highlighting Nick Mamer's military achievements. From these, and augmented by newspaper clippings, Princeton University, Ancestry.com, and our researches of other historical sources, we were able to trace his military activities. It must be acknowledged as well, however, that significant gaps exist.

Our search was not helped by the necessity of determining the accuracy of a newspaper article in the *Seattle Post-Intelligencer's* "Pacific Northwest Pictorial" of Sunday, January 26, 1964. The four-page article, titled "Saga of the Spokane Sun God," beginning on page five, includes the following entry regarding his military career:

"Mamer won his wings and his lieutenant's bars at Kelly Field, Tex. And he served with the American Expeditionary Forces in France during World War I.

"'It is my pleasure to certify that Lt. N. B. Mamer was attached to the 187th aero Squadron, A.E.F., on active duty as pursuit pilot from July 14, 1918 to December 1, 1918,' his commanding officer wrote afterward.

"'He contributed to the valor of the squadron by being awarded the French Croix de Guerre with Palms, in addition to three citations. Lieutenant Mamer is officially credited with the destruction of three enemy planes.

"'His plane was shot down in flames in combat with three enemy Fokker planes near Dun sur Meuse, France, November 2, 1918, during the Argonne battle. By skillful judgment and superb cool-headedness, he managed his plane in such a way so to protect himself, during the descent, from the flames.

"'The plane being demolished upon landing, his presence of mind enabled him to extricate himself from the wreckage, thereby saving his life and escaping with minor injuries.'"

We found this story appealing, and tried diligently to confirm it. We also noted several other publications which referenced, either the above story, or other stories featuring Mamer exploits in France.

Our searches uncovered no record of Mamer as a member of the 187th Aero Squadron. No involvement by him in the A.E.F., nor any award of the Croix de Guerre, with or without Palms, was found. We could not locate any record of debarkation of him for France, or a return from that country.

However, we did find a reference indicating that Mamer had attended the School of Military Aeronautics at Princeton University in 1918. Our inquiry to the Seeley G. Mudd Manuscript Library at Princeton University in May of 2018 was answered by Digital Archivist Annalise Berdini. She confirmed Nicholas Bernard Mamer attended (and graduated from) the U.S. School of Military Aeronautics at Princeton University from July 13, 1918 to October 5, 1918 (ref#117). Additional confirmation of Nick's attendance is his Certificate of Graduation from the MFA, dated October 5, 1918, "By direction of the Director of Military Aeronautics." (ref#207)

Mamer's attendance at Princeton overlaps the period stated in the *Intelligencer* for attachment to "the 187th aero Squadron, A.E.F., on active duty as pursuit pilot" by twelve weeks—major evidence that the *Intelligencer* story is false.

Also in the MFA, dated April 22, 1919 on letterhead "Headquarters, Air Service Flying School, Kelly Field, San Antonio, Texas" is the appointment of Nicholas Bernard Mamer to "2nd Lieutenant, Aviation Section, Signal Reserve Corps" as of April 19, 1919. It is signed by B.B. Buttler, Lt. Colonel, Commanding. Also in the archives is the Certificate headed by "The President of the United States of America, etc." appointing Nicholas Bernard Mamer "Second Lieutenant, Aviation Section (flying status) Signal Officers Reserve Corps of the Army of the United States" as of the "nineteenth day of April" 1919.

Nick Mamer's appointment as a 2nd Lieutenant therefore occurred more than nine months later than the attachment of "Lt. N. B. Mamer" on July 14, 1918 to the "187th Aero Squadron A.E.F.,"—as stated in the *Intelligencer* story. As other records verify, on July 14, 1918, and during the entire period in question, Nick Mamer actually held the enlisted rank of Private.

Further proof that the *Seattle P. I.* story of overseas service is erroneous is found on Mamer's Honorable Discharge (effective May 1, 1919) certificate (ref#211) issued at Kelly Field, which contains the annotation, "Completion of primary flying training per auth letter Nov. 30, 1918 fr. A. G. O. to D. M. A." This training took place at Kelly Field during the period the *Post-Intelligencer* reported Mamer being in France.

We have not been able to determine the source of the overseas narrative in the 1964 *Seattle Post-Intelligencer* edition, nor the identity of the "commanding officer" quoted. Unfortunately, attachment to the 187th Squadron, awards and the heroic accounts have been picked up by many other sources, from magazines to newspapers, and are frequently encountered. All such accounts are mistaken.

Before Nick enlisted in the Army, he apparently secured a position with the Duesenberg Motor Company of Minneapolis as a "racing mechanician" or mechanic. (ref#280) He said he attended high school for only three years, so he did not graduate. (ref#280) During that period, according to the *Minneapolis Star Tribune*, he was well known to attendees at county fairs for "daring feats in motorcycle races and parachute jumps."

At enlistment and throughout his Army service, Mamer lied about his date of birth, adding three years to his actual age. This is seen on documents in the archives such as his request for flying status (he claims to be 23, actually 20) (ref#280) and his Honorable Discharge certificate ("21-5/12 years of age" at enlistment, actually 18) (ref#211). He may have been enabled by the military's acceptance of a simple declaration by an enlistee rather than requiring separate documentary evidence. His motivation for lying is unknown, although the requirement for parents' permission for men younger than twenty-one to enlist may have influenced this action.

On Monday, June 26, 1916, Mamer took "the federal examination at Minneapolis." (ref#247, item 1) This presumably included a physical examination by a physician, as well as tests to determine general intelligence, knowledge and aptitude. According to the *Hastings Democrat* of July 6, 1916, (ref#247, item 2), "Out of twenty who took the examination, he was the only one that passed, and he stood 100 per cent (*sic*) in the mechanical section."

The sequence of training following enlistment is given in the *Hastings Democrat* article: "...he will receive instructions in the art of flying an aeroplane. After a number of months of training he will again be examined and if he passes he will be advanced to a position in the Aviation Section, similar to that of second lieutenant in the army with the same pay." (ref#247, item 2) The benefits listed possibly derive from recruitment advertising. Nick probably found them appealing.

The next evidence of military status is a July roster of the army's "School Detachment of the Aviation Section" in San Diego. Its heading reads "ENLISTED MEN

WHO ARE TO BE ACCOUNTED FOR BY NAME." Mamer is number eleven in a list of seventeen "PRIVATES Joined fr Recruit Depot" (ref#53). The date behind his name is July 19, 1916, more than two weeks after his enlistment. It's unclear where he was during the interim.

The full text of the May 9, 1919 article on Mamer's military service in the *Hastings Democrat* follows:

> "Second Lieut. Nicholas B. Mamer, reserve military aviator, arrived here Sunday [May 4, 1919] on a visit with his mother, Mrs. Mary Mamer, on East Seventh Street, after an absence of three years. He left Hastings in June, 1916, enlisting at Minneapolis, in the aviation section, signal corps, (*sic*) sent to San Diego, Cal., and attached there to the 1st aero squadron, (*sic*) and in September of that year transferred to New Mexico, remaining on the Mexican border until January, 1917, and then sent to the Panama Canal zone where he served as aerial patrol engineer, and in June 1918, was sent to the officers' training camp at Princeton, N.J. and from thence assigned to Camp Dix, Dallas, Tex., being commissioned second lieutenant, (*sic*) November, 6th, 1918 and since November 28th, of last year [1918], has been engaged as flying instructor at Kelley Field, Tex." (ref#247, item 3)

Disregarding the misplaced Camp Dix (it was in New Jersey) and "Kelley" Field for Kelly Field, the run-on sentence is a fair summary of Mamer's military sojourn. Less-obvious errors include: 1) Nick was commissioned as 2nd Lieutenant at Kelly Field on April 19, 1919, rather than at Camp Dix on November 6, 1918; and 2) the "officers' training camp at Princeton, N.J." should be correctly identified as the School of Military Aeronautics at Princeton University, Princeton, N.J.

The November 28, 1918 date as the start of his duty as a flying instructor in the *Hastings Democrat* differs slightly from the annotation on his Honorable Discharge indicating he completed "primary flying training" on November 30, 1918. This discrepancy may not be significant.

The association of the 1st Aero Squadron with New Mexico in the *Hastings Democrat* article is reasonable, since the 1st Aero Squadron spent more than a year there providing reconnaissance, scouting, intelligence and logistical support for General Pershing's forces pursuit of Pancho Villa during the period. [ref#131]

If we believe the date in the *Hastings Democrat* summary, Mamer arrived at the Canal Zone early in 1917 as the 7th Aero Squadron was being organized by Capt. H. H. Arnold. (ref#407) By March of 1917, the 7th consisted of 51 men. (refs#83, 133) However, it was hardly a flying defense for the Atlantic entrance to the Canal, since it was stationed on the Pacific side and it had no aircraft.

During March through May, the squadron moved from Ancon to Corozal to Empire, all on the Pacific side. (ref#83) Their duties are not known. Not until August did the squadron take residence at Ft. Sherman at the Atlantic side of the Panama Canal. (ref#133) By this time, the U.S. had been at war for four months.

Little is known of Private Nick Mamer's activities on the Isthmus until October of 1917. On October 3, Maj. W. W. Wynne was named Commander of the 7th Aero Squadron. (ref#409) Ten days later, Private Mamer was promoted to Corporal. (ref#208) And, nine days after that, he flew for the first time as Observer with Major Wynne piloting a "practice flight." (ref#282-A) Apparently, Major Wynne early recognized Nick's contributions to the squadron. It was not until December, however, that the squadron received updated aircraft. On December 10th, two Curtiss R-4s were tested; at the end of the month, they received two R-3 seaplanes. (ref#83)

In the new year of 1918, the squadron finally moved operations from the parade grounds of Ft. Sherman across Limon Bay to a site that later became France Field Reservation, an actual airfield. (ref#133) Shortly thereafter, on February 22, they received Curtiss R-6s (supplied by the U.S.Navy). (ref#83) Not long after that, on March 1, Mamer was promoted to Sergeant, (ref#209) and on March 14, to Master Signal Electrician (M.S.E.). (ref#210)

It's clear from these rapid promotions that Nick was not only a skilled mechanic and responsible leader, but that he had gained the respect of the flying officers. According to a later letter from his Commander, he "acted as First Sergeant and Noncommissioned Officer in charge of flying and operation of hangars,"—obviously a heavy responsibility. (ref#206)

It was at this time (March 30, 1918) that M.S.E. Mamer petitioned the Chief Signal Officer in Washington to be placed "on flying status." (ref#280) His letter was accompanied by Major Wynne's memo to the Chief Signal Officer "recommending approval," while adding "I have examined Master Signal Electrician Nicholas B. Mamer, and find that he has all the qualifications prescribed by the Chief Signal Officer necessary to become a pilot." (ref#414)

During March, April, May and June of 1918, M.S.E. Mamer was regularly included as observer on flights with Lieutenants Burnight, Dawson, Winslow, Evans, and Malloway. (ref#282A) In mid-June Adjutant-General Henry P. McCain in Washington ordered Brigadier General Richard M. Blatchford, Commander of the Panama Canal Department, to send Master Signal Electrician Nicholas B. Mamer from the 7th Aero Squadron to the School of Military Aeronautics in Princeton, N. J. (ref#413) This order, a positive response to Nick's petition and Major Wynne's supporting memo, was followed by General Blatchford's order for Nick's reduction in grade and transport via New York to Princeton University (ref#413):

> "C.O., 7th Aero Squadron, Signal Corps, Cristobal, C.Z., who will in compliance with above instructions, reduce this noncommissioned officer to grade of private first class and send him to Princeton via New York City, by Panama Railroad Steamer, sailing from Cristobal, C.Z. on or about June 27, 1918...The Quartermaster Corps will furnish the necessary transportation. The journey is necessary for the public service. By command of Brigadier General Blatchford. (signed) Frank C. Wood, Capt., Acting Adjutant."

Three letters of recommendation, from 1st Lieutenant Winslow (ref#204), 1st

Lieutanant Dawson (ref#205), and Major Wynne (ref#206) attest to their support and the esteem Mamer had earned. This constituted a big win for Nick, who was willing to give up the equivalent of a Master Sergeant's rank, the added pay, and the approval he'd earned in the squadron, for the opportunity to become a military pilot.

Later in June, he got a chance to try his hand piloting. On three flights, with Lt. Malloway as observer, he was at the controls. (ref#282A) These piloting flights were probably intended as training exercises, and may have occurred in aircraft with dual controls.

He left the port of Cristobal, C.Z., on June 25 aboard the *S.S. Panama*, a Panama Railroad Steamer, and arrived in New York on July 13, 1918. He checked in the same day at the School of Military Aeronautics at Princeton University. (refs#63, 117)

A copy of the photograph of his graduating class from the School of Military Aeronautics at Princeton University (ref#252), courtesy of the Pioneer Room at Hastings, Minnesota, shows all 48 of the graduates stiffly attired in Army dress tunics with high collars, epaulets, and five buttons centered in front. They are arrayed closely in front of the entrance to what appears to be a college building, between two large outdoor lamps.

Each man wears a small button on his left chest with a two-digit identifying number on it. They wear knee breeches and canvas puttee-gaiters that lace up over their calves and the top of their boots. One man in the front row has a wide-brimmed hat with its crown creased into four sections, on his lap. The men are mostly clean shaven, though a number of moustaches are seen.

Each man has been numbered 1 to 48 on the surface of the photograph, which numbers correspond to those on an accompanying sheet of names, labeled "PHOTOGRAPHS OF CLASS DUE TO GRADUTE OCTOBER 5, 1916." Nick, looking very sober, is number six. (ref#252)

From Princeton, Private Mamer was apparently processed through Camp Dix and sent to Kelly Field outside San Antonio, Texas, where he went through "primary flying training." His name appears in the "Roster of Detachment of Flying Cadets," in *Kelly Field in the Great World War* by Harry David Kroll. (ref#54)

He's described in a letter from Major L. A. Walton, "Officer in Charge of Flying" dated April 23, 1919 as having completed the "course required by a Reserve Military Aviator [R.M.A.] and is classified as a Pursuit Pilot." (ref#215)

Mamer's promotion to 2nd Lieutenant (ref#213) as of April 19, 1919 is well-documented (above). Ten days later, on May 1, he received his Honorable Discharge, with its notations regarding back pay and travel money. (ref#211)

18. The Stormer

The material on the formation and personnel of Federated Fliers, Inc., comes from two sources. The newspaper clipping in the MFA titled "Peterson Goes With the Federated Fliers" (ref#416) headlines the capture of the two Army Lieutenants (Harold Peterson and Paul H. Davis) by the Mexican bandits and their eventual rescue and return, with emphasis on Peterson, who had just joined Federated.

Much of the material on Federated (with the exception of the Peterson episode) is duplicated in the second reference, "Ten Most Important State Pioneers," February 1, 2014, by Noel Allard, accessed 5/9/2018 from the Internet edition of *Minnesota Flyer*, (ref#124), with one notable exception: The Peterson clipping spells the founder's surname as Hinch, rather than the correct Hinck.

Other differences between the references are minor, except the Peterson clipping states that Lt. Mamer joined Federated in June of 1918 rather than the actual year of 1919. The addition of Rask and Tattersfield to Federated's pilot roster is covered only in the Peterson clipping, while the Allard article adds Al and Clarence Opsal, and Elmer Hinck, three pilots not mentioned in the Peterson clipping.

An interesting sidelight is that the Peterson clipping refers to Mamer as "one of the old timers (sic) in the flying game," although Nick was just 21 years old, had received his R.M.A. from the Army only a few months before, and had been flying as a pilot for less than a year.

Most of the information on the JN-4 "Jenny" is from *Wikipedia* on the Internet, (ref#418). Originally built by the Curtiss Aeroplane and Motor Company, many were built by other firms during and after WWI. Because thousands were sold after the war at bargain prices, the Jenny is referred to in the article as the "backbone of American postwar [civil] aviation." The article points out that the lack of regulation fostered the stunt flying and aerobatic displays of the barnstorming era, in which the Jenny was a major factor.

The reference to Mamer as winning the prize of $600 (and a silver cup) at the Minnesota State Fair on September 4, 1919 comes from the *Hastings Democrat* of Friday, Sept. 12, 1919, headed "'Nick' Mamer, King of Flyers." His August trip under the "High Bridge" at Hastings is from the *Hastings Gazette* of Friday, August 8, 1919, (ref#247, item 24).

The collision of Pete Rask's airplane with Mamer is from *St. Paul Pioneer Press*, Friday, Sept. 5, 1919 in the article headed, "Aerial Derby Starts Boom to Bring All-American Event Here Next Year," which described the success of the derby and stunt contest the day before during the State Fair. This article (ref#247, item 21) also repeats some of the material given in ref#247, item 24, above.

Nick Mamer's employ with United States Air Craft Corporation, C. H. Messer, President, is from the original typed and signed agreement in the MFA (ref#420). It is signed by Messer and Mamer, dated April 9, 1920, and signed by witness C. E. Robinson.

Clarence W. Hinck, President of Federated Fliers, Inc., on his letterhead, composed the typed letter of April 15, 1920, lauding Nick's service. The original is in the MFA, (ref#415). Headed "TO WHOM IT MAY CONCERN," and signed "Very truly yours C. W. Hinck," it is the source of all the quotations beginning "...his purpose in leaving our company..."

Mamer's stunt, including the landing and take-off of Vamp on Main Street, Kalispell, Montana is from two newspaper clippings of July 16, 1920 in the MFA, (ref#419). Vamp is believed to have been a new Lincoln-Standard airplane in the United States Air Craft Corporation's fleet of the time.

C. H. Messer's quotations on stunts by United States Air Craft Corporation pilots and descriptions of the stunts themselves are from two unidentified and un-dated newspaper clippings in the MFA, (ref#421). The first is headed "NEW AIR STUNTS FOR LOCAL FANS." The second is headed "HANGS BY TOES FROM AIRPLANE."

The plunge into the Spokane River is from two sources: The August 30, 1922 SDC, page 1, with banner "AIRPLANE PLUNGES INTO RIVER," (ref#423) and the August 31, 1922 SR story headed, "HE MISSES DEATH, BUT IS ARRESTED" (ref#424).

The SDC "Airplane Plunges" in the MFA retains the banner headline with a large, above-the-fold, photograph (by Nelson) showing the upended airplane stuck, tail up, in the water. The SDC's abbreviated story—the crash occurred just hours earlier—appears in the caption below the photograph. It incorrectly identifies the mechanic as Bobbie Anderson instead of Robert Henderson, but furnishes the time (1:30 p. m.).

The SR story that appeared the day after the crash provided most of the details for the story. To the crash narrative it adds the "arrest" story. It is also from the MFA. According to the SR article, Mamer said the airplane's motor quit because rain had short-circuited its ignition system. The airplane was disassembled and returned to the Foster Russel airfield. (Note: The O.W.R. & N. in the story is the Oregon Washington Railroad & Navigation Company.)

Mamer's aerial displays over Newman Lake for the benefit of Faye Carey, Nick's future wife, is taken from a newspaper clipping in a scrapbook from the MFA, next to which appears, in a neat handwriting, "July – 1921 – When Faye was at Newman lake for vacation – Nick dropped Notes & flowers every afternoon – (We kept his identity a secret from the Spokane Newsboys -)"

The clipping, creased and torn, but pasted with care, is headed "Out of the Sky Each Day Parachutes with Flowers and Letters Are Dropped" (ref#245). It is quoted in full.

Information on the wedding of Faye and Nick is from the original Marriage Certificate, No. 10031, dated July 7, 1923, in the MFA (ref#235), signed by Clergyman F. C. Whitney, N. B. Mamer, Faye Carey Mamer, and witnesses Mr. and Mrs. Chas. A. Martin.

A newspaper clipping of a photograph of the newly-married couple standing next to an open-cockpit, 2-place airplane is included in the MFA, (ref#422). On the left of the photograph is Mrs. Mamer in a printed, over-the-knee frock with a sash. It looks like she is wearing white shoes. She wears a short leather flying jacket and a leather helmet, unfastened, topped by flying goggles. Nick stands to her left, arms folded. He wears flying jodhpurs, knee-high lace-up boots, and a cardigan over his sport shirt. His unfastened leather helmet is topped by flying goggles.

The clipping is captioned, above the photo, "SPENT HONEYMOON IN THE CLOUDS." Below the photo is an eleven-line description, beginning, "A honeymoon in the clouds was spent by Pilot and Mrs. Nick B. Mamer, who are shown here with their airplane upon their return to Spokane, where they will make their home." This description is the source of the other marriage-related material.

19. Earthquake, Wildfires, a Prizefight

The Great Kanto Earthquake of Japan occurred September 1, 1923. The estimated death toll of 140,000 is almost nine times greater than deaths during the more recent Japan earthquake and tsunami at Fukushima on March 11, 2011. "The Great Japan Earthquake of 1923" by Joshua Hammer, in the online *Smithsonian* Magazine, May, 2011(ref#425) provides a good summary of the 1923 earthquake, fires and tsunami.

Because the facility for transmitting images was very limited in 1923, considerable delay was experienced in communicating the magnitude and extent of the disaster. Mamer quickly found himself engaged to speed the transport of both still photographs and movie films by air.

Undated and unidentified newspaper clippings from the MFA on his trip to Salt Lake include one headed "MAMER FLIES WITH EARTHQUAKE FILMS," (ref#426). A second clipping is headed "FLYERS TO RUSH FILMS OF QUAKE," and a third "MAMER HAS LUCK ON PHOTO TRIP," (ref#427). Mamer was under contract to both *The New York Times* and *Wide World Magazine* for this service. In the first clip he is said to describe the trip as "a tough ride, through forest fire smoke and adverse winds."

The $50,000 cost figure for transporting moving pictures of the disaster to New York is from page 26 of the *St. Louis Post-Dispatch* of September 25, 1923, headed "PLANE SPEEDING EASTWARD WITH JAPANESE QUAKE FILMS," where it is called, "a race across the continent," (ref#429). On the same date, the *Springfield Leader and Press* headlined the story "HEAVY STAKES FOR AVIATORS IN FILM RACE" on a page 1 story datelined Great Falls, Montana, (ref#428). It describes the race: "The prize for which the rival pilots are competing is that of being the first to take to New York the moving picture films of the Japanese earthquake disaster." Other details came from the *Great Falls Tribune* (Montana) of the same date, on page 12 (ref#430).

The story of Mamer locating the body of Pearl Romelly, or Romilly, is from three undated and unidentified Spokane newspaper clippings (ref#431) in the MFA. One includes a double banner headline, "AIRPLANE PILOT FINDS BODY OF GIRL DROWNED IN THE SPOKANE RIVER." A second is headed, "AIRPLANE PILOT LOCATES BODY OF DROWNED GIRL FROM MID-AIR," and a third, in which the name is spelled Romilly, is headed, "AVIATOR FINDS DROWNED GIRL." The girl's age is also given as 16 or 17.

Four newspaper clippings from the MFA are sources for the 1923 Potlatch Timber Association aerial patrol story (ref#432). One, believed to be from the *Coeur d'Alene Evening Press* of March 3, 1923 is headed, "CONTRACT FOR AERIAL PATROL." Other details come from undated and unidentified clippings headed "USE PLANES FOR FOREST PATROL," "START AERIAL FOREST PATROL OVER ASSOCIATION'S TIMBER," and "FOREST PATROL PLANE IS IN COEUR D'ALENE."

Much of the information on the prizefight in Shelby, Montana comes from "Dempsey vs. Gibbons: 'The Fight that Ruined a Town'", by Norman Marcus, dated

November 21, 2012, on the boxing.com website. Mamer's transport of the photos is from an undated *Spokane Press* newspaper clipping in the MFA headed, "AVIATOR RISKS LIFE TO BRING FIGHT PHOTOS" (ref#434), which also displays two photos of the fight under the heading "FIRST FIGHT PHOTOS." The road situation was derived from *Paved Roads of the Nation*, the Clason Map Company, 1924, p.40.

Appointment of Nick Mamer as forest fire patrol pilot for the United States Forest Service in 1925 is from "Missoula Smokejumpers History Facts, Early Aerial Recon" on the Missoula Smokejumpers' Fire and Aviation Management website (ref#318) and from *The Static Line* (National Smokejumpers Association), vol. 3 Quarterly, July 1998, Edition 5, (ref#68). The DH-4B information is from *Smithsonian* National Postal Museum site, "The de Havilland DH-4" by Nancy A. Pope, April, 2004, (ref#319). The (USFS Photo) photograph of the U. S. Forest Fire Patrol DeHavilland DH-4B is from *Touch & Go* (Society for Aviation History), newsletter p.36, on the Society's website. Other information is from an unidentified newspaper clipping from the MFA dated August 1, 1925 and headed "MUST TELL JUST WHERE EVERY FOREST FIRE IS," (ref#317)

Two undated and unidentified newspaper clippings from the MFA supplied information on aerial photography (ref#435): One is headed "PILOT NICK MAMER, SUPERVISOR FLINT, PHOTOGRAPH FIRE-DAMAGED FOREST," the second, "TO FILM RUINS OF FOREST FIRE."

Mamer's plans for the future are derived from an undated and unidentified newspaper clipping from the MFA headed "LT. MAMER WINS FAME WITH EX-PLOITS," (ref#436).

20. Races, Crashes, and an Air Circus

The wire quote "Big DH with 400-..." is from an unidentified newspaper clipping in the MFA with the heading "MAMER STARTS FLIGHT NORTH" and subhead "Landed at Hollywood Last Night—Continues Trip Today" (ref#437). The remainder of the Easterbrook and Mamer flight is from two other unidentified newspaper clippings in the Mamer archives: One headed "AIRPLANE FORCED DOWN" with a subhead "Landing Made by Spokane Fliers Near Hubbard, Or." and a second headed "BIG PLANE LANDS IN OREGON FOG" with a subhead "Aviators Bringing De Haviland [sic] Machine Here Fly Low" (ref#437).

The news photograph of Major John Fancher, Captain Lawrence Albert and Nick Mamer is from an unidentified newspaper clipping in the MFA. It is headed "UP IN THE AIR AGAIN—FIRST TIME SINCE WAR" with subhead "Commander of National Guard Unit Finds the Air of Spokane Something Like That Over German Lines" (ref#438).

The September 20, 1925 air circus and death of Lt. Schuyler Priestley is from *One Man's Opinion of the Spokane Aviation Story*, J. P. McGoldrick II, Ye Galleon Press, Fairfield, Washington, 1982, pp. 69-72, (ref#114).

The crash of Mamer and two students in the Alexander Eaglerock aircraft is from four sources. Unidentified clippings from the MFA are 1) headed "2000-Foot Fall in Plane Doesn't Halt Day's Work, and 2) headed "FALLS 2000 FEET; MAMER IS UNHURT" with subhead "Plane Carries Three Passengers Safely Through Harrowing Dash" dated Wednesday, June 23, 1926, (ref#440). The E. Harve Partridge article headed "Spokane, Washington" is from *Aviation*, July 12, 1926, p.68 (ref#440). The fourth source is a typed draft of a letter with handwritten annotations, dated July 3, 1926 and signed by "N. B. Mamer," addressed to "Editor, *Aviation*, 225 Fourth Ave., New York City," with a return address "N. B. Mamer, Airplane Forest Patrol, 211 Trent, Spokane, Wash." (ref#258). It is unclear whether Mamer mailed this letter (ref#258), or any letter to the Editor of *Aviation* magazine. My search of *Aviation*'s archives for Mamer in 1926 came up null.

In his letter, Mamer credits the Eaglerock's handling as "one of the nicest performing jobs I have flown." He blames the loading conditions for the spin: "[It] is due I understand by the flying center of gravity being too far to the rear." As for the inability to stop the spin: "The prop blast isn't forceful enough to reach the tail. The control surfaces are absolutely helpless..." (ref#258)

It is impossible to know how far the fliers were above ground when they leaped to safety. Mamer's letter says 20 feet (above), but E. Harve Partridge, in *Aviation*, said it was 10 feet.

The initial downward speed of the men at the instant they leap free of the aircraft would approximate that of the falling airplane. In his letter, Mamer credits the slow descent of the craft for the fliers' survival: "the vertical speed was estimated to be about equivalent to parachute speed," meaning about the same speed as that of a parachutist in a round, 1926 parachute at the moment of impact. (A round parachute produces much higher impact force upon landing than a properly-deployed modern parachute such as those used in skydiving.)

Once free of the aircraft, the men who jumped were subject to the acceleration of gravity. Jumping off a ledge from a height of six feet is sometimes considered the equivalent of a "hard" landing in a (round) parachute. Thus even if the fliers' height above ground were only ten feet at the time of their jump, they could easily have sustained sprains, broken bones or worse. It is therefore remarkable that all three escaped unhurt—"without a scratch."

Partridge's estimate of ten feet, however, is minimal, considering the geometry of the plane's impact with overhead wires and the railroad track. The men's surprise at surviving unhurt is therefore warranted, although Mamer's later quote that the 2,000-foot fall was "rather exciting," says more about the aviator's bravado than it does about the spin/crash.

It appears possible the men's impact may have been reduced to sustainable levels by what I will term a 'glide' conversion. Today's skydivers reduce their impact with the ground by this technique: when approaching the ground, the skydiver manipulates the parachute's control lines in a manner that converts the skydiver's downward momentum into a (nearly) horizontal glide. Momentum is conserved, but energy that would otherwise appear as downward force—a hard landing—is instead converted to kinetic energy parallel to the ground—a glide.

This process, converting downward momentum into horizontal energy, however, requires auxiliary action. The skydiver, by manipulation of the parachute's control lines, alters the aerodynamics of the parachute (the auxiliary action), and thus the momentum vector. A somewhat similar auxiliary action may have occurred during the final phase of Mamer's crash when the wing contacted the overhead wires.

Assuming a wing contacted the wire(s) of the power line before the aircraft contacted the ground (and thus before the electric arc), it provided a substantial lever arm (the Eaglerock's wingspans were more than thirty feet). Contact of a wing with the wire, combined with the rotating and descending aircraft, might have forced the airframe into a substantial sideways motion. In a manner analogous to the skydiver's skilled manipulation, this motion might have forced the aircraft's downward momentum to occur largely or partly as horizontal kinetic energy, analogous to the skydiver's 'glide.'

Thus, if the men were in fact swung sideways at the time they leaped clear of the plane, they might have experienced less forceful impacts with the ground, resulting in the lack of injury that was observed. This is at least a plausible scenario for how a spin from 2,000 feet resulted in three men surviving a fiery crash "without a scratch."

Patricia Ann Mamer's birth and comments are from Ancestry.com (ref#62) and from an unidentified newspaper clipping in the MFA headed "NEW AIR PILOT AT MAMER HOME" (ref#435).

Lieutenant James Buell Felts death and the naming of Felts Field is from Mc-Goldrick's book (above), p. 96. (ref#114) and from Robert Lambeth's blog post of Monday, November 19, 2012, "Felts Field" (ref#14).

The background of the 1927 National Air Derby and Air Races in Spokane is from the SR site, www. Spokesman.com, "Spokane takes flight," by Jim Kershner, published Oct. 8, 2006, (ref#56/445); from HistoryLink.org Essay 7924, "Spokane hosts National Air Derby and Air Races beginning on Sept. 21, 1927", Laura Arksey, posted August 31, 2006 (ref#182); and from McGoldrick's book (above), pp. 95-96, (ref#114).

The photo of Nick in his Swallow is from an unidentified newspaper clipping in the MFA labeled "Type of Plane Mamer Will Fly in Air Derby," (ref#441). It was powered by the Curtiss OX-5 motor. Juptner discusses the design at length on pp. 66-68, *U.S. Civil Aircraft Series, Volume 1*, Joseph P. Juptner, 1993, (ref#307). The label on this news photograph is misleading because the airplane Nick flew in the 1927 Derby was a Buhl Airster powered by a radial Wright Whirlwind, rather than the water-cooled OX-5 as in the Swallow.

Jimmy Doolittle earned a doctorate in aeronautical science, and later would pioneer "blind flying," or the art of safely navigating a route without reference to anything more than the instruments in the airplane's cockpit. He went on to military glory, especially for the famous WWII raid on Tokyo, Japan. Doolittle's feats and background are described and mapped in *The Aviators*, Winston Groom, 2013, (ref#444). His stunt flyover of downtown Spokane is from Laura Arksey's HistoryLink Essay above (ref#182) in which she writes he "buzzed downtown Spokane upside down in one of his trademark 'loops.'"

Charles A. Lindbergh's famous flight to Paris and subsequent developments, including a map that shows his 1927 visit to Spokane, comes from *The Spectacle of Flight: Aviation and the Western Imagination*, Robert Wohl, 2005, (ref#159); his visit is also pictured in McGoldrick's book (above) on p. 84 (ref#114).

The 1927 Derby race information is from "Spokane Air Derbies a big hit in 1927," Dennis Parks, Nov. 8, 2015 on the aviationnews.com website, (ref#17), the Laura Arksey article (above), (ref#182), and McGoldrick's book (above), p.100, (ref#114). "Airplanes Race to Spokane!", by Brian Shute, in *Nostalgia Magazine*, September-October 2010 issue, pp. 24-33, contains useful information on the Derby, but misidentifies Mamer's 1927 race companion as Art Walker (it was Bruce McDonald), and misidentifies the 1927 airplane as the Sun God (the Sun God was a special Buhl Airsedan CA-6 first delivered to Felts Field from the Buhl factory in 1929 and subsequently flown on the 1929 record flight). Consult the Appendix for discussion of how the Sun God has been confused with other airplanes in reports and articles.

The 1927 race results are from the Dennis Parks General Aviation News article (above), (ref#17) and from *Aviation* magazine, October 3, 1927, p. 306 fol.,"C. W. Holman Wins Class A Derby" (ref#160), and from McGoldrick's book (above), p. 95, (ref#114). The winning time for C. W. Holman of 19 hours, 42 minutes is misstated in the *General Aviation News* as 16 hours, 42 minutes. The *Aviation* article includes a photograph of Mamer and McDonald standing in front of Mamer's third-place Buhl Airster. Other photographs of the race are included in the MFA (ref#442).

The loss of the tire from Holman's airplane and other incidents at Butte are from unidentified, September 1927 newspaper clippings in the MFA (ref#443). Apparently, the tire was observed flat during Holman's stop for gas, but was not repaired.

The death of Major John Fancher is from "A bomb explosion fatally injures Spokane pioneer aviator Major John T. Fancher during an air show in East Wenatchee on April 29, 1928", Jim Kershner, Sept. 26, 2010, HistoryLink.org Essay 9555.

Information on the 1928 National Air Derby and National Air Races and Mamer's participation is from the SDC, Sept. 13, 1928, from *The Casper Herald*, Casper Wyoming, Sept. 14 (ref#448) and 15, 1928, (ref#405), *The Denver Evening News*, Sept 14, 1928 (ref#449) and from the *New York Daily News*, Sept. 13, 1928, (ref#447) all of which are in the MFA, folder A#7. This folder also contains black-and-white photographs of Mamer's aircraft, the peculiarly-modified Buhl Airsedan with the 300-gallon tank in the front, and the pilot's control station far back in the Airsedan's cabin.

George Kivel's report in the *New York Daily News* was particularly helpful. This edition of the New York paper also furnished the p.2 photograph that showed Nick's takeoff from Roosevelt Field., the trailing dust cloud, the crowds and the parked cars.

21. Tin Geese to Sky Future

Much of the St. Paul-Seattle-St. Paul record flight of 1930 is from the July 19, 1930 SR headlined "MAMER WINS; FLIES ST. PAUL TO SEATTLE, DAY ROUND TRIP" (ref#458). The airplane involved, the Buhl CA-1 sport model designed as a racer by Etienne Dormoy (ref#20), was one-of-a-kind. It was a low-wing, single-seat, open cockpit, "streamlined" airplane with a cowled motor. *Wikipedia* (ref#462) indicates a second CA-1 was built with two tandem seats, but neither of them sold. The MFA holds two photographs from Mamer's flight which shows the single-seater with installed wheel spats shaped like teardrops. Other coverage is from the July 19, 1930, *Seattle Post-Intelligencer* "MAMER MAKES ST. PAUL ROUND TRIP IN 24 HRS" (ref#459).

The Spoils Conference and subsequent Airmail Scandal were included in this Chapter because they explain the government's influence in the early development of the airlines in the U.S. My coverage is from a paper by Grant Cates, "Airmail and the Evolution of the U.S. Aviation Industry in the 1920s and 1930s," presented at the May 2, 2000 Space Congress, and from airlinefiles.com, the article titled "Air Mail scandal" (ref#457).

Mamer's second-place finish in the 1930 Derby race is from *The Dayton Herald*, Aug. 26, 1930 (ref#492)

The nonstop record flight of 1928 is from an unidentified St. Paul newspaper clipping, probably Oct. 24, 1928, in the MFA headlined "NICK MAMER BLAZES TRAIL FROM COAST," (ref#465) and from an Associated Press story in SR dated October 24, 1928 headlined "MAMER SUCCEEDS IN NONSTOP HOP" (ref#466). Mamer was returning the special Airsedan flown in the 1928 race to the Buhl factory in Marysville, Michigan. Mrs. C. I. Paulsen left Mamer in St. Paul and continued on to Cincinnati, Ohio. It is surprising that the news coverage failed to note the irony of Mrs. Paulsen riding with Nick on this journey while Mr. Paulsen's planned ride with Nick the previous month at Roosevelt Field was abandoned on the ground.

Purchase of the Ford Tri-Motor "West Wind," and the tour that followed are from the gray linen-bound, 142-page blank ledger in which Nick pasted news clippings during the 1929 tour. It is from the MFA, labeled by hand in ink "MAMER-FORD TOUR of the TRI-MOTOR WEST-WIND," and retains a pencil inscription "PRESS BOOK" on its cover. The pages are numbered from 1 to 148 including the inside front and rear covers. Pages 22-25 have been inserted (glued in) and were not bound in the original binding. They were inserted later, apparently to accommodate clippings from the *Miles City Star* (Miles City, Montana). These inserted clippings are also identified with a different handwriting (not Nick's).

This volume contains an estimated three-hundred clippings. Clippings on the first four-dozen or so pages are identified and dated in Nick's handwriting in pencil. Few of the remainder are identified or dated. (ref#453, 454, 456, 460, 463, 464, 469)

The Mamer flying school information comes from the school's twelve-page printed brochure in the MFA labeled "MAMER Air Transport Approved School of Flying" (ref#489). The brochure contains course descriptions, prices, and other details. It apparently dates from 1929 or 1930. The graduation rate from the school is from a Spokane newspaper clipping of unknown date in the MFA headed "VAST GAINS IN AVIATION MADE AT SPOKANE FIELD" (ref#488).

Although not much is known of Nick's finances, he apparently lost money in the market crash of October, 1929. Some information comes from "Saga of the Spokane Sun God," by William Schulze in Sunday's PICTORIAL REVIEW, January 26, 1964, *Seattle Post-Intelligencer,* (ref#75). On p.7, the article quotes Mrs. Leo Lee—Nick's daughter Patricia Ann—saying Nick "did lose 'a great deal of money' in the stock market crash."

Mrs. Lee is also quoted as saying, "My father hardly ever smiled." This characterization conflicts with recollections by others as well as numerous photos showing

Nick's smile, but may reflect what his daughter, almost aged 12 years at his death, recalled of her father during her formative years (ref#75).

The depression discussion is from *Daily Life in the United States, 1920-1940*, David E. Kyvig, Ivan R. Dee, Chicago, 2002, revised 2004, especially Chapter 10, "Crisis: The Impact of the Great Depression" (ref#470). Activities during this period are from *The Missoula Sentinel*, Feb. 8, 1930, headlined "MISSOULA IS ON AIR LINE" (ref#471), and from *St. Paul Daily News*, June 15, 1930, headed "ST. PAUL BECOMES AVIATION HUB WITH NEW SERVICE TO SPOKANE" (ref#472). The government appropriation of 1930 is from *Billings Gazette*, Nov. 19, 1933, headed "NICK MAMER, SPOKANE PILOT OF SUN GOD FAME, LAYS OUT EMERGENCY STATE PORTS" (ref#481).

The September 11, 1930 crash is from *Billings Gazette*, Sept. 12, 1930, headed "MAMER AIRLINE PLANE WRECKED AT IDAHO PORT" (ref#473).

Mamer Air Transport's cessation of operation is from *Billings Gazette*, Nov. 22, 1930, (ref#474) and from Frank Wiley's book, *Montana and the Sky*, p. 223 (ref#115). Possible resumption of the St. Paul service is from *The Missoulian*, Mar. 23, 1931, headed by "Spokane-Seattle Air Service Will Be Doubled Soon" (ref#476). The forest service bid is from *The Montana Standard*, May 13, 1931, headed "MAMER AIR TRANSPORT LOW BIDDER ON FOREST PATROL WORK IN WEST" (ref#477). The observer (Jack Jost) and lack of regular trips are from *The Montana Standard*, July 26, 1931, headed "Airplanes Used to Spot Forest Fires When Smoke Is Too Thick for Lookouts" (ref#478). The meeting with Dempsey is from *The Eugene Guard*, Sept. 4, 1931, (ref#479).

The 1932-33 depression news is from Kyvig, *Daily Life in the United States, 1920-1940*, Ivan R. Dee, Chigago, 2002, revised 2004 (ref#470). Mamer's optimistic plan is from an unidentified and undated (likely 1932) newspaper clipping from the MFA headed "MAMER SAYS FAST PLANES AID TRAVEL" and "Development of Northern Airway Foreseen by Veteran Pilot" (ref#475).

The 1933 Ferguson report is from *The Sunday Missoulian*, Nov. 19, 1933, headed "AIRWAYS ADVANCE MISSOULA ROUTE" (ref#480). The Mamer quote about emergency fields is from *The Billings Gazette*, Nov. 19, 1933 (above) (ref#481).

Croil Hunter's announcement is from *The Minneapolis Star*, Nov. 20, 1933, headed "NEW N.W. AIRWAYS CRUISERS ARE FAST" (ref#482). Mamer's first flight for Northwest into Seattle is from an unidentified and undated clipping from the MFA headed "WHO'S WHO IN AIR" and "Nick Mamer Pioneer Pilot" (ref#483). The second Croil Hunter announcement is from *Billings Gazette*, Dec. 7, 1933, headed "AIRWAY OFFICER ANNOUNCES NEW FAST SCHEDULE" and "Seattle-Spokane Link Marks End of Long Fight for Through Northwest Service" (ref#484).

The airmail statistics for 1933 and Roosevelt's action are from airlinefiles.com, the article titled "Air Mail scandal." The Army's tragic response and the public outcry are from *The Aviators*, Winston Groom, National Geographic Society, 2013, p.177-79, (ref#444).

Mamer's Orion flight and Croil Hunter's "half-a-continent" remarks are from an undated (probably early 1934) Billings, Montana, newspaper clipping from the

MFA headed "NEW SPEED SHIP OF NORTHWEST AIRWAYS IN CITY" and "MAMER BRINGS CRAFT TO CITY" (ref#485).

Sale of the Tri-Motors, attendance at the honoring dinner, etc., is from unidentified and undated newspaper clippings from the MFA: One is headed "MAMER PLANES GO ADVENTURING", a second, "Fords Sail Skies of Guatemala and Alaska" (ref#490), and a third, "MAMER RETAINS FLYING SCHOOL" (ref#491).

Nick's remarks celebrating his 10,000 hours in the air are from SR, July 5, 1936, headed "MILLIONTH MILE FOR NICK MAMER" and "Friends of Famous Pilot Give Glimpses of Career He Won't Talk About" (ref#217). The *Northwest Airliner*, a glossy magazine put out by Northwest Airlines (probably in 1936) is from the MFA (ref#486). It is the source of the Mamer profile quote.

22. The Final Flight

The flight, timing, and radio call are from "NICK MAMER, EARLY AERIAL FIRE PATROL PILOT," in *The Static Line* quarterly of the National Smokejumpers Association, Vol. 3, July 1998, Edition 5 (ref#68). The crash is from *Early Aviation Disasters*, David Gero, The History Press (UK), p.52-53 (ref#37) and from the Gen-Disasters Internet site, "Bozeman, MT Plane Crash, Jan 1938" (ref#493). The weather is from an unidentified newspaper clipping dated Jan. 19, 1938 from the MFA datelined Bozeman, Mont., Jan. 18, 1938, and headed "SKIES WERE BAD, BOARD IS TOLD", (ref#494).

Those killed, besides Nick B. Mamer, pilot and Frederick W. West, Jr., copilot, were T. Anderson, I. E. Stevenson, G. A. Anderson, L. Levin, Walter Ton, A. Croonquist, Douglas McKay, and W. E. Borgenheimer.

The airplane information is from *Early Aviation Disasters* (above) (ref#37), from *Wikipedia*, "Model 14 Super Electra," (ref#495) and from a MFA newspaper clipping, Seattle Post-Intelligencer of January 11, 1938 (no dateline) headed "Airliner Falls Near Bozeman; Nick Mamer Pilot" (ref#498). The latter reference contains a cutaway drawing illustrating the interior of "the eleven-passenger 'Sky Zephyr' of *Northwest Airlines*." (The Lockheed 14-H is variously stated as seating 9 to 14 passengers, probably depending upon the configuration of the cabin.)

The crash site search parties, posting of guards, and photographs are from a MFA newspaper clipping, *The Seattle Daily Times*, datelined Bozeman, Mont., Tuesday, Jan. 11, 1938 (AP), and headlined "FIRST AIR CRASH PHOTOS" (ref#496). One photo shows Coroner Howard Nelson "as he brushed snow from a fragment of sleeve to identify Pilot Nick Mamer." A second photo shows two men near the snow-covered wreckage.

The grounding of the Lockheed 14-Hs, partial inquest results and the schedule for the board of investigation is from MFA newspaper clipping, *Seattle Post-Intelligencer* of Jan. 13, 1938 (no dateline) headed "LINE GROUNDS NEW AIRPLANES PENDING PROBE" (ref#261). This clipping also includes photographs headlined "WHERE 10 DIED IN PLANE CRASH," one of which shows about twenty men (also a horse), behind the pile of wreckage. Its caption includes the following: "The plane landed on its nose, telescoped to its tail, then turned over, as shown here." Close examination of the photo, however, shows the tail of the aircraft upright, rather than "turned over." The horizontal stabilizer is clearly visible, together with the extreme rear part of the fuselage and both of the rounded lower sections of the vertical stabilizers. This photograph confirms the absence of the vertical stabilizers from the tail of the crashed airplane, a clear indicator of an anomaly.

More results of the inquest are from the *Independent-Record* (Helena, Montana) of Jan. 13, 1938 datelined Bozeman, Jan. 12, 1938 (AP), headlined "PLANE CRASH INQUEST IS OPENED; SAID ALL KILLED BEFORE BLAZE BROKE OUT" (ref#497).

The certificate of death for Nick Mamer is from the MFA (ref#51). The burial site is from the APPLICATION FOR HEADSTONE dated March 22, 1938 from the MFA (ref#52).

Faye's illness and the funeral information for Nick is from the MFA newspaper clipping, *Seattle Post-Intelligencer*, probably Jan. 14, 1938 (no dateline), headed "MAMER FUNERAL TO BE SATURDAY" (ref#260). The telegram quoted from Faye Mamer to James Mamer is from the MFA (ref#499). We do not know how Faye became aware, on Jan. 11, the day following the accident, of "mechanical trouble of new ship."

Telegrams of condolence are from the MFA, and the Governor's call for a memorial is from a MFA unidentified and undated newspaper clipping datelined Spokane, Jan. 14, 1938 (AP) headed "Mamer Memorial Urged by Martin" (ref#502). Additional funeral information is from a MFA unidentified and undated newspaper clipping datelined Seattle, Jan. 15, 1938 (AP) headed "MOURN AT BIER OF NICK MAMER" (ref#511).

Board of inquiry, radio condition, radio "beam," and Niemeyer's testimony, "I soon found..." are from a MFA unidentified and undated newspaper clipping datelined Bozeman, Mont., Jan. 20, 1938 (AP) headed "MAMER'S PLANE SHOOK OFF BITS" (ref#502). The futile search for the missing parts and Whittemore's testimony, "He was rated..." are from (ref#494, above). The engines' conditions and Gerschler's testimony, "the Lockheed Company..." are from the *Montana Standard* newspaper of Jan. 21, 1938 datelined Bozeman, Jan. 20, 1938 (AP) headed "GONE BEFORE SHIP HIT" (ref#501).

The questioning of pilot Smith and the further testimony of Niemeyer on his prior trip in a plane of the same type are from "MAMER'S PLANE SHOOK OFF BITS" (ref#502, above). Gerschler's testimony "I am quite sure...", K. O. Larson's agreement, and Gerschler's telephone call to Lockheed are all from (ref#262, above).

Niemeyer's testimony, "There were holes..." is from the *Arizona Republic*, Jan. 21, 1938 datelined Bozeman, Mont., Jan. 20, 1938 (AP) headed "Tail Assembly Blamed For 10-Death Crack-Up" (ref#503).

The $50 reward offer is from a MFA unidentified newspaper clipping dated Jan. 20, 1939 datelined Bozeman, Mont., Jan. 19, 1938, headed "REWARD POSTED FOR PLANE TAIL" (ref#504). The first finding, a rudder, is from a MFA unidentified and undated newspaper clipping datelined Bozeman, Mont., Feb. 7, 1938 (AP) headed "Rudder of Wrecked N. W. Plane Found" (ref#502, above). The second finding is from the *Casper Star-Tribune* of Feb. 20, 1938, datelined Bozeman, Mont., Feb. 19, 1938, headed "Section of Tail Assembly Found" (ref#505).

Added information on the Lockheed 14-H airplane is from the *Wikipedia* (ref#495, above). The "twisting motion" is from the earlier Niemeyer quote regarding his prior trip in a plane of the same type. The analysis of the airplane's compromised stability and the pilots' hypothetical countering actions is from the author's engineering background and aeronautical experience. Others' analyses and theories may differ.

Rancher Diteman's observation "I first saw the plane..." is from the *Seattle Post-Intelligencer* of Jan. 11, 1938 (no dateline) headed "SEATTLE PLANE CRASHES NEAR BOZEMAN; 9 DIE" (ref#512). I have altered the order of the sentences, which the newspaper reported partly in reversed chronological order.

Mrs. Vogel's letter is from the MFA (ref#264). Mr. (Lt.) Winslow's letter is from the MFA (ref#263).

The Bureau of Air Commerce's pending authorization to resume is from the *Billings Gazette* of Feb. 9, 1938 datelined Washington, Feb. 8, 1938 (AP) headed "Northwest Airlines Starts Proving Runs" (ref#508).

The Internet letter of August, 1999 by Mary Lou Williams, Nick's niece, "about the Mamer family" is from an angelfire.com site (ref#167). Research was able to find only one lawsuit by heirs of victims, that by heirs of Walter Borgenheimer, filed Sept. 12, and reported in the *Billings Gazette* of Sept. 13, 1938 datelined Butte, Sept. 12, 1938, headed "File Crash Suit" (ref#509). Borgenheimer's heirs sued Northwest Airlines for $113,000; Carl Remmil, air lines inspector, was named co-defendant.

The Mamer memorial tower and dedication at Felts Field are from two MFA unidentified and undated newspaper clippings, one headed "W.P.A. Clock Memorial Will Honor Mamer" and the other a photograph of Faye and Patricia Mamer headed "Nick Mamer's Widow Attends Ceremony" (ref#506). Other information on the memorial is from the e-edition of the SR dated Sept. 20, 2007, headed "Felts Field clock honors aviator Nick Mamer" (ref#507). The bronze plaque inscriptions were recorded from personal observation (ref#375).

Nick Mamer's philosophy of aviation is excerpted from a MFA unidentified and undated newspaper clipping headed "VETERAN PILOT IS MISSOULA VISITOR" (ref#510), in which he addressed a question about the deaths of Army aviators after the Air Mail Scandal. I have changed the order of the sentences, but not the thought behind them.

23. Seeking the Sun God

The first Kellogg trip is from the *Battle Creek Enquirer* newspaper dated September 9, 1929 (no dateline) headed "Plane Which Spanned U. S. Twice Without a Stop, Is Visitor Here" (ref#513). The second Kellogg trip is from the *Battle Creek Enquirer* newspaper dated February 16, 1930 (no dateline) headed by "SKY-LINES: Notes About Kellogg Airport, etc." (ref#514).

The photo of the Sun God inside the St. Louis Arena in 1930 is from www.dawgshed.com, March 29, 2017, page 3590 of 4430, accessed November 14, 2018. The photo clearly shows the repainted Sun God and change from NR9628 to NC9628. (ref#523)

The dedication of Buhl Airport, sometimes called Buhl Field, in 1931 is from the *Port Huron Times Herald* (Michigan) of June 13, 1931 datelined "St. Clair (Michigan) June 13 under the banner "THOUSANDS ON FIELD TO SEE ALTITUDE FLIGHT" and headed "NOTED FLYERS HELP DEDICATE BUHL AIRPORT" (ref#515). The newspaper said Jack Story was the announcer for the day's program.

The Air Tour for the Ford Reliability Trophy is from Chapter VII, *The Ford Air Tours, 1925-1931* by Lesley Forden, 1972, Aviation Foundation of America (ref#15). The "intensive and exhaustive" is from (ref#515, above), and the Bull Pup information is from *Wikipedia*, "Buhl Bull Pup" (ref#517). Herbert Hughes obituary is from *Port Huron Times Herald* (Michigan) of September 6, 1932 (no dateline) headed "Former Manager of Buhl Aircraft Corporation Dies" (ref#389).

The six stockholders petition is from *Port Huron Times Herald* (Michigan) of June 14, 1932 (no dateline) headed "Buhl Aircraft Co. Dissolution Asked" (ref#394). The legal notice of October 6, 1932 is from *Port Huron Times Herald* (Michigan) of October 20, 1932 (no dateline) headed "Auctions—Legals, Legal Notices" (ref#387). The auction sale is from *Port Huron Times Herald* (Michigan) of October 31, 1932 datelined "St. Clair (Michigan), Oct. 31, 1932 headed "Brothers Bid In Buhl Property For $80,000" (ref#516). The equivalent of 1932's $80,000 in 2018 dollars is about $1.35 million.

The history of the Buhl family wealth and tragedy is from *Detroit Free Press* of December 24, 1932 (no dateline) headed "Name of Buhl Long Famous" and "Intensifies Interest in Pointe Tragedy" (ref#519).

The OPAS seaplanes, George Ponsford and Buhl aircraft are from the Canadian Bushplane Heritage Museum website, "Ontario Provincial Air Service" section (ref#391). The museum assisted in researching this book.

The sale of Buhl Sons Co. is from *Detroit Free Press* of January 8, 1960 (no dateline) headed "Buhl Bros. Sells Hardware Firm" by James B. Glynn (ref#518). This sale ended the business dynasty of the Buhl men that was begun in 1855 by Christian Henry Buhl and Charles Ducharme.

Addison Pemberton's recollection is from a personal communication to the author on August 13, 2018 (ref#397).

APPENDIX

A Mistaken Caption

A photograph of Nick Mamer at the controls of an airplane appears in J. P. McGoldrick II's original 1982 book on page 173, and in the revised edition (2007) on page 154 (ref#114). The camera is aimed at the interior left side and forward, inside the airplane. Nick is seated several feet behind the windshield (slanted pillar at the extreme right of the photo).

In this photo, the interior space frame structure of welded steel tubes is visible. In particular, one diagonal tube slants downward across the window next to the instrument panel, ending near Nick's left hand. His hand is on the throttle lever while his right hand grips the stick.

In the 1982 edition, the caption for this photograph reads, "Nick inside the Sun God. Note the large tank ahead of the panel." In the 2007 edition, the first sentence of the caption reads, "Nick Mamer inside the Sun-God." (ref#29) The photos are substantially identical in both volumes.

During the research phase for this book, we saw no reason to question the authenticity of the caption. We therefore assumed that the photograph showed Nick Mamer at the controls of the "Spokane Sun God," NR-9628, the specially-equipped CA-6 Airsedan built by the Buhl Aircraft Company in 1929 for the now-famous flight.

We finally became suspicious of the caption on the McGoldrick photo for two reasons:

1. Films of the air-to air refueling of the *Spokane Sun God* over New York (ref#1A, 1B, and 347) show Art Walker sticking out of the opening in the top of the fuselage, handling the dropped gas hose at the rear of the top wing of the aircraft. If Nick's pilot station were located at the rear of the wing, Art would be right on top of Nick.

2. These films clearly show Nick piloting the aircraft from the normal control station directly behind the windshield.

Only months later did we realize the photograph actually shows Nick Mamer at the controls of the special Buhl Airsedan, NX-6874, built by Buhl Aircraft for the transcontinental nonstop race of 1928. Three other photographs of this 1928 airplane in the Mamer family archives (folder labeled "1928 NAT'L AIR RACE") confirm its identity.

These three photographs from the family archive, and the one in the McGoldrick book, clearly show the control station located to the rear of the plane's wing structures. They also show the identical diagonal tube bracing ending near the throttle handle.

A close-up photo from the Mamer Family Archives (MFA) with the photo credit "Wide World Photos" shows the outside left side of this plane, with two large windows. Nick is seated at the controls looking at the camera, his left elbow hanging out the rearmost large window and his right hand on the stick. He is seated several feet behind the trailing edge of the lower wing which appears on the left hand side of the photograph. The fuselage is lettered. Lettered to the rear and below the rear window is "N. B. MAMER." Lettered beneath the two large windows is "MAMER FLYING SERVICE INC. SPOKANE, WASH" (ref#520).

Glued to the bottom of this photograph is the following Teletyped message: "#25-26-120 - -LOCAL..ROOSEVELT FIELD..10 BIG PLANES READY TO START ON TRANSCONTINENTAL NONSTOP RACE.- - PHOTO SHOWS N. B. MAMER WHO IS PILOTING A BUHL SPECIAL AIRSEDAN IN THE NONSTOP DERBY. 9-11-28"

A second photo from the MFA with the same "Wide World Photos" credit shows a more distant view with Nick standing in front of the left side of the airplane. This photo shows the lettering, a circled insignia for Buhl on the side of the fuselage, and a large "25" painted near the tail. This photograph has the same message, datelined Roosevelt Field, attached to its lower edge (ref#521).

A third photo from the MFA with a different credit—"From *That Picture Man* Denkelberg, Port Huron, Mich."—shows the right side of the same airplane with a large "25" painted near its tail. This photograph shows the Mamer Flying Service lettering, the circled Buhl insignia, and NX-6874 painted on the vertical stabilizer, and Nick and another man standing before the airplane (ref#522).

Also present in the MFA folder labeled "1928 NAT'L AIR RACE" is a newspaper clipping from the Casper Herald (Casper, Wyoming) of September 15, 1928, which describes the pilot's position (ref#405). "The pilot flies 'blind,' though a great amount of light is admitted into the cockpit through cabin windows. *A 300-gallon gasoline tank is between the pilot and the power unit* and two reserve tanks, one in each wing, provide emergency fuel" (emphasis added). This is significant for two reasons: the Sun God had a 200-gallon tank in its cabin, and also, the pilot in the Sun God was seated directly behind the power unit (motor).

Daniel Rust, in his 2008 article "Flight of the Spokane Sun God" for *Aviation History Magazine* (ref#163), describes the Sun God interior: "The two men [Mamer and Walker] squeezed into the cabin, where a custom-made 200-gallon fuel tank…replaced passenger seats in the middle of the cramped interior. Mamer occupied a small cockpit in front of the tank…A narrow passage between the tank and the side of the fuselage allowed the two men to trade places."

We examined the original Libby photo (identical to the one in the Mc-Goldrick books) in the online archive file of the Museum of Arts and Culture, Joel E. Ferris Research Library. The caption below the photo says "Nick Mamer in the Spokane Sun-God, 1928. Mamer poses in the cockpit the year before the record breaking flight. Image L87-1.37508-28 courtesy of the Northwest Museum of Arts and Culture" (ref#29A). The important number here is *1928*. The label "Spokane Sun-God" is incorrect, but the date, 1928, is correct. This photo had been mislabeled for many years. The actual Sun God airplane was not built, specially-equipped, or named, until 1929. It was delivered to Nick Mamer in Spokane on August 12, 1929, (ref# 335).

It is now clear. Two Airsedans were built and specially-equipped by Buhl for Nick Mamer. One (NX-6874) was painted with the Mamer Flying Service emblem for the 1928 National Air Race transcontinental nonstop race from Roosevelt Field, New York to Los Angeles. It had a 300-gallon gas tank between the pilot's station and the motor, so the controls were far to the rear of the airplane.

The second (NR-9628) was painted red with the "SPOKANE SUN GOD" emblem and the Texaco Star for the 1929 nonstop Spokane-San Francisco-New York and return, air-to-air refueling flight. The pilot's station was up front behind the windshield and motor. The cabin held a 200-gallon gas tank.

These two airplanes should not be confused.

Distance Flown Between Refueling Points (Est.)

Subleg	Straight Line	Road	Distance Flown (Est.)
Spokane – Pasco	126	137	130
Pasco – Umatilla	25	N.A.	25
Umatilla – Boardman	16	N.A.	16
Boardman – Biggs	57	66	66
Biggs – Portland	N.A.	104	104
Portland – Eugene	109	115	109
Eugene – Roseburg	62	71	65
Roseburg – Grants Pass	55	68	58
Grants Pass – Medford	23	30	26
Medford – Weed	70	81	73
Weed – Redding	59	71	64
Redding – Red Bluff	29	31	30
Red Bluff – Fairfield	35	N.A.	135
Fairfield – Mills Field	48	N.A.	50
TOTAL, LEG 1			961

In the above table, distances are in statute miles and N.A. = Not Applicable.

Leg 2 distance flown from the "Air Navigation Maps" (ref#81):

San Francisco – Reno, map #35	184 mi
Reno – Elko, map #34	232 mi
Elko – Salt Lake City, map #33	200 mi
Salt Lake City – Rock Springs, map #14	155 mi
TOTAL (Leg 2)	771 mi

Leg 3 distance eastbound from "Distances on the Transcontinental Route" (ref#165):

Rock Springs – Cheyenne	258 mi

Leg 4 distance eastbound from "Distances on the Transcontinental Route" (ref#165):

Cheyenne – North Platte	216 mi

Leg 5 distance eastbound from "Distances on the Transcontinental Route" (ref#165):

North Platte – Cleveland	1013 mi

Leg 6 distance eastbound from "Distances on the Transcontinental Route" (ref#165), plus the detour to Armonk, N.Y. before reaching Roosevelt Field, Long Island:

Cleveland – Newark	399 mi
Newark – Armonk, N.Y.	37 mi
Armonk – Roosevelt Field	25 mi
TOTAL (Leg 6)	461 mi

Leg 7 distance westbound from "Distances on the Transcontinental Route" (ref#165), plus the distance from Roosevelt Field, Long Island to Newark:

Roosevelt Field – Newark	27 mi
Newark – Cleveland	399 mi
TOTAL (Leg 7)	426 mi

Leg 8 distance westbound from "Distances on the Transcontinental Route" (ref#165), plus the estimated distances along the airway from Chicago to St. Paul:

Cleveland – Chicago	327 mi
Chicago – Milwaukee	81 mi
Milwaukee – Madison	71 mi
Madison – Portage	31 mi
Portage – Mauston	34 mi
Mauston – LaCrosse	60 mi
LaCrosse – St. Paul	116 mi
TOTAL (Leg 8)	720 mi

Leg 9 distance westbound over the new Northwest airway. Estimate comes from straight-line (S.L.) miles and/or road (R) miles, railroad track variance considered:

St. Paul – Aberdeen, S.D., (S.L.= 270 mi, R= 275 mi)   275 mi

Leg 10 distance westbound over the new Northwest airway. Estimate comes from straight-line (S.L.) miles and/or road (R) miles, railroad track variance considered:
Aberdeen – Miles City, Mont., (S.L.=365 mi, R=473mi)   400 mi

Leg 11 distance westbound over the new Northwest airway. Estimate comes from road (R) miles that parallel the Yellowstone river and railroad tracks:
Miles City – Belgrade, Mont., (R=297 mi)   297 mi

Leg 12 distance westbound over the new Northwest airway. Estimate comes from road (R) miles:
Belgrade – Missoula, Mont. (R=190 mi)   190 mi

Leg 13 distance westbound over the new Northwest airway. Estimate comes from road (R) miles through passes and paralleling railroad tracks:
Missoula – Spokane via Wallace (R=232 mi)   232 mi

SUM of distances between refueling points: 6,210 mi
Subtotal, San Francisco to Newark: 2,657 mi (this table) vs the 1924 published distance of the Transcontinental Air Mail Route (ref#165): 2,669 mi.

REFERENCES

1. 1.a, *British Pathe'*, "Petrol Stations in the Sky Soon? Spokane fliers in 'the Sun God' make non-stop flight from Coast to Coast and back non-stop – refueling in the air!" www.youtube.com/watch?v=NVoqILzEibg/ Also 1.b,"Refueling the Spokane Sun-God", New York, 18 Aug 1929, *Fox Movietone News*, story 3-434, U of South Carolina, University Libraries, Moving Image Research Collections, Digital Video Repository, mirc.sc.edu/islandora/object/usc 0/0 3A28381. (See also, Ref#347.)

2. Bakse, Colin, "Across the Continent and Back Again", *Airlift Tanker Quarterly*, Winter 2012, Vol. 20, Number 1, pp 6-12.

3. "Refueling Non-Stop Tour Planned", *The New York Times,* 26 Jul 1929.

4. "Plans Refueling Flight", *The New York Times,* 3 Aug 1929.

5. "Begins Non-Stop Flight", *The New York Times,* 15 Aug 1929.

6. "Non-Stop Flyers Fuel Twice", *The New York Times,* 17 Aug 1929.

7. "Sun God Refueled, Off to Cleveland", *The New York Times,* 18 Aug 1929.

8. "Sun God Hovers Here and Flies Back West", *The New York Times,* 19 Aug 1929.

9. "Sun God Reported at Aberdeen S.D.", *The New York Times,* 20 Aug 1929.

10. "Completing Refueling Round-Trip Flight To New York, Sun God Lands at Spokane", *The New York Times,* 21 Aug 1929.

11. Optical Heritage Museum Advertisement "Pilot Mamer Says, 'I Found Them Restful to My Eyes'", www.opticalheritagemuseum.com/special-exhibit-relaxation.

12. Passehl-Stoddart, Erin "US Army Consolidated 0-17 NG28-360" Photo of Airplane, Nick Mamer, pilot. *The Yellow Pine Times*, (Yellow Pine, Idaho), 2014. Photo from Stonebraker Photograph Collection, U of Idaho Library Digital Initiatives, 21 Aug 1928.

13. Stonebraker Photograph Collection, Photo of Nick Mamer next to his airplane on Stonebraker Ranch, Idaho, U of Idaho Library Digital Initiatives, 21 Aug 1928.

14. Lambeth, Robert, "Felts Field", Robert Lambeth History 596, 19 Nov 2012 (blog).

15. Forden, Lesley, The Ford Air Tours, c1972, Ch. 7 "The Last Tour", 2003 Edition Issued by Aviation Foundation of America, New Brighton MN. www.nationalairtour.org/pdf/ford_pdf_files/chapter_7. PDF

16. Buhl Air Sedan CA-6, *Wikipedia.* Accessed April 2018. Photo of Sun God at Felts Field, Aug 1929.

17. Parks, Dennis, "Spokane Air Derbies a big hit in 1927", *General Aviation News,* 8 Nov 2015, generalaviationnews.com/2015/11/08/flight-flyers-

for-21/ Accessed Apr 2018.

18. Mutschler, Charles V, *Spokane's Street Railways,* 1987.

19. "Felts Field History," *Wikipedia.* Accessed Apr 2018.

20. Buhl Aircraft Company, *Wikipedia.* Accessed 6 Apr 2018.

21. Buhl Sesquiplane, *Wikipedia*, Photo. Accessed Apr 2018.

22. Buhl Sesquiplane, *Wikipedia,* Photo. Accessed Apr 2018.

23. Buhl Sesquiplane, *Wikipedia,* Photo. Accessed Apr 2018.

24. Nick Mamer, *Wikipedia.* Accessed 6 Apr 2018.

25. Meister, Richard L. Jr, "Flight of the Sun God", *Our Community Today* (Spokane WA) Feb 2000. Accessed from *Aerofiles* Apr 2018.

26. "A Tribute to Nick Mamer" Photos, www.angelfire.com/theforce/ echo1946/mamer/MamerTributePage.html.

27. Cover Art, "The Saga of the Sun God", by Schulze, William, *Seattle Post-Intelligencer*, 26 Jan 1964.

28. Smith, Anita L. and Smith, Robert E, bibliography and source references for info on Nick Mamer. Accessed April 2018. http://www.angelfire.com/ theforce/echo1946/mamer/acknowledgements.html

29. Libby, Charles A, (photo of Nick Mamer), 1928, Northwest Museum of Arts and Culture (Spokane), No. L87-137508-28, mislabeled: "…in the Spokane Sun-God, 1928." This photo is also mislabeled in the McGoldrick books (ref#114). See Appendix "Mistaken Caption."

30. *Seattle Post-Intelligencer*, Photo, "Nick Mamer in airplane receiving photos to deliver to Seattle, 1934". "Saga of the Sun God" by Schulze, William, 26 Jan 1964, *Sunday Pictorial Section.*

31. Mamer Air Transport Brochure, cover and inside, 1930. Airline Timetable Images, Bjorn Larsson and David Zekria. Accessed April 2018.

32. Library of Congress, Mamet, Julien 1877-1932 , Photo, at end of "Circuit de l'Est" in France between 1910-1920. Identified as Nick Mamer by Library of Congress, but is actually Julien Mamet. Correct info is at www. flyhistoricwings.com/2013/08/the-circuit-de-lest.

33. Plehinger, Russell *Marathon Flyers*, Photos, "Nick Mamer", "Nick Mamer, wife and daughter", "Arthur E. Walker".

34. U of Idaho Digital Memories "Preparing for fire spotting", January 2003. Accessed 22 Apr 2018.

35. Tinsley, Jesse "Remembering pilot Nick Mamer", *The Spokesman-Review*,19 Mar 2018.

36. "Parkwater Municipal Aviation Field", *Aerial Age Weekly,* 15 May 1922.

37. Gero, David, *Early Aviation Disasters*, The History Press, Stroud, Glouces-tershire, UK, 2011.

38. N.A.

39. "Spokane Aviation", *The Spokesman-Review*, 23 Dec 2007.

40. Arksey, Laura, "Nick Mamer and Art Walker take off from Spokane's Felts Field on a history-making feat of endurance flying on August 15, 1929". HistoryLink.org Essay 8899, 27 Jan 2009.

41. Jack Knight log/Nick Mamer, http://www.angelfire.com/theforce/ echo1946/mamer/JKbib.html

42. Shute, Brian, "Airplanes Race to Spokane!" *Nostalgia,* Sept-Oct 2010.

43. Libby, Charles, "Spokane 1929", No. 39410, Northwest Museum of Arts and Culture, Spokane WA.

44. N.A.

45. "Mamer Flying Service", *Aero Digest*, Sept & Nov 1927.
46. "Ten Killed As Airliner Hits Peak Of Montana Mountain", *The New York Times,* 11 Jan 1938.
47. Google Maps ContemporaryAerial View of Felts Field, Spokane Washington.
48. "Air Service of the AEF", *Wikipedia.* Accessed Apr 2018.
49. "Nicholas Bernard Mamer" (gravestone photo) *Billiongraves.com* Accessed Apr 2018.
50. "Nicholas Mamer in Northwest Airlines Uniform", Northwest Airlines.
51. State of Montana Bureau of Vital Statistics Standard Certificate of Death, Book 3, Page M-6. Filed 13 Jan 1938, Bozeman Montana.
52. Application For Headstone, Veterans Memorial Cemetery. Nicholas B. Mamer, War Dept. O.Q.M.G. Form 623. Application Date 22 Mar 1938.
53. Roster of Recruit Depot, 19 Jul, 1916, Mamer, Nicholas B., Records of the Adjutant General's Office, 1780-1917, Record Group 94, Nat'l Archives, Washington D.C.
54. Kroll, Harry David, Ed., *Kelly Field in the Great World War*, "Roster of Flying Cadets", p 150. Nicholas B. Mamer listed.
55. City of Hastings Minnesota History, www.hastingsmn.gov/visitors/about-hastings/-history. Hastings Area Chamber of Commerce Directory of Clubs, Organizations, Churches and Schools. Accessed 6 June 2018.
56. Kershner, Jim, "Felts Field History", *The Spokesman-Review*, 8 Oct 2006.
57. "Clarence M. Young appoints committee to study air transportation safety regulations", *Aviation Week,* 8 Feb, 1930.
58. N.A.
59. "187th Aero Squadron", Air Force Historical Research Agency, U.S. Air Force, Maxwell AFB, Alabama. Accessed Apr 2018.
60. 1930 Census, Dept. of Commerce –Bureau of the Census—Fifteenth Census of the United States: 1930, Roosevelt Apts 68-100, 4-5 Apr 1930, Spokane Washington.
61. Ancestry, Nicholas Bernard Mamer 1898-1938.
62. Ancestry, Patricia Ann Mamer, 1927-1995.
63. List of United States Citizens sailing on *S.S. Panama* from Cristobal, Canal Zone, June 26, 1918 to Port of New York arriving July 13, 1918.
64. Levin, Anne, "Preparing For The Trenches—Princeton's Role in WWI", 2008. Accessed April 4, 2018.
65. Shen, Spencer '16, "Princeton University During WWI" Posted on Mudd Manuscript Library Blog 13 Jan 2016 by April C. Armstrong.
66. Roberts, Chad, "Dakota County History 101: Aviator Nick Mamer (1898-1938)", 16 Jul 2011, Posted on *Patch.com,* https://patch.com/minnesota/mendotaheights/dakota-county-history-101-aviator-nick-mamer-1898-1938
67. "School of Military Aeronautics", *Princeton Weekly Bulletin,* Vol 98 (2008-09) Number 28 June 1.
68. "Nick Mamer, Early Aerial Fire Patrol Pilot", *The Static Line* (National Smokejumpers Assn.) Vol 3 Quarterly July 1998 Edition 5.
69. "Mamer Flying Across Continent and Back", *Aero Digest*, Sept. 1929*,* p. 218, Internet Digitization (OCR) of *Aero Digest* article (1929).
70. "Refueling Endurance Flights, Spokane Sun God", *The Aircraft Year Book For 1930*, Vol Twelve, pp153-154, D. Van Nostrand Company, Inc., New

York, 1930.

71. Mamer, Lt. Nick, "First Flyer to Make Non-Stop Round Trip Trans-Continental Flight", *Montana Standard* and the North American Newspaper Alliance, 21 August 1929.

72. Haskell, F.K. "Twelve-Hour daily passenger and express service", *Aero Digest* Nov 1929.

73. N.A.

74. "Soaring 20s: Races and Sun God", *The Spokesman-Review,* 8 May 1965.

75. "Saga of the Spokane Sun God", Pictorial Review, *Seattle Post-Intelligencer,* 26 Jan 1964.

76. "Flaming Arrow", *Time,* 17 Jan 1938.

77. French, E.C., "We Are Over The Peak---Nothing Worries Us Now", 11 January 1938 unidentified newspaper clipping. Northwest Museum of Arts and Culture.

78. "Bodies of Air Tragedy Victims Found", unidentified newspaper, datelined Bozeman MT, 11 Jan 1938, Northwest Museum of Arts and Culture.

79. "Parkwater", unidentified newspaper, undated. Northwest Museum of Arts and Culture.

80. R.B.C., "Soaring 10,000 Feet Above Spokane", *The Spokesman-Review,* unknown date. Northwest Museum of Arts and Culture.

81. University of Connecticut Libraries Map and Geographic Information Center – MAGIC. (2012). *United States Air Navigation Maps Index 1923 – 1935.* Retrieved from http://magic.lib.uconn.edu/.

82. List of American Aero Squadrons, *Wikipedia.* Accessed 1 May 2018.

83. 7th Aero Squadron, WWI, *Wikipedia.* Accessed 1 May 2018.

84. "Aviation Section U.S. Signal Corps", *Wikipedia.* Accessed May 1, 2018, https://en.wikipedia.org/wiki/Aviation_Section_U.S._Signal_Corps

85. May, Mike, "Gas Stations In The Sky", *Invention and Technology Magazine,* Spring 2004, Vol. 19, Issue 4, American Heritage.com

86. "The Birth of the United States Air Force", Air Force Historical Research Agency, 9 Jan 2008.

87. "Rushing Emergency Fuel to Mamer", *Spokane Daily Chronicle,* 16 Aug 1929.

88. "Refueling Sun God at North Platte", *Spokane Daily Chronicle,* 17 Aug 1929.

89. Mamer, Nick Lt.,"Mamer Tells of Troubles on Trip", *Spokane Daily Chronicle,* 17 Aug 1929.

90. "Sun God Refueled After Hard Fight", *Spokane Daily Chronicle,* 17 Aug 1929.

91. "Spokane Sun God Given More Gas at Cheyenne", *Spokane Daily Chronicle,* 17 Aug 1929.

92. "Sun God Barely Avoids Being Forced to Land", *Spokane Daily Chronicle,* 17 Aug 1929.

93. "Sun God Has Narrow Escape From Being Forced to Land", *Spokane Daily Chronicle,* 17 Aug 1929.

94. "Sun God Future Left to Mamer", *Spokane Daily Chronicle,* 19 Aug 1929.

95. "Sun God Back Tomorrow", *Spokane Daily Chronicle,* 19 Aug 1929.

96. "Mamer Passes Cleveland", *Spokane Daily Chronicle,* 19 Aug 1929.

97. "Examine Record of Engine of 'Angeleno'", *Aviation,* 27 Jul 1927.

98. Goldsborough, Brice, "The Earth Inductor Compass", *Aero Digest,* June

1927.

99.   Pioneer Instrument Company, "for Air Travelers the Earth Inductor Compass", advertisement.

100.   Titterington, Maurice M, "The Earth Inductor Compass", *Aviation Week*, 20 Jun 1927.

101.   "Mamer Crosses Nation In Refueling Flight Test", *Aviation*, 24 Aug 1929.

102.   Buhl Aircraft Company "Buhl Air Sedan No. CA-6-42 is the first to fly from Coast to Coast and back again without a stop", Advertisement, *Aviation*, 28 Dec 1929.

103.   Buhl Aircraft Company, "Buhl Standard Air Sedan", *The 1930 Aircraft Year Book*, p. 337. Accessed May 2, 2018.

104.   "Lindbergh's Wright Whirlwind a Result of Seven Years' Development", *Aviation Week*, 20 Jun 1927.

105.   "Sun God Flight A Distance Mark", *Aviation Week*, 31 Aug 1929.

106.   "Mamer Makes Non-Stop Trip", *Aviation,* 3 Nov 1928.

107.   Partridge, E. Harve, "The Northwest Forest Patrol", *Aviation*, 17 Jan 1927.

108.   "Aviation Advance Noted in Spokane", *Aviation*, 15 Sep 1928.

109.   "Question Mark (aircraft)", *Wikipedia.* Accessed May 5, 2018.

110.   "Cross section drawing of Question Mark refueling", *Aviation*, 19 Jan 1929.

111.   Orzel-Gryglewska, Jolanta, "Consequences of Sleep Deprivation" *International Journal of Occupational Medicine and Environmental Health*, University of Gdansk, Poland, Dept. of Animal Physiology, August 25, 2009. Accessed May 28, 2018.

112.   Theobald, Mikel, "What Happens to You When You don't Sleep for Days", *Every Day Health* website https://www.everydayhealth.com/conditions/ what -happens-when-you-dont-sleep-days/ Updated Jan 31, 2018. Accessed May 28, 2018.

113.   "Mamer Passes Cleveland", *Spokane Daily Chronicle*, 19 Aug 1929.

114.   McGoldrick, J.P. II, *One Man's Opinion of the Spokane Aviation Story*, Ye Galleon Press, Fairfield WA, 1982.   Also 114B, McGoldrick J.P. II, *The Spokane Aviation Story*, Tornado Creek Publications, 2007.

115.   Wiley, Frank W., *Montana and the Sky*, Montana Aeronautics Commission, First Edition, 1966.

116.   Plehinger,Russell, *Marathon Flyers*, Harlo Press, Detroit, 1989.

117.   Berdini, Analise, email confirming Mamer attendance at U.S. School of Military Aeronautics at Princeton University, received by Anya Carlson, May 8, 2018.

118.   Princeton Weekly Bulletin, "School of Military Aeronautics", Princeton University Vol. 98 (2008-09) No. 28 (June 1).

119.   "Pilots and Ship Ready For Great Flight", *Spokane Daily Chronicle*, 16 Aug 1929.

120.   "Sun God Refuels and Speeds East", *Spokane Daily Chronicle,* 16 Aug 1929.

121.   "Sun God is Ordered to Land", *Spokane Daily Chronicle*, 20 Aug 1929.

122.   Guilfoil, Michael, "Front & Center: The long and fulfilling days of Addison Pemberton, president of Liberty Lake manufacturer Scanivalve", *The Spokesman-Review*, 19 Mar 2017.

123.   "Minnesota's first recruit in the army aviation corps is Nicholas B. Mamer of Hastings, Minn.", *Aerial Age Weekly*, 17 Jul 1916.

124. Allard, Noel, "Ten most important state aviation pioneers", *Minnesota Flyer*, 1 Feb 2014.

125. "Nick Mamer, Spokane Aviator, tonight was laying plans to smash three records on flight", *Klamath News* (Klamath Falls Oregon) 31 Jul 1929.

126. Corrigan, Mike, "The Spokane Sun God", *Pacific Northwest Inlander*, 9 Aug 2001.

127. "Mamer Crosses Nation In Refueling Flight Test", *Aviation Week,* 24 Aug 1929.

128. Yockelson, Mitchell, "The United States Armed Forces and the Mexican Punitive Expedition: Part 2", Genealogy Notes, Winter 1997, Vol. 29, No. 4.

129. Frank, Sam Hager, "American air service observation in World War I", Dissertation presented to Graduate Council of University of Florida in partial fulfillment of the requirements for degree of Doctor of Philosophy, U of Florida, 1961.

130. N.A.

131. McClung, Stuart. Review of *An Illustrated History of the 1st Aero Squadron at Camp Furlong: Columbus, New Mexico 1916-1917*, by John L. Dueble, Albuquerque, N.M., 2016. *Guest Blog*, Nov 23, 2017.

132. History.com Staff "Pancho Villa attacks Columbus, New Mexico", History.com 2009. Accessed May 08, 2018. http://www.history.com/this-day-in-history/pancho-villa-attacks-columbus-new-mexico

133. "An American Legacy in Panama". Accessed May 8, 2018. http://ufdc.ufl.edu/AA00022175/00001

134. Center of Military History, United States Army, "The Panama Canal An Army's Enterprise", Washington D.C. 2009. Accessed May 08, 2018. https://history.army.mil/catalog/pubs/70/70-115.html

135. CZ Images "The Early Days of Fort Sherman Panama Canal Zone" *Wikipedia*. Accessed May 08 2018. www.czimages.com/CZMemories/VAP/Sherman/fort_sherman_index.htm

136. Tender Tale, "Deployments-The Early Years. The Panama Canal Zone approaches and sea lanes" MAP Panama Canal Zone 1916. Accessed May 08, 2018. http://www.tendertale.com/ttd/ttd4/ttd4.html

137. "CA-6 Airsedan, Special 1929 (CA-6 Special, Spokane Sun God)," *Aerofiles,* http://www.aerofiles.com/_buhl.html (Note: Approved Type Certificate contains incorrect registration number NR9629, should be NR9628.)

138. Novak, Matt, "The 'Highway of Light' That Guided Early Planes Across America", Nov 18, 2013. Accessed May 07, 2018. https://paleoffuture.gizmodo.com/the-highway-of-light-that-guided-early-planes-across-1466696698 Also "The Evolution of Airway Lights and Electronic Navigation Aids," https://www.centennialofflight.net/essay/Government_Role/navigation/POL.13.htm Also "Transcontinental Airway System," *Wikipedia*. Accessed 7 May 2018.

139. Map from Reference 134.

140. "Sun God And Refueler Yesterday" Photo, *Spokane Daily Chronicle*, 21 Aug 1929.

141. "Weather Forecast", *Oakland Tribune*, 15 Aug 1929.

142. "History of SFO" (Mills Field) /San Francisco International Airport. Accessed May 15, 2018. http://www.flysfo.com/about-sfo/history-sfo

143. San Francisco International Airport, History, *Wikipedia*. Accessed May 15,

2018.

144. N.A.

145. Simmons, Daniel, "The Spokane Sun-God", *Fairchild Air Force Base Newsletter,* 92nd Air Refueling Wing Historian, 18 Aug 2009. Accessed May 15, 2018.

146. "Mamer and Walker Will Leave Within 48 Hours On Nonstop Refueling Hop To Cleveland", *Spokane Daily Chronicle,* 22 Aug 1929.

147. "Mamer Reaches St. Paul", *Spokane Daily Chronicle,* 19 Aug 1929.

148. "Mamer Breaks Plane Records", *Spokane Daily Chronicle,* 22 Aug 1929.

149. "Sun God Being Hindered By Montana Forest Fire", *Spokane Daily Chronicle,* 20 Aug 1929.

150. Mahan, H.E., "Lighting of Airways and Airports", *Transactions of the American Institute of Electrical Engineers* (Vol: 48, Issue:3, Jul 1929, pp:849-854).

151. "History of the Elko Regional Airport", http://www.flyelkonevada.com/index.php/history-of-elko-regional-airport/

152. "Hole in the Mountain Peak", *Wikipedia.* Accessed May 19, 2018

153. "Rock Springs, Wyoming Airfield", Southwest Regional Airport (RKS) site. Accessed May 15, 2018. http://www.flyrks.com/about-rks/history/

154. Freeman, Paul, "Abandoned and Little Known Airfields", Rock Springs Wyoming Hanger, Photos. http://www.airfields-freeman.com/WY/Airfields_WY.htm#rocksprings

155. Freeman, Paul, "Abandoned and Little-Known Airfields: Wyoming", Revised 30 Dec 2017, http://www.airfields-freeman.com/WY/Airfields_WY.htm#rocksprings

156. Meekhof, Marla, "Spokane's Famous Aviator, Nick Mamer", *Nostalgia Magazine* July 2001 pp10-15. Photos supplied by Ralph Nortell.

157. "Record Is Set In Night Air", *The Spokesman-Review,* 20 Aug 1929.

158. "Spokane Sun-God Flight All Set", *The Spokesman-Review,* 16 Aug, 1929.

159. Wohl, Robert, *The Spectacle of Flight, Aviation and the Western Imagination 1920-1950,* Yale University Press, New Haven and London, 2005.

160. "C.W. Holman Wins Class A Air Derby", *Aviation,* 3 Oct 1927.

161. 397th Bombardment Squadron, *Wikipedia.* Accessed May 20, 2018.

162. Kiecker, G.L., *Invention of Duct Tape,* 2012. https://www.slideshare.net/glkiecker/invention-of-duct-tape-49605053

163. Rust, Daniel L, "Flight of the Sun God", *Aviation History,* January 2008, reprinted May 23, 2018. *Aviation History Magazine on History Net,* http://www.historynet.com/flight-spokane-sun-god.htm

164. Pacific Air Transport (PAT) (1926-1928) www.worldhistory.biz 11-07-2015, 11:13—http://www.worldhistory.biz/contemporary-history/78597-pacific-air-transport-pat-united-states-1926-1928.html Accessed May 29, 2018.

165. Arrow and Beacon Locations - DreamSmithPhotos.com http://www.dreamsmithphotos.com/arrow/arrows.html

166. Weingroff, Richard F, "The Lincoln Highway", Federal Highway Administration Website www.fhwa.dot.gov/infrastructure/lincoln.cfm Accessed May 29, 2018.

167. Williams, Mary Lou "Letter from Mary Lou Williams about Mamer Family", Angelfire.com August 1999. http:www.angelfire.com/theforce/echo1946/mamer/NicksFamily.html

168. Smith, Robert E, "The Flight of the Spokane Sun God 1929", Jack Knight

"Air Log", angelfire.com/theforce/echo1946/mamer/BobMamerarticle.html Accessed June 1, 2018.

169. Nelson, Cliff, "Comments on Articles about Nick Mamer" angelfire.com/theforce/echo1946/mamer/articles.html Accessed June 1, 2018.

170. "The Northern Airway" Flyer for Mamer Air Service (author unknown) angelfire.com/theforce/echo1946/mamer/memorabilia.html Accessed June 1, 2018.

171. The Clason Map Company, *Atlas of the Best Roads of the United States, 1924.*

172. N.A.

173. N.A.

174. N.A.

175. N.A.

176. Nelson, James A, "Airborne", *Wheat Life*, pp.67-70, April 2012.

177. Progressive Management Publications, *Seventy-Five Years of Inflight Military Aircraft Refueling Highlights 1923-1998, Compiled from U.S. Gov't, U.S.Military, DoD, U.S.A.F.,* 1998. Richard K. Smith compiler.

178. Holder, Gill & Wallace, Mike, *Range Unlimited, a History of Aerial Refueling*, A Schiffer Military History Book, 2000.

179. Mamer, N.B. "Nick", "Texaco Across the Sky", *The Texaco Star,* vol. 16, pp. 3-6, August 1929.

180. Leinberger, Lisa, "Museum Honors 1927 Air Race", *The Spokesman-Review*, 20 Sep 2014.

181. Kassa, Thomas, "1927 National Air Races At Felts Field", *Spokane Historical*, http://www.spokanehistorical.org/items/show/544 Accessed June 7, 2018.

182. Arksey, Laura, "National Air Derby and Air Races beginning on September 21, 1927", HistoryLink.org/File/7924 Accessed June 7, 2018.

183. National Air Derby Association of Spokane, "National Air Races 1927 Spokane Air Port", Handbook or Manual/Program, A#9 Mamer Family Archives.

184. North Platte Regional Airport, History "North Platte Airport", *Wikipedia*. https:Wikipedia.org/wiki/North_Platte_Regional_Airport. Accessed June 8, 2018.

185. Wishart, David J, Ed. *Encyclopedia of the Great Plains*, University of Nebraska Press, 2004.

186. Hardie, George, "Mystery Plane", *Vintage Airplane*, Magazine of EAA Antique Classic Division-April 1993, p. 25. https://issuu.com/vintageeaa/docs/va-vol-21-no-4-april-1993 Accessed June 11, 2018.

187. Price, Catherine, "The Healing Power of Compressed Yeast", article adapted from *Vitamania:Our Obsessive Quest For Nutritional Perfection*, Penquin Press, 2015.

188. Aeronautical Chamber of Commerce of America, *The Aircraft Year Book For 1930* Vol. 12, D. Van Nostrand Co. Inc. New York, 1930.

189. Pemberton, Addison, Personal email to J.B. Rivard, June 11, 2018.

190. "Barnstormers Aeronautics Random", Barnstmr Blogspot Feb 1995, "reprinted" online Saturday December 21, 2013. http://barnstmr.blogspot.com/2013/

191. "Deuel County Where Wheat Is King", Deuel County History (Nebraska) http://www.co.deuel.ne.us/webpages/about/history.html Accessed June 10,

2018.

192. Ruzich, Joseph, "Lindbergh helped make Maywood a key site in aviation's early days", *Chicago Tribune*, 20 May 2014. Maywood Field http://www.chicagotribune.com Accessed June 12, 2018.

193. Air Mail Pioneers website, "Hadley Field". http://www.airmailpioneers.org/index.htm Accessed June 12, 2018.

194. Weather Report for August 17, 1929, *Des Moines Register,* 17 Aug 1929, Sunrise 5:24 AM, Sunset 7:45 PM.

195. "Lindy Sees Rosy Years Ahead of Aviation In U.S.", *Des Moines Register,* 17 Aug 1929.

196. Timeanddate.com, Sunrise/ Sunset, Moonrise/Moonset Calculator. https://www.timeanddate.com/moon/usa/omaha?month=8&year=1929 Accessed June 15, 2018.

197. Williams, J.R., *IFR By The Book: Techniques of Instrument Flying*, General Aviation Press, Snyder, Texas. First Printing March 1980.

198. "Sun God Flies Over Nebraska On Way To East", *Lincoln Evening Journal*, 17 Aug 1929.

199. Van Tassel, David. (author), Brabowski, John J. (editor) *Encyclopedia of Cleveland History*, Indiana University Press, December 1987.

200. Mamer, Nicholas B., Notes dropped from *Spokane Sun God*, 18 Aug 1929. A#6 Mamer Family Archives A-6.1 to A 6.6. Transcribed from original notes June 23, 2018 by A. Carlson.

201. Mamer, Nick, "Introducing An Advanced Phase of Endurance Flying", *Aero Digest*, October 1929.

202. Nicholas B. Mamer Appointment to 2nd Lieutenant, 22 Apr 1919, Headquarters Air Service Flying School, Kelly Field, San Antonio, Texas, A#13 Mamer Family Archives.

203. *Memorandum of Information,* information concerning appointment to reserve officer for active duty or non-active duty, A#13 Mamer Family Archives

204. Winslow, Kenelm Jr., 1st Lieutenant 7th Aero Squadron, Panama Canal Zone, Recommendation of N.B. Mamer as Mamer leaves 7th Aero Squadron for U.S. School of Military Aeronautics, Princeton, N.J., 21 Jun 1918, A#13 Mamer Family Archives.

205. Dawson, Athol A., 1st Lieutenant, 7th Aero Squadron, Panama Canal Zone, Recommendation of N.B. Mamer "for any position that requires an able, trustworthy man". 24 Jun 1918, A#13 Mamer Family Archives.

206. Wynne, Walter W., Major 7th Aero Squadron, Panama Canal Zone, Recommendation of N.B. Mamer "for any position requiring good judgement, responsibility or trust". 25 Jun 1918, A#13 Mamer Family Archives.

207. Certificate of Graduation, United States Schools of Military Aeronautics, Princeton University, October 5, 1918, A#13 Mamer Family Archives.

208. N.B. Mamer, Promotion Certificate to *Corporal*, 7th Aero Squadron of the Regular Army, 13 Oct 1917, A#13 Mamer Family Archives.

209. N.B. Mamer, Promotion Certificate to *Sergeant*, 7th Aero Squadron of the Regular Army, 25 Feb 1918, A#13 Mamer Family Archives.

210. N.B. Mamer, Promotion Certificate to *Master Signal Electrician*, 7th Aero Squadron of the Regular Army, 14 Mar 1918, A#13 Mamer Family Archives.

211. Honorable Discharge from The United States Army, Nicholas B. Mamer,

#348467, 1 May 1919, A#13 Mamer Family Archives.

212. Appointment of Nicholas Bernard Mamer to *Second Lieutenant*, Aviation Section (flying status) Signal Officers Reserve Corps of the Army of the United States, 10 May 1919, Certificate, A#13 Mamer Family Archives.

213. N.B. Mamer, Appointment to *Second Lieutenant*, Aviation Section, Signal Reserve Corps Headquarters, Air Service Flying School, Kelly Field, San Antonio, Texas, 19 Apr 1919, A#13 Mamer Family Archives.

214. Special Order No. 112, Appointment of Nicholas Bernard Mamer as Reserve Military Aviator (R.M.A.), and to Second Lieutenant (as of 19 Apr 1919) dated 22 Apr 1919. Headquarters Air Service Flying School, Kelly Field, San Antonio, Texas, A#13 Mamer Family Archives.

215. Walton, L.A., Major JMASC, Officer In Charge of Flying, Certifying N.B. Mamer "has had a total of 63 hours, 10 minutes flying time at Kelly Field and is classified as a Pursuit Pilot, A#13 Mamer Family Archives.

216. "How to get a stiff Neck," *The Inland Veteran*, Vol. VII, No. 21, Spokane Washington, 25 Jun 1925, A#17 Mamer Family Archives.

217. "Millionth Mile For Nick Mamer", *The Spokesman-Review*, 5 Jul 1936, A#17 Mamer Family Archives.

218. Bean, Margaret, "Spokane's Flying Community at Parkwater Is Prosperous", *The Spokesman-Review*, 26 Sep 1920, A#17 Mamer Family Archives.

219. Hinck, C.W., Federated Flyers Inc., Letter of Introduction for Nicholas B. Mamer who was associated with F.F.I. June 1919 to April 1920, A#15 Mamer Family Archives.

220. Kitt, Bruce, *Uniform History Project,* 4 letters to Leo Lee Oct 6, 1997, March 23, 1998, March 31, 1998, Jan 27, 1999, A#50 Mamer Family Archives.

221. Kitt, Bruce, *Uniform History Project*, 2 letters to Leo Lee, Sept 22, 2002, Oct 16, 2002, A#50 Mamer Family Archives.

222. "Tupper, Doc and Buddy", letter to Mr.& Mrs. James Mamer of Hastings, Minn., visit to Spokane Sept 20, 1942, A#52 Mamer Family Archives.

223. Mamer, James, Mamer, Rose, Letter to Patty (Patricia) Mamer Lee Oct 28, 1973, concerning the death of Regina Mamer (Jean) and other topics, A#54 Mamer Family Archives.

224. Connick, Elmer, "Record is set in Night Air," undated unidentified newspaper clipping, A#21 Mamer Family Archives.

225. Mamer, Nicholas B, undated unidentified newspaper clipping recollecting Rock Springs Wyoming refueling, A#21 Mamer Family Archives.

226. Greeley, Carlos, telegram to Lt. Nick Mamer 15 Aug 1929, from San Francisco, A#21 Mamer Family Archives.

227. Greeley, Carlos, Telegram to Lt. Nick Mamer 8 Aug 1929, A#21, Mamer Family Archives.

228. Mamer, Nick, "Local Aviators Refuel Sun God with Rope, Cans," undated unidentified Miles City, Montana, newspaper clipping, A#21 Mamer Family Archives.

229. Mamer, Nick, "Mamer Plane Arrives Over Montana City," unidentified newspaper clipping, August 19, 1929, for North American Newspaper Alliance (NANA), A#21 Mamer Family Archives.

230. Mamer, Nick Lt., "Home Greeting Thrills Mamer", *The Spokesman-Review*, 21 Aug 1929.

231. "Tanks Are Full Of Gas…" unidentified newspaper clipping, 17 Aug 1929.

A#21, Mamer Family Archives, also "…For Cleveland During Night Some Time," unidentified newspaper clipping, 17 Aug 1929, A#21, Mamer Family Archives.

232. "Made Five Refueling Contacts," unidentified newspaper clipping, Rock Springs Wyoming, dateline Aug. 16, 1929, also "Air Derby Dispatches Refueler for Emergency Contact," undated unidentified newspaper clipping, A#21 Mamer Family Archives.

233. Mamer, Nick Lt., "Coughing Motor Thrilled Flyers", *The Spokesman-Review*, 16 Aug 1929.

234. E.C. French, telegram to Wilson Refueling Plane, also "Mamer's Stories of Flight Thrilling –Again Nears Cleveland Port", unidentified newspaper clipping, dateline Cleveland, Ohio Aug. 19, 1929, also "Sun God Refueled at New York Heading West" undated unidentified newspaper clipping, also "New York Spires Thrill Flyers" unidentified newspaper clipping, datelined Roosevelt Field, N.Y., Aug. 18, 1929, A#21, Mamer Family Archives.

235. Marriage Certificate, Nicholas B. Mamer and Faye C. Carey, July 7, 1923, Yakima, Washington, A#56 Mamer Family Archives.

236. Miscellaneous Papers and Photos, "White Notebook", A#56 Mamer Family Archives.

237. N.A.

238. Application for Appointment as Pilot Aerial Mail Service, 6 Sep 1919 and two letters of recommendation, Nicholas B. Mamer applying, A#56 Mamer Family Archives.

239. Pilot Licenses, copies, "Federation Aeronautique Internationale – Aero Club of America No. 4715, also "United States of America Department of Commerce Aeronautics Branch Pilot's Identification Card No. 817, also Mechanic's License No. 111, A#56 Mamer Family Archives.

240. *Aviation*, Vol. 22 no. 16, 18 Apr 1927.

241. Palmer Method, *Wikipedia*. https://en.wikipedia.org/wiki/Palmer_Method. Accessed June 28, 2018.

242. "Mamer-Walker Established Four New Records—Scene at Air Field Impressive", *The Spokesman-Review,* 21 Aug 1929, pp. 1-2.

243. Weather Conditions for day and night, *Pittsburgh Press*, 19 Aug 1929.

244. *Bellefonte Historical and Cultural Association*, Fred D. Smith Collection. http://www.bellefontearts.org/Smith_pages/Smith_airfield.htm Accessed July 1, 2018.

245. "Out of the Sky Each Day…", unidentified newspaper clipping, Jul 1921, A#3 Mamer Family Archives.

246. CommAv: Mamer; Newspapers: Idaho, Minnesota, Montana, Washington, Wisconsin. Accessed January 18 &19, 2001, Pioneer Room, Hastings, MN, 2018.

247. ComAvHis: Mamer; nzpaper; Minnesota. A#37 Mamer Family Archives.

248. "Spiral Bridge", early 20th Century Photo, *Historic Minnesota Highways*. Accessed July 2, 2018. http://www.deadpioneer.com/routes/US61/historicus61se/spiralbridge/spiralbridge.htm

249. Newspaper clippings, *Hastings Gazette, Hastings Democrat,* including obituaries for Lt. James Mamer and Jacob H. Mamer. P#2 Pioneer Room, Hastings MN

250. Obituary, Marie Mamer McLaughlin, *Hastings Gazette*, 9 Oct 1980. P#3, Pioneer Room, Hastings, MN.

251. Obituaries, Joseph W. Cavanagh, Bertha B. Cavanagh, *Hastings Gazette*. P#4, Pioneer Room, Hastings, MN.

252. U.S. School of Military Aeronautics, Princeton University, Graduating Class October 5, 1918, photo. Keyed list of graduates attached. P#5, Pioneer Room, Hastings, MN.

253. Nicholas B. Mamer, undated photograph, infant in baptismal gown. P#6, Pioneer Room, Hastings, MN.

254. Nick Mamer Memorial Clock at Felts Field, and Plaque, photos. Obituaries for Mrs. Mary Mamer and Mrs. Faye Mamer. P#7, Pioneer Room, Hastings, MN.

255. Newspaper clippings, *Dakota County Tribune, Hastings Gazette, Bozeman Daily Chronicle*, all 1938, Nick Mamer's death. P#8, Pioneer Room, Hastings, MN.

256. Newspaper clippings, *Hastings Gazette, Dakota County Tribune*, P#9, Pioneer Room, Hastings, MN.

257. Buhl Aircraft Company, for OPAS, Ontario Canada, Proposed Modification of Buhl CA-6 for Provincial Air Service, Soo, Ontario Canada, Oct 31, 1931(?)

258. "Falls 2000 feet; Mamer Is Unhurt", unidentified Spokane newspaper clipping, 23 Jun 1926, also letter to *Aviation* editor from Nick Mamer 3 Jul 1926 concerning the airplane and crash, A#20 Mamer Family Archives.

259. "Goes 15,200 Feet Above City", unidentified Spokane newspaper clipping, April 1920, A#17 Mamer Family Archives.

260. "Mamer Funeral To Be Saturday", *Seattle Post-Intelligencer*, 14 Jan 1938, A#4 Mamer Family Archives.

261. "Where 10 Died In Plane Crash" story, captioned photos, *Seattle Post-Intelligencer,* 13 Jan 1938, A#4 Mamer Family Archives.

262. "'Flutter' Cause of Plane Crash", *Seattle Post-Intelligencer*, 21 Jan 1938, A#4 Mamer Family Archives.

263. Winslow, Kenelm Jr., letter to Faye Mamer, no date, A#4 Mamer Family Archives.

264. Vogel, Mrs. C.C., Letter to Faye Mamer, 14 Jan 1938, A#4 Mamer Family Archives.

265. Tinsley, Jesse,"Then and Now: The Desert Hotel", *The Spokesman-Review,* 19 Sep 2016, www.spokesman.com/stories/2016/sep/19/then-now-desert-hotel/ Accessed July 5, 2018.

266. "Mamer Refuels In Montana for Last Leg of Hop", *Minneapolis Star*, 20 Aug 1929.

267. "Sun God Gets Gas in St. Paul and Soars On", *Minneapolis Star Tribune*, 20 Aug 1929.

268. "National Air Races 1927," A#9 Mamer Family Archives,.

269. "Nick Mamer Celebrates 20 Years of Flying", *Seattle Times,* 1936 (?), also letter from Nick Mamer to Croil Hunter (Gen. Mgr., Northwest Airways), December 25, 1933, also copy of page 13, *Northwest Airliner*, date unknown, also "Happy Landings," captioned photo, *Seattle Sunday Times*, 1937 (?), A#5 Mamer Family Archives.

270. Map, Center for Great Plains Studies, University of Nebraska, https://www.unl.edu/plains/about/Map.shtml

271. "Spokane Fliers Now On Last Leg of Flight", *Rapid City Daily Journal*, 20 Aug 1929.

272. "Visibility is Poor", *Daily Missoulian,* 20 Aug 1929.

273. Mamer, Nick, "As I start to write this dispatch…" dispatch from Nick Mamer, *Montana Standard*, 19 Aug 1929.

274. Mamer, Nick Lt., "Over Chicago," and "Run Into Storm," NANA dispatches dropped for *Montana Standard,* 20 Aug 1929.

275. Yellowstone Trail, *Wikipedia*, https://en.wikipedia.org/wiki/Yellowstone_ Trail Accessed July 9, 2018.

276. Milwaukee Road Map (Chicago, Milwaukee, St. Paul & Pacific Railroad), *Wikipedia.* https://en.wikipedia.org/wiki/Chicago_Milwaukee_St.Paul_ and_Pacific_Railroad Accessed July 9, 2018.

277. "Feminine Air Derby Contestant Killed…",*Great Falls Tribune*, 21Aug 1929, also "Saw Plane Dive in Arizona Trees", *The Boston Globe,* 20 Aug 1929.

278. "Both New to Flying", *The Boston Globe,* 20 Aug 1929.

279. Loughmiller, Athol Lt., letter to his mother, July 16, 1918 from 7th Aero Squadron Cristobal Canal Zone, *Austin American*, 18 Aug 1918.

280. Mamer, Nicholas B., letter to Chief Signal Officer, Air Personnel Division, Washington DC, requesting flying status, March 13, 1918, A#13 Mamer Family Archives.

281. *Janes Aircraft*, WW I Aircraft Recognition, http://flyingmachines.ru/Site2/ Crafts/Craft25884.htm Accessed July 11, 2018.

282. War Department Aviation Section, Signal corps, U.S. Army, *Weekly Airplane Report* (Mamer, Nicholas B., records of flight time, 10-22-1917 to 6-21-1918, 7th Aero Squadron), A#13 Mamer Family Archives.

282B Wynne, W.W. Major, 7th Aero Squadron, Panama C.Z. Commander, Letter to certify dates, duration and purpose of flights participated in by MSE Nicholas B. Mamer 10-22-1917 to 6-21-1918, A#13 Mamer Family Archives.

283. Curtiss Model R, *Wikipedia,* https://en.wikipedia.org/wiki/Curtiss_ Model_R Accessed July 11, 2018.

284. "U Boats Are Answered", *Pittsburgh Daily Post,* 7 Jun 1918.

285. Maurer, Maurer, compiled & edited, *The U.S. Service In WW I, Vol II: Early Concepts of Military Aviation,* The Albert F. Simpson Historical Research Center, Maxwell AFB Alabama, The Office of the Air Force History Headquarters USAF, Washington 1978.

286. "Government Purchases Huge Seaplanes For Use In Canal Zone", *San Bernadino County Sun,* 02 Feb 1917.

287. "Aircraft Service Needs Pilots and Mechanics", *Evening Star* (Washington D.C.) 19 Sep 1918.

288. "Duesenberg Motor Company Moves Plant to Chicago", *Star Tribune* (Minneapolis) 21 Apr 1916.

289. "France Air Force Base", *Air Force Historical Research Agency* website. Accessed July 11, 2018. http://www.afhra.af.mil

290. "Sun God Refueled Here, Speeds West", unidentified newspaper clipping, A#21 Mamer Family Archives.

291. "Mamer's Plane Shook Off Bits", unidentified newspaper clipping, 20 Jan 1938, A#44 Mamer Family Archives.

292. "Part of Plane Lost In Flight", unidentified newspaper clipping, 21 Jan 1938, A#44 Mamer Family Archives.

293. "Department of Commerce Investigators Seek Reason for Disastrous Air Crash in Montana" (Northwest Airlines Lockheed Zephyr), captioned photo, unidentified newspaper clipping, A#44 Mamer Family Archives.

294. "All North America Learns of Spokane Through Sun God's Epoch-Making Trip", unidentified Spokane newspaper clipping, A#21 Mamer Family Archives.

295. "Leave at Dawn", "Non Stop to Cleveland", unidentified newspaper clipping, A#21 Mamer Family Archives.

296. "What America Thought of Spokane Sun God Epoch-Making Air Trip" montage of newspaper clippings, A#21 Mamer Family Archives.

297. "Local Aviators Refuel Sun God With Rope, Cans", *Miles City Daily Star,* A#21 Mamer Family Archives.

298. Map of Sun God Flight with photos of Mamer and Walker and Sun God, p.12-13, unidentified magazine, A#21 Mamer Family Archives.

299. "Miles City As A Two-Railroad Town", *Montana Historic Landscape.* Accessed July 15, 2018. https://montanahistoriclandscape.com/2014/12/29/mile-city-as-a-two-railroad-town/

300. Eight newspaper clippings, undated and unidentified, Hastings MN newspapers, A#43 Mamer Family Archives.

301. "Forty men trapped near Cedar …", datelined Kalispell, Aug 19—*The Missoulian,* 20 Aug 1929, also "Idaho Flames threaten 400 Million…", *Bismarck Tribune,* 20 Aug 1929.

302. *Rand McNally New Universal World Atlas,* Rand McNally Corp., 1994.

303. "New Wagon Bridge", photo, Mobridge S.D. Accessed July 15, 2018. https://bridgehunter.com/sd/walworth/bh73956

304. Mamer, Nick Lt., "Refueling Plane Now at Missoula…", *The Missoulian,* 20 Aug 1929.

305. Miles City Chamber of Commerce, *Airport Master Plan.* Accessed July 16, 2018. http://milescitychamber.com/mcLuci/uploads/2013/11/Introduction-and-Facilities-Inventory-11-25-13.pdf

306. *Danger Lights*, RKO Radio Pictures, 1930. Alpha Home Entertainment. www.oldies.com

307. Juptner, Joseph P., *U.S. Civil Aircraft Series, Vol One*, TAB AERO Division of McGraw-Hill, Inc. 1962, 1993.

308. "Spokane Sun God Plane Reaches Butte, Mont", *The Boston Globe,* 20 Aug 1929.

309. "Dedication of Field Attended by Hundreds", *The Montana Standard,* 24 April 1929.

310. "Mamer And 'Sun God' Pass Over Billings…", *The Billings Gazette,* 21 Aug 1929.

311. "Bozeman Yellowstone International Airport History". (Belgrade airport name was changed to Bozeman). Accessed July 19, 2018. https://bozemanairport.com/history

312. "Reach Butte at 9:30", *The Bend Bulletin* (Bend Oregon) 20 Aug 1929.

313. "Spokane Sun God Completes Coast to Coast…", unidentified Spokane newspaper clipping, A#21 Mamer Family Archives.

314. Mamer, Nick Lt., "Coughing Motor Thrilled Flyers", undated clipping, *The Spokesman-Review,* datelined 16 Aug 1929, A#21 Mamer Family Archives.

315. "Mamer Refueling Plane in Top Shape", undated unidentified newspaper clipping, captioned photo, also Libby, Charles A., Libby No. 40121,

Bookwalter and Coppula, also Libby No. 40087, interior of airplane, A#21 Mamer Family Archives.

316.   "Spotting Forest Fires By Air Is Risky (THRILLING) Stunt". Handwritten note on margin, "You can take the risk out of this story", signed, N.B.M. Unidentified newspaper clipping, A#21 Mamer Family Archives.

317.   "Must Tell Just Where Every Forest Fire Is", unidentified newspaper clipping, 1 Aug 1925, A#43 Mamer Family Archives.

318.   "Missoula Smokejumpers", USDA Forest Service. Accessed July 21, 2018. https://www.fs.fed.us/fire/people/smokejumpers/missoula/History/General/index.htm

319.   Pope, Nancy A, April 2004, *Smithsonian National Postal Museum,* DeHaviland DH-4. Accessed July 21, 2018. https://postalmuseum.si.edu/collections/object-spotlight/de-havilland-dh-4.html

320.   "Cooler weather yesterday came to the aid…", p.1, *The Missoulian,* 21 Aug 1929.

321.   "USFS Aircraft", *Touch & Go Society for Aviation History,* Vol.5 No.4, July 2010. http://www.sfahistory.org/SampleNewsletter.pdf

322.   "Remodeled Mail Plane Tried Out", *The Washington Times* (Washington D.C.) 05 May 1919.

323.   Kraemen, Kristin M., "First Commercial Airmail Flight 90 Years Ago Put Pasco In History Books", *Tri-City Herald,* (Pasco, Richland, Kennewick WA) 05 Apr 2016.

324.   "Man Is Killed Fighting Fires", *Lebanon Daily News* (Lebanon PA) 15 Aug 1929.

325.   "U.S. Army To Help Battle Forest Fires", *LeGrande Observer,* (LeGrande Oregon) 16 Aug 1929.

326.   "Northwest Fires", p.1, *Arizona Republic,* 16 Aug 1929.

327.   "Rushing Emergency Fuel to Mamer", *Spokane Daily Chronicle,* 16 Aug 1929, also "Sun God Departs on Return Trip of Spokane-N. Y. Flight", undated, unidentified clipping, A#21 Mamer Family Archives.

328.   Mamer, Nick, "Introducing An Advanced Phase of Endurance Flying", *Aero Digest*, Oct 1929.

329.   "Sun God Feat Better Realized", *Spokane Daily Chronicle,* 29 Aug 1929, A#21 Mamer Family Archives.

330.   "Colorful Ceremonies Just Before Take-Off At Felts Field Yesterday", *Spokane Daily Chronicle,* 16 Aug 1929.

331.   "Mamer Fixing Refueler For Nonstop Hop", undated Spokane newspaper clipping, A#21 Mamer Family Archives.

332.   Photo, "Seven of the Men Behind the Mamer Flight Scenes", undated Spokane newspaper clipping, captioned photo, A#21 Mamer Family Archives.

333.   Greeley, Carlos S, telegram to Nick Mamer, 8 Aug 1929, A#21 Mamer Family Archives.

334.   Greeley, Carlos S, Telegram to Nick Mamer, 15 Aug 1929, A#21 Mamer Family Archives.

335.   "'Miss Spokane' Here For Flight" *Spokane Daily Chronicle,* 12 Aug 1929, A#21 Mamer Family Archives.

336.   N.A.

337.   "Spokane Sun-God and Refuelers of Endurance Flight" undated unidentified Spokane newspaper clipping, captioned photo, A#21 Mamer Family Archives.

338. "Spokane Sun God Is Non Stop Ship", undated unidentified Spokane newspaper clipping, A#21 Mamer Family Archives.
339. "'Up-In-The-Air' is Right Phrase", undated unidentified Spokane newspaper clipping, A#21 Mamer Family Archives.
340. "'Sun God' Flies Eastward With Gas Tanks Full", *Chicago Tribune* clipping, 18 Aug 1929, A#21 Mamer Family Archives.
341. "Smoke Holds Up Portland Plane", *The Spokesman-Review* clipping, 15 Sep 1929, A#21 Mamer Family Archives.
342. Mamer, Nick, "Mamer Outlines Refueling Ideas", *Spokane Daily Chronicle* clipping (NAN A) 21 Aug 1929, A#21 Mamer Family Archives.
343. Mamer, Nick, "'Here We Are' Says Nick Mamer", *The Spokesman-Review* clipping (NANA), also "Sun God Aviators Return to Spokane", *The Spokesman-Review* clipping, 21 Aug 1929, A#21, Mamer Family Archives.
344. "Spokane Sun-God Flight All Set", *The Spokesman-Review* clipping, 14 Aug 1929, A#21, Mamer Family Archives.
345. "Mamer Ready For Circuit of Country", *p.15, Great Falls Tribune*, 11 Aug 1929.
346. "U. S. Okeh on Ship", undated unidentified newspaper clipping, A#21 Mamer Family Archives.
347. Grinberg, Paramount, Pathe' Newsreels, Getty Clip #841821404, Collection Sherman Grinberg Library, www.gettyimages.com/detail/video/airplane-spokane-sun-god-flying-vs-it-flies-overhead-news-footage/841821404
348. "Mamer Goes East After Refueling in California", unidentified newspaper clipping and captioned photograph, datelined Mills Field, San Francisco, 16 Aug 1929, also "Mamer Sun God Flies to East" unidentified newspaper clipping, datelined Mills Field, San Francisco, 16 Aug 1929, A#21 Mamer Family Archives.
349. "Spokane SunGod Passes Its Test", *Spokane Daily Chronicle* clipping, probably 14 Aug 1929, A#42 Mamer Family Archives.
350. "Mamer Flight Schedule Fixed" unidentified Spokane newspaper clipping, probably 11 Aug 1929, also "Mamer's Flight Set August 15", unidentified Spokane newspaper clipping 7 Aug 1929, also "Famous Aviator to Aid Mamer", unidentified Spokane newspaper clipping Aug 1929, A#42 Mamer Family Archives.
351. "Mamer Fixing Refueler For Non-Stop Hop", undated unidentified newspaper clipping, Aug 1929, A#21 Mamer Family Archives. See Ref#331
352. "Get Barograph For Big Flight", undated unidentified newspaper clipping, Aug 1929, A#21 Mamer Family Archives.
353. Air Derby Association, program for Nick Mamer Day (Send-Off, August 7, 1929), Marie Antoinette Room, Davenport Hotel, Spokane Washington, A#21 Mamer Family Archives.
354. N.A.
355. "Los Angeles Mail Plane Hits In Fog", p.1, *The Los Angeles Times,* 03 Oct 1928.
356. "Local Aviator to Attempt Coast to Coast…" unidentified newspaper clipping, also "Speed Record Try For Mamer", undated unidentified newspaper clipping, A#1 (Mamer-Ford Tour Ledger) Mamer Family Archives.
357. "Mamer Chooses Plane's Co-Pilot", undated unidentified newspaper clipping, A#1 (Mamer-Ford Tour Ledger) Mamer Family Archives.

358. "Thirty Spokane Businessmen In Meeting Today Sponsor Flight—Route Now Being Worked Out", *Spokane Daily Chronicle* (?), July 1929, A#1(Mamer-Ford Tour Ledger) Mamer Family Archives.

359. "Mamer Flight Aides Organize", undated unidentified Spokane newspaper clipping, July 1929, A#1 (Mamer-Ford Tour Ledger) Mamer Family Archives.

360. "Mamer Flies With Yeast to Village Isolated By Snow", undated unidentified newspaper clipping, A#1 (Mamer-Ford Tour Ledger) Mamer Family Archives.

361. "National Flyers Here to Attend Airmen's Dance", undated unidentified Minnesota newspaper clipping with captioned photo, A#1 (Mamer-Ford Tour Ledger) Mamer Family Archives.

362. "Refuel Points Are Scheduled", undated unidentified newspaper clipping, A#1 (Mamer-Ford Tour Ledger) Mamer Family Archives.

363. "Mamer's Record As A Flier Impressive As Results Are Studied", probably *Miles City Star,* 8 Apr 1929, A#1 (Mamer-Ford Tour Ledger) Mamer Family Archives

364. "Coast to Coast Pilots Train", undated unidentified newspaper clipping, A#1(Mamer-Ford Tour Ledger) Mamer Family Archives.

365. "Veteran Airmen Meet Again In Spokane First time Since War", undated unidentified newspaper clipping, A#1(Mamer-Ford Tour Ledger) Mamer Family Archives.

366. Photo Caption: "Thirty minutes after meeting of prominent Spokane businessmen", undated unidentified newspaper clipping, A#1(Mamer-Ford Tour Ledger) Mamer Family Archives.

367. "'West Wind' Winging West to Valley", *Valley City Peoples Opinion* (Valley City N.D.), 4 Apr 1929, A#1 (Mamer-Ford Tour Ledger) Mamer Family Archives.

368. "Big Mamer Ship Plans Trip Over Mount Rainier", undated Seattle newspaper clipping, A#1 (Mamer-Ford Tour Ledger) Mamer Family Archives.

369. "Sun God Sits Down In St. Paul", Spokane unidentified newspaper clipping, 25 or 26 Aug 1929, A#21 Mamer Family Archives.

370. Turner, Clint, "Restoring My Atwater Kent Model 20", www.ka7oei.com/ak20c.html

371. "Sun-God Pilots Presented $1000", *The Spokesman-Review* clipping, 23 Aug 1929, A#21 Mamer Family Archives.

372. Libby, Charles A., photograph No. 3850, interior of Sun God, A#21 Mamer Family Archives.

373. Libby, Charles A., photograph No. #40138 , interior of Sun God, A#21 Mamer Family Archives.

374. "Wonderful Start For Mamer Plane", *The Spokesman-Review* clipping, probably 16 Aug 1929, A#21 Mamer Family Archives.

375. Carlson, Anya, photograph of Felts Field Mamer Clock Tower Memorial and plaque, 30 Jun 2018.

376. Fisher, Bob, "Aviation History: Ford Tri-Motors", geochache: www.geocaching.com/geocache/GC43KMV_aviation-history-ford-tri-motors?guid=45b691d8-d3e2-466e-bfd2-909450a626f8

377. Mamer, N.B. "Nick", letter to A.E. Hurst, Camas Hot Springs, Hot Springs, Montana, December 17, 1933. Accessed August 9, 2018. http://www.earlyaviators.com/emamer.htm

378. "Sun-God Pilots Leave at Dawn", *Spokane Daily Chronicle* clipping 24 Aug 1929 (?), A#21 Mamer Family Archives.

379. "Sugar Factory Begins First run", Sugar Beet Section, *The Sunday Missoulian*, 14 Oct 1928.

380. "Zooming over the crest…", p.2, *Billings Gazzette,* 21 Aug 1929, datelined Butte, Aug. 20.

381. "Spokane Pilot Drops Note Expressing Regret…", p.1, *The Montana Standard,* 21 Aug 1929.

382. "Anaconda Smelter Stack", *Wikipedia.* Accessed August 11, 2018. https://en.wikipedia.org/wiki/Anaconda_Smelter_Stack

383. N.A.

384. Missoula International Airport, history. Accessed August 11, 2018. https://flymissoula.com/about-mso/mso-history/

385. "Refueled Twice Here", p.2, *The Missoulian,* 21 Aug 1929.

386. "Circling above a curtain of smoke…", p.1, *The Billings Gazette,* 21 Aug 1929.

387. "Auctions—Legals", p. 13, *The Times Herald* (Port Huron, Michigan) 20 Oct 1932.

388. "To Sell Planes At Buhl Auction", p.14, *The Times Herald* (Port Huron, Michigan) 29 Oct 1932.

389. "Former Manager Of Buhl Aircraft Corporation Dies", p.5, *The Times Herald* (Port Huron, Michigan) 06 Sep 1932.

390. "Motive In Man's Suicide Is Sought", p. 11, *Lansing State Journal* (Lansing, Michigan) 23 Dec 1932.

391. Ontario Provincial Air Service Buhl Air-Sedans, *Canadian Bushplane Heritage Centre.* Accessed August 12, 2018. http://www.bushplane.com

392. "Mamer And Walker May Bring Sun God To Marysville Soon", p.7, *The Times Herald* (Port Huron, Michigan) 23 Aug 1929.

393. "Mamer to Fly to Marysville" p.1, *The Times Herald,* (Port Huron, Michigan) 04 Sep 1929, also, "Mamer Changes Plans, Marysville Visit Canceled" p.2, *The Times Herald,* 05 Sep 1929.

394. "Buhl Aircraft Co. Dissolution Asked", p.7, *The Times Herald* (Port Huron, Michigan) 14 Jun 1932.

395. Northern Pacific Railroad Map Circ. 1900. *Wikimedia Commons.* Accessed Aug 12, 2018. https://commons.wikimedia.org/wiki/File:Northern_Pacific_Railroad_map_circa_1900.jpg

396. "Dangerous Leg", p.1, *The Montana Standard,* 21 Aug 1929.

397. Pemberton, Addison, email to J.B. Rivard. Addison Pemberton's recollection of his trip to find the Sun God, received August 13, 2018.

398. National Personnel Records Center, National Archives, St. Louis, MO., letter to Anya Carlson from Derek Springmeyer, Archives Technician (AFN-MC2A) Re: Mamer, Nicholas B., SSN/SN: 348467, August 8, 2018, includes copies of documents.

399. "Just After Spokane Sun-God Landed", *The Spokesman-Review* clipping, captioned photo, 21 Aug 1929, A#42 Mamer Family Archives.

400. Hindley, W.W., "3-Mile-a-Minute Glimpse of City Provides Thrills", undated *Spokane Daily Chronicle* clipping, also "Fast Lockheed N. W. Liner Here" undated unidentified newspaper clipping, A#21 Mamer Family Archives.

401. "A Record And A Wire", *Aero Digest,* Oct 1929, advertisement for Buhl

Aircraft Co.

402.   Hoover, Herbert, President of the United States, Telegram to Mamer and Walker, 20 Aug 1929, A#21 Mamer Family Archives.

403.   National Personnel Records Center, 26 Jul 2018, Letter, Request #2-21657788780. Service Record for Nicholas B. Mamer SN 348467, (Destroyed by fire July 12, 1973).

404.   Leatherwood, Art, revised by Jasinski, Laurie E., *Handbook of Texas Online,* "Kelly Air Force Base". Accessed August 20, 2018. https://tshaonline.org/handbook/online/articles/qbk01

405.   "Mamer Has Plane Serviced Here For Flight to Spokane" and "Mamer To Leave For Home Today", *The Casper Herald* (Casper WY) clipping 15 Sep 1928, A#7 Mamer Family Archives, also three photographs of Buhl Special Airsedan with attached notations: "Roosevelt Field 10 Big Planes Ready to Start…9-11-28", A#8 Mamer Family Archives.

406.   "Hastings Aviator First Minnesotan to Enlist for Army Plane Work", p. 17, *Star Tribune* (Minneapolis MN) 01 Jul 1916.

407.   "Overseas Aviation Defenses", p. 3, *The Washington Post,* 25 Feb 1917.

408.   "Aero Squadron For Panama", p. 3, *El Paso Herald,* 08 Mar 1917.

409.   "Aero Squadron New Commander", p. 8, *Dayton Daily News* (Dayton Ohio) 03 Oct 1917.

410.   "SS Aleutian", *Wikipedia.* (Aleutian is the S.S. Panama, renamed). Accessed August 22, 2018 https://en.wikipedia.org/wiki/SS_Aleutian

411.   "Mrs. Mary Mamer…received a letter…", undated Hastings MN newspaper clipping, A#43 Mamer Family Archives.

412.   Glines, C.V. "General Henry H. "Hap" Arnold: Architect of America's Air Force", *Aviation History Magazine* June 12, 2006. HistoryNet.com Accessed August 23, 2018.

413.   McCain, Henry P, Major General, Adjutant General, Cablegram to Blatchford, Richard M, Brigadier General, Panama Canal Dept. Commander, and response: Re: Nicholas B Mamer, A#13 Mamer Family Archives.

414.   Wynne, Walter W, Major RMA Signal Corps, letter of approval of Mamer's request to be sent to pilot training, March 30, 1918, A#13 Mamer Family Archives.

415.   Hinck, C.W. Letter of introduction for N.B. Mamer, April 15, 1920, A#15 Mamer Family Archives.

416.   "Peterson Goes With the Federated Fliers", undated unidentified Minnesota newspaper clipping, June 1919, A#43 Mamer Family Archives.

417.   "Lt. Paul H. Davis, Whose Fate Held a Nation in Suspense, Describes His Experiences…", *Madera Mercury* (Madera, California), No. 79, 10 Sep 1919.

418.   "Curtiss JN-4 'Jenny'", *Wikipedia.* Accessed August 28, 2018.

419.   "Airplane Lands On Main Street and Does Stunts", undated unidentified Kalispell, Montana newspaper clipping, 16 Jul 1920, A#43 Mamer Family Archives.

420.   Messer, C. H., agreement by Nicholas B. Mamer and United States Aircraft Corp., April 9, 1920, A#17 Mamer Family Archives.

421.   "Hangs by Toes from Airplane", undated unidentified Spokane newspaper clipping, April-May 1920, A#43 Mamer Family Archives.

422.   "Spent Honeymoon In The Clouds", undated unidentified newspaper clipping, captioned photograph of Mamer and wife, A#43 Mamer Family

Archives.

423. "Airplane Plunges Into River", *Spokane Daily Chronicle,* 30 Aug 1922, A#17 Mamer Family Archives.

424. "He Misses Death But Is Arrested", *The Spokesman-Review* clipping and photo, captioned "Air Plane Dives Into Spokane River", probably 31 Aug 1922, A#43 Mamer Family Archives.

425. Hammer, Joshua, "The Great Japan Earthquake of 1923", *Smithsonian Magazine,* May 2011.

426. "Mamer Flies With Earthquake Films", undated unidentified newspaper clipping, A#43 Mamer Family Archives.

427. "Spokane Pilot Rushes Quake Pictures to New York Times Plane", undated unidentified newspaper clipping, A#43 Mamer Family Archives.

428. "Heavy Stakes For Aviators In Film Race", p.1, *Springfield Leader and Press* (Springfield Missouri) 25 Sep 1923.

429. "Plane Speeding Eastward With Japanese Quake Films", p. 26, *St. Louis Post Dispatch,* 25 Sep 1923.

430. "New York In 24 Hours", p. 12, *Great Falls Tribune* (Great Falls Montana) 25 Sep 1923.

431. "Cruises Along Over Water and Discovers Remains of ..." and "Airplane Pilot Locates Body of Drowned Girl From Mid-Air", two undated unidentified newspaper clippings, A#43 Mamer Family Archives.

432. "Use Planes for Forest Patrol", "Contract for Aerial Patrol" and "Start Aerial Forest Patrol Over Association's Timber" three undated unidentified newspaper clippings, early 1923, A#43 Mamer Family Archives.

433. Marcus, Norman, "Dempsey vs Gibbons: The Fight that Ruined A Town", boxing.com November 21, 2012. Accessed Sept 2, 2018.

434. "Aviator Risks Life to Bring Fight Photos", *Spokane Press* clipping and captioned photographs, 5 Jul 1923, A#43 Mamer Family Archives.

435. "Pilot Nick Mamer, Supervisor Flint, Photograph Fire-Damaged Forest", "To Film Ruins of Forest Fire", and "New Air Pilot at Mamer Home" (13 Feb 1927), three unidentified newspaper clippings, A#43 Mamer Family Archives.

436. "Lt. Mamer Wins Fame With Exploits", undated unidentified newspaper clipping, A#43 Mamer Family Archives.

437. "Big Plane Lands In Oregon Fog", "Mamer Starts Flight North", and "Airplane Forced Down", three undated unidentified newspaper clippings, A#43 Mamer Family Archives.

438. "Up In The Air Again—First Time Since War", undated unidentified newspaper clipping, captioned photograph, 1924, A#43 Mamer Family Archives.

439. President of the United States of America, Certificate appointing NB Mamer as Second Lieutenant Air Service effective from April 19, 1924, dated Feb 27, 1925, A#16 Mamer Family Archives.

440. Partridge, E. Harve, *Aviation,* July 12, 1926, p.68, "Airports and Airways, Spokane, Washington"

441. "Type of Plane Mamer Will Fly in Air Derby", undated unidentified newspaper clipping, captioned photograph (incorrect information) A#9 Mamer Family Archives.

442. "Gassing Up at Cleveland, New York-Spokane Class 'A' Derby", three photographs of New York-Spokane Class "A" Derby, 19 Sep 1927, A#9 Mamer

Family Archives.

443. "Third Into Butte And Third In The Derby", undated unidentified newspaper clipping captioned photograph, and undated unidentified newspaper clipping "'That's all right; we're leaving now,' Holman answered.", A#43 Mamer Family Archives.

444. Groom, Winston, *The Aviators,* National Geographic Society, 2013.

445. Kershner, Jim, "A bomb explosion fatally injures Spokane pioneer aviator Major John T. Fancher during an air show in East Wenatchee on April 29, 1928.", HistoryLink.org Essay 9555.

446. "Crash of a Sikorsky S-35 in Rooosevelt Field; 2 Killed" *Bureau of Aircraft Accidents Archives.* Accessed Sept 9, 2018. https://www.baaa-acro.com/crash/crash-sikorski-s-35

447. "5 Mishaps In Plane Race", p. 1,4, & p.2, *New York Daily News* clippings and captioned photographs, 13 Sep 1928, A#7 Mamer Family Archives.

448. "All Fliers Fail In Non-Stop Race", *The Casper Herald,* 14 Sep 1928, A#7 & 8 Mamer Family Archives.

449. "Art Goebel added to the…", *Denver Evening News* clipping 14 Sep 1928, datelined Los Angeles, 13 Sept 1928, A#7 Mamer Family Archives.

450. Partridge, E. Harve, "Local Air Pilot Flies Long Hours", undated unidentified clipping, A#43 Mamer Family Archives.

451. "Three Fall 900 Feet", p.1, *Morning Register* (Eugene Oregon) 23 Jun 1926.

452. National Guard of the United States, Honorable Discharge certificate, also letter of commission to 2nd Lieutenant Nicholas Bernard Mamer from Maurice Thompson, Brigadier General, also President of the United States, Appointment as 2nd Lieutenant, Air Corps, A#16 Mamer Family Archives.

453. "Nick Mamer Completes Purchase of Ford Tri-Motored Plane", *Spokane Daily Chronicle* clipping captioned photograph, 21 Mar 1929, A#1 (Mamer-Ford Tour Ledger) Mamer Family Archives.

454. "Ford Tri-Motored Airplane to Visit Bismarck In April", *Bismarck Tribune* clipping 27 Mar 1929, A#1 (Mamer-Ford Tour Ledger) Mamer Family Archives.

455. "Mamer Has Enviable Nation-Wide Reputation In Flying Business; Has Been In Air Game Since War", undated unidentified newspaper clipping, late 1929, A#21 Mamer Family Archives.

456. "Mamer to Get Indian Name", undated unidentified newspaper clipping A#1 (Mamer-Ford Tour Ledger) Mamer Family Archives.

457. Cates, Grant, "Paper Session I-A Airmail and the Evolution of the U.S. Aviation Industry in the 1920s…", paper presented at *The Space Congress 2000*, 02 May 2000. http://commons.erau.edu/space-congress-proceedings

458. "Mamer Wins; Flies St. Paul to Seattle, Day Round Trip", *The Spokesman-Review* clipping, 19 Jul 1930, A#21 Mamer Family Archives, also two photos of Buhl CA-1, A#10 Mamer Family Archives.

459. "Mamer Makes St. Paul Round Trip In 24 Hrs", *Seattle Post-Intelligencer* clipping with captioned photograph, 19 Jul 1930, A#10 Mamer Family Archives.

460. *Ford Tri-Motor Tour, Press Book*, Ledger A#1 Scrapbook, A#1 Mamer Family Archives.

461. Mamer, Nicholas B "Nick", three clippings on 1929 Air Races In Cleveland, A#21 Mamer Family Archives.

462. Buhl CA-1 Airster, *Wikipedia*. Accessed Sept 14, 2018. https://wikipedia.

org/wiki/Buhl_CA-1_Airster

463. "Pilot Mamer Is Guest At Dinner Meet", undated unidentified newspaper clipping, LaGrande Oregon, A#1 (Mamer-Ford Tour Ledger) Mamer Family Archives.

464. "Tri-Motored Ford Plane to Visit Local Airport May 28", undated unidentified Longview WA newspaper clipping, 1929, A# 1 (Mamer-Ford Tour Ledger) Mamer Family Archives.

465. "Nick Mamer Blazes Trail From Coast", unidentified St. Paul MN newspaper clipping, 24 Oct 1928, A#19 Mamer Family Archives.

466. "Mamer Succeeds In Nonstop Hop", *The Spokesman-Review,* 25 Oct 1928, A#19 Mamer Family Archives.

467. "Family Tree-Northwest Airlines" Delta Flight Museum. Accessed Sept 16, 2018. https://www.deltamuseum.org/exhibits/delta-history/family-tree/northwest-airlines

468. Howard, Frank and Gunston, Bill, *The Conquest of the Air,* Random House, 1972.

469. "Big Ford Plane Service Ready", undated unidentified newspaper clipping, 1929, A#1 (Mamer-Ford Tour Ledger) Mamer Family Archives.

470. Kyvig, David E, *Daily Life in the United States 1920-1940,* Ivan R. Dee, Chicago 2002/2004.

471. "Mamer Will Open Service From Spokane to St. Paul", *The Missoula Sentinel,* 8 Feb 1930, A#30 Mamer Family Archives.

472. "St. Paul Becomes Aviation Hub With New Service to Spokane", *St. Paul Daily News* clipping, 15 Jun 1930, A#42 Mamer Family Archives.

473. "Mamer Airline Plane Wrecked at Idaho Port", p.1, *The Billings Gazette,* 12 Sep 1930.

474. "…the Mamer company had operated…"p.3, *The Billings Gazette,* 22 Nov 1930.

475. "Mamer Says Fast Planes Aid Travel", undated unidentified newspaper clipping, probably 1932, A#30, Mamer Family Archives.

476. "Spokane-Seattle Air Service Will Be Doubled Soon", p.5, *The Missoulian,* 23 Mar 1931.

477. "Mamer Air Transport Low Bidder on Forest Patrol Work In West", p.16, *The Montana Standard,* 13 May 1931.

478. "Airplanes Used to Spot Forest Fires When Smoke Is Too Thick For Lookouts", p.1, *The Montana Standard,* 26 Jul 1931.

479. "Dempsey came into Eugene on the 1:20 train…" p.1, *The Eugene Guard* (Eugene Oregon) 04 Sep 1931.

480. "Airways Advance Missoula Route", *The Sunday Missoulian,* 19 Nov 1933.

481. "Nick Mamer, Spokane Pilot of Sun God Fame, Lays Out Emergency State Ports", p.3, *The Billings Gazette,* 19 Nov 1933.

482. "New N.W. Airways Cruisers Are Fast", p.2, *The Minneapolis Star,* 20 Nov 1933.

483. "Who's Who In Air, Nick Mamer Pioneer Pilot", undated unidentified newspaper clipping, A#42 Mamer Family Archives.

484. "Airway Officer Announces New Fast Schedule", p.1, *The Billings Gazette,* 07 Dec 1933.

485. "New Speed Ship of Northwest Airways In City", *The Billings Gazette,* early 1934, A#21 Mamer Family Archives.

486. *Northwest Airliner,* 14-page booklet for passengers, probably 1936, A#5

Mamer Family Archives.

487. "Air Mail Scandal", *airlinefiles.com* Accessed Sept 12, 2018. https://airline-files.com/airline-profile-drop-down-box/historic-milestones-item/221-air-mail-scandal.html

488. "Vast Gains In Aviation Made At Spokane Field", undated unidentified Spokane newspaper clipping, 1929, A#21 Mamer Family Archives.

489. Mamer, N.B., *Mamer Air Transport Approved School of Flying,* 12-page booklet, probably 1929-1930, A#30 Mamer Family Archives.

490. "Mamer Planes Go Adventuring", undated unidentified Spokane newspaper clipping, probably Nov-Dec, 1934, A#21 Mamer Family Archives.

491. "Mamer Retains Flying School", undated unidentified Spokane newspaper clipping, A#21 Mamer Family Archives.

492. "Blum was followed in elapsed time by Nick…" p.9, *The Dayton Herald* (Dayton Ohio) 26 Aug 1930.

493. Beitler, Stu, "Bozeman, MT Plane Crash, Jan 1938", *GenDisasters; Events that touched our Ancestors' lives.* Accessed Sept 20, 2018. http://www.gendisasters.com/montana/423/bozeman-mt-plane-crash-jan-1938?page=0,7

494. "Skies Were Bad Board Is Told", p.3, unidentified Montana newspaper clipping, 19 Jan 1938, A#4 and A#44 Mamer Family Archives.

495. "Lockheed Model 14 Super Electra", *Wikipedia.* Accessed Sept 20, 2018.

496. "First Air Crash Photos", p.1 & 4, *Seattle Daily Times* clippings with captioned photographs, 11 Jan 1938, A#4 Mamer Family Archives.

497. "Plane Crash Inquest Is Opened; Said All Killed Before Blaze Broke Out", p.1, *The Independent Record* (Helena Montana) 13 Jan 1938.

498. "Seattle Plane Crashes, Burns; 10 Believed Dead"- "Sketch of Doomed Airliner", p.2, *Seattle Post-Intelligencer,* 11 Jan 1938, A#4 and A#44 Mamer Family Archives.

499. Mamer, Faye C, Western Union Telegram to Capt. James Mamer and Family, Jan 11, 1938. A#4 Mamer Family Archives.

500. "Mamer Funeral To Be Saturday", undated unidentified Seattle newspaper clipping, Jan 1938, A#44 Mamer Family Archives.

501. "Gone Before Ship Hit", p.1, *The Montana Standard,* 21 Jan 1938.

502. "Mamer's Plane Shook Off Bits", undated unidentified newspaper clipping, datelined Bozeman Mont. 20 Jan 1938, also "Mamer Memorial Urged by Martin", undated unidentified newspaper clipping, datelined Spokane, 14 Jan 1938, also "Rudder of Wrecked N. W. Plane Found" undated unidentified newspaper clipping, datelined Bozeman, Mont. 7 Feb 1938, also "Part Of Plane Lost In Flight" unidentified newspaper clipping dated 21 Jan 1938, datelined Bozeman, Mont. 20 Jan 1938, A#44 Mamer Family Archives.

503. "Tail Assembly Blamed For 10-Death Crack-Up", p.13, *Arizona Republic,* 21 Jan 1938.

504. "Reward Posted For Plane Tail", undated unidentified newspaper clipping, datelined Bozeman, Mont. 19 Jan 1938, A#4 and A#44 Mamer Family Archives.

505. "Section of Tail Assembly Found", p.10, *Casper Star-Tribune* (Casper Wyoming) 20 Feb 1938.

506. "Governor Pays Flyer Tribute", unidentified Spokane newspaper clipping, 31 May 1939, also undated unidentified newspaper captioned photograph of Faye & Patricia, A#4 Mamer Family Archives.

507. Pettit, Stefanie, "Felts Field clock honors aviator Nick Mamer", *The Spokesman-Review* 20 Sep 2007. Accessed Sept 22, 2018. http://www.spokesman.com/stories/2007/sep/20/felts-field-clock-honors-aviator-nick-mamer/

508. "Northwest Airlines Starts Proving Runs",p.7, *The Billings Gazette,* 9 Feb 1938.

509. "File Crash Suit.", p.9, *The Billings Gazette,* 13 Sep 1938.

510. "Veteran Pilot Is Missoula Visitor", undated unidentified newspaper clipping, probably 1934, A#21 Mamer Family Archives.

511. "Mourn At Bier of Nick Mamer", undated unidentified Seattle newspaper clipping, datelined Seattle, 15 Jan 1938, A#44 Mamer Family Archives.

512. "Seattle Plane Crashes Near Bozeman; 9 Die", *Seattle Post-Intelligencer* clipping, 11 Jan 1938, A#4 Mamer Family Archives.

513. "Plane Which Spanned U.S. Twice Without a Stop, Is Visitor Here", p.2, *Battle Creek Enquirer,* 19 Sep 1929.

514. "Three visiting planes stopped at Kellogg airport last week…" p.3, *Battle Creek Enquirer,* 16 Feb 1930.

515. "Thousands On Field To See Altitude Flight", p.1, *The Times Herald* (Port Huron Michigan) 13 Jun 1931.

516. "Brothers Bid In Buhl Property For $80,000", p.1, *The Times Herald* (Port Huron Michigan) 31 Oct 1932.

517. "Buhl Bull Pup", *Wikipedia.* Accessed Sept 25, 2018.

518. Glynn, James B.,"Buhl Bros. Sells Hardware Firm", p.9, *Detroit Free Press,* 8 Jan 1960.

519. "Name of Buhl Long Famous", p.3, *Detroit Free Press,* 24 Dec 1932.

520. Wide World Photos, photograph with attachment: "10 Big Planes Ready to Start On Transcontinental Nonstop Race. Photo Shows N.B. Mamer [seated in plane]Who Is Piloting A Buhl Special Air Sedan In The Nonstop Derby", (Local Roosevelt Field, N.Y.) 11 Sep 1928, A#8 Mamer Family Archives.

521. Wide World Photos, photograph with attachment: "10 Big Planes Ready to Start On Transcontinental Nonstop Race. Photo Shows N.B. Mamer [standing] who Is Piloting A Buhl Special Air Sedan In The Nonstop Derby", (Local Roosevelt Field, N.Y.) 11 Sep 1928, A#8 Mamer Family Archives.

522. "From that Picture Man Denkelberg Port Huron, Mich" photograph, A#8 Mamer Family Archives.

523. "The then-new St. Louis Arena in St. Louis, Missouri, where the 1930 International Aircraft Show was taking place" captioned photograph from www.dawgshed.com 29 Mar 2017, page 3590 of 4430. Accessed 14 Nov 2018.

ACKNOWLEDGMENTS

After I'd written my assignment for the magazine, the senior editor cautioned me, "The most difficult part of this will now be to remain interesting, to keep the story moving, and to tell it clearly and concisely." Nearly thirty years later, Marilyn Barrett's words continue to ricochet in my mind—getting a story on paper is only the beginning.

And one should begin at the beginning. The beginning of this book occurred February 4, 2018, when during a visit, Bob Fisher related some incidents in the life of Nick Mamer. He remarked on the many articles published about the famous aviator, but thought the absence of a book on Mamer odd. "However," he said with a smile and a pointed finger, "you're just the guy to write that book!" Although I had chapters and drawings for another book in hand, I quickly realized an opportunity—and a challenge.

Later, after deducing an address from the Internet, I wrote a letter to one of Nick Mamer's grandchildren. It explained my writing mission and sought the family's help. Some days later, my phone rang. Nick's grandson, David S. Lee, said his sister had contacted him about my letter. He said he had custody of the Mamer "family archives," and that he was open to having me view them. As it turned out, I was allowed over many months complete access to this trove of primary materials unavailable to others. Without that extraordinary privilege this book would have been less detailed, lacking in scope and limited in authenticity. My debt of gratitude to the grandchildren of Nick Mamer is deep and lasting.

During the actual course of writing this work, valuable advice and encouragement were offered by too many to name. However, I would particularly like to list Vince and Karen Azzinnaro, Russel Davis, Bob and Connie Fisher, Roger Mattson, Addison Pemberton, Ivy Rivard and Jayne Singleton.

I also thank the Pioneer Room in Hastings, MN, for their assistance. Cindy Smith of that Room was promptly cooperative and gracious in supplying information from their records.

I'm grateful to John Harper at Texaco for his aid in obtaining Nick's article written for the Texaco Star. Anna Harbine at the Joel E. Ferris Research Library of the Northwest Museum of Arts and Culture helped us copy articles on Mamer in their archives. Libby Kamrowski helped us with scans from the Spokane Daily Chronicle.

Readers of initial drafts are long suffering. Here are some who have survived this kind of treatment: Vince Azzinnaro, Bob Fisher, Cam Inglis, Addison Pemberton, Ivy Rivard, and Pat Sheldon.

This, my first attempt at a nonfiction book, benefitted from the advice of Sol Stein, the master editor of some of the most successful writers in the world. His 1995 book, Stein on Writing, was often open on my desk during the writing of this book.

My goal has been from the onset to present a fair and accurate account of the flight of the Sun God, together with as much as is available about Nick Mamer's life. Anya Carlson brings expert research persistence, indefatigable editing and proofreading, and day-to-day advice to a project. Her love, support and dedication are very much appreciated, though I hasten to add that the errors, mistakes, and omissions are entirely mine.

GLOSSARY OF AVIATION TERMS

AGL abbreviation of Above (local) Ground Level, qualifier for altitude; see **MSL**

ailerons hinged portions of the trailing edges of a wing which change the wing's lifting properties

airfoil a shape designed by its orientation and motion to control the flow of air

airspeed speed of an aircraft relative to its surrounding air mass—see **ground speed**

airspeed indicator instrument which registers speed through the air, in miles per hour or in knots.

altimeter instrument that indicates altitude by measuring air pressure

angle of attack angle of the aircraft along the flight path, i.e., pitch up, level, pitch down

attitude indicator instrument that displays **pitch** and **roll** (or **bank**) of the aircraft; also called **artificial horizon**

bank the angle of **roll** during a turn; the angle wings make with the true horizon

biplane an airplane with two wings, one above the other, of approximately equal wingspan

ceiling maximum altitude aircraft is able to reach and maintain; also the height of clouds above ground

circle to turn at a steady rate while maintaining a fixed altitude

cockpit control zone of the aircraft; may also designate the location of an observer or passenger

control surfaces movable, pilot-controlled parts, including flaps, ailerons, rudders and elevators that determine the motion and behavior of the aircraft in the air

coordinated turn combination of control inputs by the pilot that produce a maximally efficient turn

deadstick flying without the aid of engine power or thrust

ditch to land safely somewhere other than a runway

dive to descend, nose-down; this results in increasing the aircraft's forward airspeed unless countered by other pilot inputs

drag a force tending to slow an aircraft in the direction of motion

drift the angle between an aircraft's heading and its actual path of travel (**track**)

elevator hinged portion of the tail's horizontal stabilizer; it controls pitch

final proper heading, descent rate, airspeed, and altitude during approach prior to landing.

flaps hinged portions of the wing that increase the lift of the wing. Most often used to allow slower landings and shorter takeoffs. Not always present.

flare pitch-up of the nose, before landing, as the aircraft nears the ground. Its purpose is to minimize the descent rate at touchdown

FPM abbreviation of Feet Per Minute, a unit of measure of speed

fuselage body of an aircraft, usually contains cockpit, cabin, cargo space, etc.

gear landing gear, the undercarriage and wheels of an aircraft

ground speed speed of an aircraft relative to the surface of the earth; see **airspeed**

heading direction in which the nose of the aircraft is pointed; may not coincide with actual direction of travel (see **drift**)

horizontal stabilizer horizontal section of the tail that provides pitch stability (nose up, nose down)

inputs pilot's actions using the airplane's controls

knot one nautical mile per hour; approximately 1.15 statute miles per hour

lateral axis axis along the wing about which an aircraft pitches

lift force created by a moving airfoil, often refers to the lifting force of wing

liquid-cooled engine internal-combustion motor which is cooled by water flowing through a radiator

longitudinal axis axis, extending from nose to tail, about which an aircraft rolls

mixture amount of gasoline relative to the amount of air fed to an internal-combustion motor during operation; 'increase' means higher proportion of gasoline; 'lean' means reduced proportion of gasoline

MSL abbreviation for Mean Sea Level, the average height of the surface of the sea, qualifier (datum) for altitude; see **AGL**

pitch   angle of the airplane's longitudinal axis relative to horizontal

radial engine   aircraft motor in which the internal-combustion cylinders are arranged in a circle around the shaft of the propeller; usually air-cooled

rate of climb   speed (**FPM**) at which aircraft gains altitude; also (negative) speed at which it loses altitude

roll   angle of the plane's wings relative to horizontal; causes aircraft to bank

RPM   abbreviation for Revolutions (full rotations) Per Minute, rate at which propeller (or rotor, turbine, etc.) turns

rudder   hinged, movable section of the vertical (fin) stabilizer

sesquiplane   an airplane with one full wing and a second wing of half its span

side-slip   maneuver in which the aircraft loses altitude without increasing speed; alternative to diving (see **dive**)

stall   loss of lift during flight caused by insufficient speed or improper orientation of the aircraft. A stall causes a loss of altitude.

stick   lever in the cockpit which, with forward/back motion controls the elevators, and with left/right motion controls the ailerons; see **yoke**

tachometer   onboard instrument indicating engine/propeller speed in RPM

tab   small hinged surface, or other adjusting mechanism (usually in the cockpit) providing straight, level flight without a pilot's input to the controls. Also known as **trim tab**

taxi   movement of an airplane under power while on the ground

throttle   control in the cockpit, usually a lever, which adjusts the motor's power

track   actual path traveled by the aircraft over the ground

trim   adjust the tabs of an aircraft; also the state of an aircraft in which no control input by the pilot is required to maintain straight, level flight

turn and slip indicator   instrument that shows two aspects: the rate of turning of the aircraft and also whether skidding or slipping (lack of **coordinated turn**)

vertical stabilizer   vertical (fin) section of the tail, maintains the aircraft aligned along its direction of motion

vertical speed indicator   instrument which indicates rate of climb or descent, in feet per minute (**FPM**), see **rate of climb**

wing   aircraft structure designed to produce lift

wingspan   linear distance between the tips of a wing

yaw   angle of the airplane's longitudinal axis relative to its direction of motion

yaw axis   imaginary vertical axis about which an aircraft yaws

yoke   pilot's control, an alternative to **stick**. Consists of a wheel on a lever; the wheel controls the airplane's ailerons; the lever controls the airplane's elevators

BIBLIOGRAPHY

Clason Map Co., *Atlas of the Best Roads of The United States*, 1924, Clason Map Co., Chicago 1924.

Groom, Winston, *The Aviators*, National Geographic Society, 2013.

Holder, Gill and Wallace, Mike, *Range Unlimited, a History of Aerial Refueling*, A Schiffer Military History Book, 2000.

Howard, Frank and Gunston, Bill, *The Conquest of the Air*, Random House, 1972.

Juptner, Joseph P., *U.S. Civil Aircraft Series, Vol. One*, TAB AERO Division, McGraw Hill, Inc., 1962, 1993.

Kyvig, David E., *Daily Life in the United States 1920-1940*, Ivan R. Dee, Chicago 2002/2004.

McGoldrick II, J. P., *One Man's Opinion of the Spokane Aviation Story, Part I 1920-1941*, Ye Galleon Press, Fairfield WA, 1982.

McGoldrick II, J.P., *The Spokane Aviation Story*, Tornado Creek Publications, Spokane, WA 2007.

Plehinger, Russell, *Marathon Flyers*, Harlo Press, Detroit MI, 1989.

Rand McNally, *New Universal World Atlas*, Rand McNally Corp., 1994.

Smith, Richard K., (compiled by), *Seventy-five Years of Inflight Military Aircraft Refueling Highlights 1923-1998*, Progressive Management Publications, 1998.

Wiley, Frank W., *Montana and the Sky*, Holden Printing Co., Minneapolis MN, Montana Aeronautics Commission, First Edition, 1966.

Williams, J.R., *IFR By The Book, Techniques of Instrument Flying*, General Aviation Press, Snyder, TX, First Printing, March 1980.

Wohl, Robert, *The Spectacle of Flight, Aviation and the Western Imagination 1920-1950*, Yale University Press, New Haven & London, 2005.

INDEX

A

Page numbers in *italics* indicate images.

altitude and effect of load on resupply planes, 30, 35, 40, 42, 43, 176, 178. *See also* elevation
Anderson, G. A., 213
Anderson, T., 213
antenna, radio, 13, 89, 168, 169
Apple Blossom, 67–68
Armonk, NY, 55, 184
Arnold, Henry H. "Hap," 108, 189
artificial horizon, 46
attitude indicator, 46
Atwater Kent radio, 13–14, 89, 168–169
autopilot, 47
Avey, John A., Jr., 128–129
Aviation Accessories Corporation, 15, 169
Aviation Camp. See Kelly Field, TX
Aviation Corporation airmail service, 139

B
B-50 nonstop flight (1948), 4
Baker, Newton, 189
Ballough, E. E., 134
barnstorming
    Federated Flyers, 26, 115–118, 203–204
    images, 95
    success at, 164, 186–187
    United States Air Craft Corp., 117–120, 204–205
beacons, 22, 41, 177, 180
Belgrade, MT
    Belgrade to Missoula leg, 81–84, 194–195
    Miles City to Belgrade leg, 78–80, 193–194
    refueling, 80
Bellefonte, PA thunderstorms, 62–64, 185–186
Bennett, A. M., 122–123
body recovery flight, 124
Boeing Air Transport, Inc., 177
Bookwalter, Vern
    at banquet, 91
    Cheyenne refueling, 39–40, 178–179
    concerns about making Missoula, MT, 66
    North Platte refueling, 40–43, 179–180
    at Rock Springs, 28
    St. Paul refueling, 67–68
    St. Paul to Aberdeen leg, 69–71
Borgenheimer, Walter, 155, 213
Boyle, Leon, 85, 86, 87

ABOUT THE AUTHOR

J. B. Rivard served in the U.S. Navy as a ground-school instructor at the Naval Air Training Command, Pensacola, Florida. He graduated with an engineering degree from the University of Florida and retired from a 25-year staff position as a nuclear reactor specialist at a U.S. National Laboratory. He has worked as a newspaper reporter and as a feature writer for WorkBoat magazine. He's a composer, artist and illustrator, the author of essays, the novels *Handful of Air* and *Illusions of Magic*, and with Anya Carlson, *Illusions of Magic, The Movie*, based on their screenplay